W9-BXV-498

New Kittredge Shakespeare

William Shakespeare

THE TRAGEDY OF
KING LEAR

William Shakespeare

THE TRAGEDY OF
KING LEAR

Editor
Kenneth S. Rothwell

Series Editor
James H. Lake
*Louisiana State University,
Shreveport*

For a distinguished actor and friend, the late Ed Feidner

The Tragedy of King Lear
© 2012 Focus Publishing
Edited by George Lyman Kittredge.

Focus Publishing/R. Pullins Company
PO Box 369
Newburyport MA 01950
www.pullins.com

Used with permission from the heirs to the Kittredge estate.
New material by Kenneth S. Rothwell used with permission.

Cover Design by Guy Wetherbee | Elk Amino Design, New England.elkaminodesign@yahoo.com

Cover image: Cordelia comforting her father, King Lear, in prison, 1886 (oil on canvas), George William Joy (1844-1925) / Leeds Museums and Galleries (City Art Gallery) U.K. / The Bridgeman Art Library International

ISBN: 978-1-58510-265-5

All rights are reserved. No part of this publication may be reproduced, stored in a retrieval system, or transmitted in any form or by any means, electronic, mechanical, by photocopying, recording, or by any other means without the prior written permission of the publisher. If you have received this material as an examination copy free of charge, Focus Publishing/R. Pullins Company retains the title to the material and it may not be resold. Resale of any examination copies of Focus Publishing/R. Pullins Company materials is strictly prohibited.

Printed in the United States of America

10 9 8 7 6 5 4 3 2 1

0112V

TABLE OF CONTENTS

Publisher's Note

George Lyman Kittredge was one of the foremost American Shakespeare scholars of the 20th century. The New Kittredge Shakespeare builds on his celebrated scholarship and extensive notes. Each edition contains a new, updated introduction, with comments on contemporary film versions of the play, an essay on reading the play as performance, and topics for discussion, with an annotated bibliography and filmography. For this an accomplished Shakespeare and film scholar has been commissioned to modernize each volume.

The series focuses on understanding the language and allusions in the play, as well as encountering Shakespeare as performance. The audience ranges from students at all levels to readers interested in encountering the text in the context of its performance on stage or on film.

Ron Pullins, Publisher
Newburyport, 2009

Acknowledgments

I am grateful to James H. Lake and Samuel Crowl, and to Ron Pullins and Cynthia Zawalich at Focus Publishing, for helping me to navigate the murky waters. Without the interlibrary loan and reference staff, especially Patricia Mardeusz, at the University of Vermont libraries, I would not have made it to the shore.

Kenneth Sprague Rothwell
Burlington, Vermont
January 29, 2009

INTRODUCTION TO THE KITTREDGE EDITION[1]

KING LEAR was entered in the Stationers' Register on November 26, 1607: "as yt was played before the Kinges maiestie at Whitehall vppon Sainct Stephens night [December 26] at Christmas Last." The First Quarto[2] came out in 1608.[3] The Second Quarto (1619, misdated 1608) reprints the First. A Third Quarto appeared in 1655. The basis for the text is the First Folio (1623), which supplies about a hundred genuine lines that are lacking in the Quartos; but the First Quarto furnishes many good readings and supplies some three hundred lines which the Folio omits. The Fool's burlesque prophecy (3.2.76-90) in the Folio (omitted in the Quartos) is commonly regarded as a spurious insertion. Apart from this passage there is nothing in either the Quartos or the Folio that seems un-Shakespearean. Indeed, the prophecy itself is not a bad piece of jester's lingo. Even the Fool's remark, "This prophecy Merlin shall make, for I live before his time," is so riotously comic that one is tempted to accept it as Shakespeare's own defiance of chronological possibility. One remembers Hotspur's ridicule of "the dreamer Merlin and his prophecies" (*1Henry IV*, 3.1). The subject was of real political significance in Shakespeare's time. An act against seditious prophecies was debated in Queen Elizabeth's first parliament (1559) and passed in her second (1563).

Most of the omissions in the Folio are obviously mere "cuts" to shorten the play for acting. This fact comes out clearly, for example, in the quarrel between Albany and Goneril in 4.2.29-68. The Folio text, then, represents a stage version of *King Lear*, but there is no evidence that the cuts were made by the author himself. The differences

---

1 Most of Professor Kittredge's introduction is unchanged, though a few sentences have been edited or slightly modified, as necessary. [K.S.R]

2 A quarto would be comparable to one of today's paperbacks, much smaller and more affordable than a large and expensive folio. [K.S.R.]

3 M. William Shak-speare: | his | True Chronicle Historie of the life and | death of King Lear and his three Daughters. | With the vnfortunate life of Edgar, sonne | and heire to the Earle of Gloster, and his | sullen and assumed humor of | Tom of Bedlam: | As it was played before the Kings Maiestie at Whitehall vpon | S. Stephans night in Christmas Hollidayes. | By his Maiesties seruants playing vsually at the Gloabe | on the Bancke-side. | London, | Printed for Nathaniel Butter, and are to be sold at his shop in Pauls | Church-yard at the signe of the Pide Bull neere | St. Austins Gate, 1608.

between the Quarto and the Folio by no means warrant the theory that Shakespeare ever rewrote his *King Lear* or subjected it to a substantial revision.

Except for its omissions the Folio text is more nearly authoritative, but, even so, it is often wrong when the Quarto is right. In cases of doubt, where both Quarto and Folio "make sense," an editor must use his judgment.[4]

For the date of *King Lear* all the evidence would fit either 1605 or 1606. One limit is fixed by the performance at court on December 26, 1606; the other by "these late eclipses in the sun and moon" (1.2.112), which occurred in September and October, 1605. If *Macbeth* was written (as seems likely) in 1606, we may settle on 1605 for *King Lear*, since it came just before or just after *Macbeth*.[5]

To Lear (Llyr, Ler), a divine but shadowy figure in the mythology of the ancient Britons, of whose children wild tales are told in Irish and Welsh, Geoffrey of Monmouth in his twelfth-century *Historia Regum Britanniae* attached the old folk-tale of the three daughters. From Geoffrey of Monmouth the legend was taken over by Raphael Holinshed in his *Chronicle*, by Edmund Spenser in *The Faerie Queene*, and by John Higgins (1574) in *A Mirrour for Magistrates*. All these books were familiar to every Elizabethan who read anything. The tale had also been dramatized in *The True Chronicle History of King Leir*, printed in 1605.

Holinshed's narrative is, in substance, as follows: Leir's reign over Britain began "in the yeere of the world 3105." He "was a prince of right noble demeanor, gouerning his land and subiects in great wealth." He had three daughters—Gonorilla, Regan, and Cordeilla—"which daughters he greatly loued, but specially Cordeilla the yoongest farre aboue the two elder.

"When this Leir therefore was come to great yeeres, & began to waxe vnweldie through age, he thought to vnderstand the affections of his daughters towards him, and preferre hir whome he best loued, to the succession ouer the kingdome. Whervpon he first asked Gonorilla the eldest, how well shee loued him: who calling hir gods to record, protested, that she loued him more than hir owne life, which by right and reason shoulde be most deere vnto hir. With which answer the father being well pleased, turned to the second, and demanded of hir how well she loued him: who answered (confirming hir saiengs with great othes) that she loued him more than toung could expresse, and farre aboue all other creatures of the world.

"Then called he his yoongest daughter Cordeilla before him, and asked of hir what account she made of him: vnto whome she made this answer as followeth: "Knowing the great loue and fatherlie zeale that you haue always borne towards me, (for the which I maie not answere you otherwise than I thinke, and as my conscience leadeth me) I protest vnto you, that I haue loued you euer, and will continuallie (while I liue) loue you as my naturall father. And if you would more vnderstand of the loue

---

4   The differences between the Quarto and Folio versions of the play have received much attention. For discussion, see Gary Taylor and Michael Warren, eds. *The Division of the Kingdom*, Oxford: Clarendon, 1983. See also Michael Warren, ed. *The Parallel King Lear*, 1608-1623. Berekeley: University of California Press, 1989. [K.S.R.]

5   E. K. Chambers, *The Elizabethan Stage*, IV, 25, 26. [K.S.R.]

that I beare you, assertaine your selfe, that so much as you haue, so much you are worth, and so much I loue you, and no more." The father being nothing content with this answer, married his two eldest daughters, the one vnto Henninus, the Duke of Cornewal, and the other vnto Maglanus, the Duke of Albania, betwixt whome he willed and ordeined that his land should be deuided after his death, and the one halfe thereof immediatelie should be assigned to them in hand; but for the third daughter Cordeilla he reserued nothing."

After this Aganippus, "one of the princes of Gallia," sent over to Britain to ask for the hand of Cordeilla, whom he married without dowry.

When Lear became very old, the Dukes of Cornwall and Albania deprived him of his half of the kingdom, assigning him merely a regular income for life. This too they diminished from time to time, with the hearty concurrence of their wives. Gonorilla and Regan, indeed, "seemed to thinke that all was too much which their father had, the same being neuer so little: in so much, that going from the one to the other, he was brought to that miserie, that scarslie they would allow him one seruaunt to waite vpon him."

At last Leir was forced to take refuge in Gallia, where he was kindly received by Cordeilla and her husband. Upon learning of the cruelty with which he had been treated, Aganippus raised an army and invaded Britain. The rebellious dukes were slain in battle and Leir was restored to the throne. It was agreed that Cordeilla should succeed him "as the rightfull inheritour after his decesse, notwithstanding any former grant made to hir sisters or to their husbands."

Leir ruled Britain for two more years and then died in peace. He was succeeded by Cordeilla, who reigned five years. In the meantime her husband died. "About the end of those fiue yeeres" her two nephews, the sons of Gonorilla and Ragan, "disdaining to be vnder the gouernment of a woman, leuied warre against hir, and destroied a great part of the land, and finallie tooke hir prisoner, and laid hir fast in ward, wherewith she tooke suche griefe, being a woman of a manlie courage, and despairing to recouer libertie, that she slue herself."[6]

In Holinshed, in Spenser, and in the *Mirrour* the story is substantially identical. The catastrophe is quite different from that of Shakespeare's tragedy. Lear dies peacefully, two years after his restoration. It is the life of Cordelia, not the life of Lear, that comes to a tragic end.

Shakespeare was dealing with a history which came to no proper dramatic conclusion—which had, in fact, two catastrophes (one happy and one tragic); and these were separated by an interval of seven years. He combined the two in a single tragic catastrophe: the insurrection against Cordelia on the part of her nephews is identified with the war waged by Cordelia against the two Dukes, and the unhappy outcome of the later struggle is ascribed to the earlier. Thus, instead of succeeding in her attempt to reinstate her father, Cordelia is defeated by Albany and Edmund, and, with the King, is taken prisoner. There is, however, an opportunity for a reconciliation between

6   Geoffrey Bullough, *Narrative and Dramatic Sources of Shakespeare* (New York: Columbia University Press, 1973) 7: 317-19. [K.S.R.]

father and daughter. The death of Cordelia is a murder under the guise of an execution. She is hanged, and King Lear escapes by violent resistance. The strength of his earlier manhood returns for the moment: he kills the hangman and comes in with the body of Cordelia in his arms. But the physical and mental sufferings that he has endured are too much for his enfeebled frame and he dies peacefully, like the going out of a candle. Shakespeare, we note, has preserved all such incidents of the two catastrophes as in any way served his purpose or lent themselves to tragic unity. He has brought the play to the only end that is conceivable after the long agony which the King had suffered. It is Lear who is the central figure of the whole, and the drama properly ends with the death of the main personage.

The anonymous old play is, as its title indicates, a "chronicle history," not a tragedy. It ends happily with the triumph of Cordelia and Lear's restoration to the throne. Shakespeare owes little to the old play except the impulse to write a new one. In various matters Shakespeare abandons the novel devices of his predecessors. To Spenser, for example, Shakespeare owes nothing except, perhaps, the form "Cordelia" (for "Cordeilla" or "Cordella"). And in the old play Lear means to divide his kingdom equally, and the test of affection is merely to "resolue a doubt which much molests [his] mind."

Gloucester and his two sons do not appear in the ancient legend. Their story Shakespeare adapted from the episode of the King of Paphlagonia in Sidney's *Arcadia.*. This he has so dexterously interwoven with the legend that Edmund's villany becomes the determining factor in the tragic catastrophe. Edgar's description of the fiend that led his father to the edge of Dover Cliff (4.6.69 ff.) recalls Horatio's warning to Hamlet (*Hamlet* 2.4). For the resemblance of his mad talk to passages in Harsnett's account of cases of supposed demoniacal possession in *A Declaration of Egregious Popish Impostures* (1603) see footnotes within the text.

Eminent critics have done their best to reconcile Cordelia's character with her refusal to compete with her sisters' lies by speaking the truth her father longs to hear. The inconsistency, however, is not chargeable to Shakespeare. It is the essential point in the ancient story and goes back to a time long anterior to any ideal of probability in narrative. If Shakespeare had changed the tale here, his tragedy would have come to a happy ending in the first act.

King Lear's Fool is clad in motley (particoloured attire) and wears the regular fool's cap crested with an imitation of a cock's comb. In real life the professional fool was usually a "natural"—that is, in plain terms, an idiot or half-wit; or he might be not idiotic but crack-brained—a harmless paranoiac. Rarely was he, either in fact or in the drama, a clever fellow who, with all his wits about him, played the jester's part for a livelihood. In the case of Lear's Fool it was insanity that had qualified him for his profession. Something had thrown his fine mind off its balance; but he retained no small part of his gifts of nature, and his genius flashes with that uncanny brilliance which often marks the intellect that has escaped from normal control. Thus he is qualified to be the chorus in a tragedy.[7]

---

7   For more information on early-modern stage fools see Enid Welsford, *The Fool, His Social and Literary History*, London: Faber & Faber, 1935. [K.S.R.]

Lear's madness has no place in the old story; it is Shakespeare's own invention. Eminent alienists have diagnosed it as senile dementia. His mind was failing, they contend, at the beginning of the play. To the Elizabethans, however, irascibility was not insanity. Nothing can be clearer than that Shakespeare intended Lear's madness to be simply an attack of feverous delirium, brought on by exposure to the storm and superinduced by the terrible strain to which his emotions had been subjected. The physician actually cures him. Even the dreadful events that follow do not overthrow his restored reason, for, when he enters with the murdered Cordelia in his arms, he is not mad. At the moment of death when his powers fail utterly, so that he cannot recognize his nearest friends, it is not madness but dissolution.

The character of King Lear is all Shakespeare's. In the chronicle Lear has no character: he is merely the king in a fairy tale—a child's figure of royalty—the kind of monarch who always wears his crown and never lays aside his sceptre. In the old play he is hardly more than that. Indeed, he is rather less; for the feebleness which he displays after the opening scene is almost provocative of contempt. He is distinctly senile. He has all the futilities of old age with none of its dignity. But in Shakespeare Lear becomes colossal. His character defies analysis because it needs none. He is a man; he is a father; he is a king—and he is old. That is the whole account. He must have love; but he requires obedience too, and veneration, as befits the kingly office. Always and everywhere he must be king. He has reigned too long and too well to be able to give up reigning. He tries to resign his kingdom, but he cannot, even in his madness. "Prithee, nuncle, tell me," asks the Fool, "whether a madman be a gentleman or a yeoman." And Lear's reply is inevitable: "A king! A king!"

INTRODUCTION TO THE FOCUS EDITION

King Lear in Print and on Stage

The well-known folktale of King Lear and his three rebellious daughters, upon which *The Tragedy of King Lear* is based, fits neatly into the general sense of melancholy characteristic of the Jacobean age, especially given the unbearably sad fate Shakespeare assigns to Cordelia in his version of the story. As Thomas P. Roche, Jr. says, "The ending of *Lear* is as bleak and unrewarding as man can reach outside the gates of hell."[1] Indeed at the time Shakespeare wrote *King Lear* and in the years following, the era itself seemed bleak. Queen Elizabeth (1558-1603) had been dead for five years and after an initial euphoria, her replacement, King James of Scotland, had begun to disappoint his new subjects.

This troubled atmosphere left the door open for a "cult of melancholia" that soon replaced "Elizabethan optimism" with "Jacobean pessimism." Leading writers and thinkers helped to popularize the Elizabethan versions of revenge plays, including Shakespeare's *Titus Andronicus* (1593-94) and *Hamlet* (1599), with its melancholy Prince. Fashionable works like Robert Burton's *Anatomy of Melancholy* (1621) contributed to the malaise; essays rooted in Neo-stoic values, like those of Michel de Montaigne (1533-92), further encouraged the belief that "for one to enure himself to melancholy, there is some kind of purpose, of consent and mutual delight."[2] The spiritual slump among the elite was shared by the general population, which was itself beset by social and religious unrest, recurring bad weather, thin harvests, endemic plague, and other ills.

Shakespeare's *King Lear* seems almost a lamentation on the miseries of human existence, its initial focus on the scandalous theme of "bastardy," the stain falling in this case on the head of Edmund, the illegitimate son of the earl of Gloucester. The

---

1   " 'Nothing Almost Sees Miracles': Tragic Knowledge in *King Lear*." *Critical Essays on Shakespeare's King Lear*, ed. Jay L. Halio. (New York: G.K. Hall, 1996) 16.

2   Michel de Montaigne, "We Taste Nothing Purely." *The Essays of Montaigne*. Transl. John Florio, Intro. J. I. M. Stewart. (New York: The Modern Library, 1933) 2.20:608.

play opens in relative tranquility but descends into turmoil when Gloucester blurts out that Edmund is illegitimate, thus casting a shadow over the scene. The chattering but genial Gloucester has tweaked the noses of the gods by boasting of a priapic foray, adding that he has spoken so often of his transgression that he has been "braz'd" [hardened] to it; he then makes matters worse by joking that this "young fellow's mother grew round-womb'd and had a son for her cradle ere she had a husband for her bed," happily chortling that "there was good sport in his [son's] making."

All of this might be dismissed as the tavern badinage of a bore who had consumed one too many; unfortunately there is a catch. Hovering in the background stands young Edmund, the bastard son himself, who, if he has overheard for the first time that "there was good sport in his making," has been given a powerful motive for loathing his father. Moreover, Edmund, a rebel with a cause, has brooded over his resentment at being a "bastard." In a first-act soliloquy central to the play's moral structure he reveals a higher commitment to Nature than to any human ethos: "Thou, Nature, art my goddess; to thy law/ My services are bound. Wherefore should / I stand in the plague of custom, and permit/ The curiosity of nations to deprive me . . . /Why bastard? Wherefore base?" (1.2.1-7).

The torment of wayward but frail persons occurs, however, not just with the story of sightless Gloucester and his sons, which Shakespeare borrowed from Sir Philip Sidney's *Arcadia* (1590), but also with the analogous story of King Lear and his three daughters. The way that the fate of one family parallels and reflects that of the other sets up a radioactive field, implying that the fate of Lear is not unique to him but may be replicated throughout the whole world. Indeed Lear's attempt to divide the kingdom strikes at the heart of the body politic. Shakespeare manages, in fact, to elevate a domestic brawl into a seismic disaster. The very word "division" and the octogenarian king's sudden decision to cast off the burdens of monarchy, "Conferring them on younger strengths, while [he]/ Unburthen'd crawl[s] toward death" (1.1.39), should have struck terror in everyone, for changes in political arrangement always spelled trouble.

The old king decides that the best method for dividing the kingdom is to have each daughter proclaim her loyalty to him and then to confer the choicest part of the kingdom on the one who most eloquently praises him. What was intended to be a happy solution turns disastrous. It seems that the king has already determined that the prize share of the kingdom (his "darker purpose") should go to his favorite, young Cordelia, a Cinderella type. But his scheme backfires when Goneril and Regan unctuously ingratiate themselves to their father, while Cordelia displays what today would be called an "attitude" (though unlike modern teen-age sullenness, her "attitude" is deeply rooted in Elizabethan codes of behavior) and abruptly rebuffs her father's question: "what can you say to draw/ A third [portion] more opulent than your sisters?" (1.1 37). Her blunt reply, "Nothing, my lord," so hurts and enrages her unstable father that he instantly disinherits her, trading her dowerless to the King of France. Foolishly ignoring her virtues, Lear embraces Cordelia's sisters, Goneril and Regan. Both Lear and Gloucester are thus duped by faithless children (Goneril and

Regan, and Edmund) and both reject those who love them most (Cordelia and Edgar). This whirligig of misunderstanding and egomania leads to Cordelia's harrowing death.

The terrifying hanging of Cordelia remains a sticking point for many. In the years following the 1660 Restoration of the exiled monarchy of King Charles II, the theatres were reopened and released from the puritanical control of Cromwell's government (1642-1660). Nahum Tate, a distinguished scholar, rewrote the play to give it the happy and moral ending congenial to a new audience, a revision that has itself been rejected today.

In the lurid sub-plot, the two wicked sisters, Goneril and Regan, enact a tale sordid enough for a checkout-counter tabloid, each falling madly in love with Edmund, the bastard. Goneril has already taken a violent dislike to her mild ("Milk-liver'd") husband, Albany; and to make matters more intricate, and unbearable, Goneril, while recruiting the obsequious Oswald as her confidant and messenger, encourages a flirtation. Oswald, dispatched with her letters, then encounters Regan, who tries to wheedle information about Goneril from him ("I'll love thee much--/Let me unseal the letter" 4.5.19).

Others in the huge cast play roles of various weight and significance. The Fool, a character who seems to follow laws of his own devising, is reminiscent of Desiderius Erasmus (1466-1536), who spoofed pomposity in learned men and exploited overtones from the Epistles of St. Paul, who urged people "to become wise in the eyes of God by becoming foolish in the eyes of the world" (1 Cor. 3:19). That bias which infiltrates the exchanges between Lear and his Fool explains why the Fool is tolerated. And there is also a biblical quotation from the *Magnificat* that puts the plight of the old king into perspective: "He hath put down the mighty from their seat, and hath exalted the humble and meek" (Luke 1:46-55).

In this disorderly world, characters in *King Lear* often seem willing to swallow the most outrageous slanders instantly. Dramatists, unlike novelists, have little space for complicated "back stories" explaining all the possible motives for a character's abrupt decisions; hence, the lightning judgments of a "decider" in Shakespeare often take the breath away. Lear immediately concludes that Cordelia is guilty of *lese majesté* (an offense against authority). Gloucester buys with astonishing speed the accusations of conspiracy against Edgar in Edmund's faked document. Edgar, with barely a squeak ("Some villain hath done me wrong"), accepts his role as a despised traitor and adopts a grotesque disguise as a madman called Tom o' Bedlam, a character Shakespeare's audience would have recognized as the type of a homeless vagabond discharged from London's notorious Bedlam hospital for the insane.

Poor Tom's bizarre vocabulary, which teeters on the edge of lunacy and makes him into a semi-comic figure, has been traced back to an anti-Catholic tract by the Rev. Samuel Harsnett (1561-1631), an Anglican clergyman and zealous anti-Jesuit who mocked papist belief in exorcism of devils from the afflicted. Mad Tom's minor devils, like Obidicut, Hoppedance, Mahu, and so forth, reek of Harsnett. And the cascade of apocalyptic language and convoluted speech offers a handy glossary of the mad folk's language at Bedlam hospital. The foul fiend haunts poor Tom in the voice of a nightingale. Hoppedance cries in Tom's belly for two white herrings: "Croak not, black angel; I have no food for thee" (3.6.31). This gibberish stands alongside such masterful incoherence as "How to prevent the fiend and to kill vermin" (3.4.163). Poor Tom serves, too, as a mirror to the madness of the old king himself, and his loony raving turns him into a choric prelude for the scene where Cornwall gouges out Gloucester's eyes. In his foul rags, Tom becomes a visual aid for the tyrannical king's own hallucinations. In his madness Lear cries out in sympathy for "poor naked wretches" (like Poor Tom?) and homiletically proclaims: "Take physic, pomp;/ Expose thyself to feel what wretches feel" (3.4.33).

The daughters are almost as adept at public speaking as their father. In the division of the kingdom scene, when Goneril, Regan, and Cordelia are summoned to pay homage to the old king, each seems aware that her fortune may depend on a talent for flattering their father. Goneril, wife to Albany and King Lear's "eldest-born," speaks first: "Sir, I love you more than words can wield the matter"(1.1.59). Next, in a scene that is often staged as a tableau (in Peter Brook's 1953 Omnibus television version there is a view of Orson Welles as King Lear, with the daughters lined up in a row like puppets); Regan, the second-born, speaks up next, by inventing a rhetorical ploy that distinguishes her as the one child who needs emotional support only from her father: "I am alone felicitate/ In your dear Highness' love" (1.1.77). After this spasm of encomia, Cordelia, who has been standing in the background muttering little sighs of uncertainty, first speaks only an aside: "What shall Cordelia speak?" (1.1.63). And to the query, "what can you say to draw/ A third more opulent than your sisters?" (1.1.87), Cordelia's bluntness staggers her father. "Nothing," says Cordelia. And her incredibly terse response highlights the excesses of her sisters and amazes the audience. Her father's reply conveys a warning: "Nothing can come of nothing" (1.1.92). The resourceful Cordelia somehow manages to conceal her true feelings, but the two older sisters become even more malevolent. Cordelia, in putting her personal standards of honesty above her old father's need for reassurance, ironically disarms herself from the tactical means to combat her sisters.

Old arguments about whether the play is essentially "Christian" or "pagan" demand the reply "all of above," since the plot deals with a pre-Christian society, but it was subsequently composed centuries later in a Christian society whose theologians and writers had embraced the pagan values of Roman stoicism. As James H. Lake has pointed out, Edgar, Kent and Albany, the potential heirs to King Lear's "gored state," would happily but myopically divide the kingdom once again, had Kent and Albany not made other plans.[3] But Stoics do not rejoice, they endure. As Edgar says to Gloucester, "Men must endure/ Their going hence, even as their coming hither;/ Ripeness is all" (5.2.8). The only victory rests in courageously living a full life, mature in its ripeness. Away in the background there is always the slim chance that faith will transcend all this bitterness. To paraphrase the prominent Neo-stoic theologian, Jeremy Taylor (1613-1667), whose edgy aphorism in *Holy Living and Holy Dying*

---

3   "The Ending of King Lear: 5.3.311-326," *Explicator* 41.4 (1983): 9-10.

(1651) expressed it all: "It is well that life is short for it is so miserable." King Lear might have understood that.[4]

King Lear on Stage

Owing to shifts in audience taste, especially during the "optimistic" eighteenth century, *King Lear* has a ragged performance history. Initially of course in the seventeenth century it played at the royal palace in Whitehall and made its way into the Globe playhouse on Bankside and the newly occupied Blackfriars indoor theatre in central London. Shakespeare's tragedy ending in the deaths of both Lear and Cordelia remained so universally repugnant that few acting companies wanted to touch it. Nahum Tate's sanitized version (see p. xv) was therefore wildly successful and dominated the stage until the early nineteenth century, when a reaction against "Tatefied" *Lear* began to set in. As G. K. Hunter has phrased it: "The staging of *King Lear* is ". . . a history of the tension between the theatrical virtues of Nahum Tate's adaptation [1681]. . . and the literary prestige of Shakespeare's play."[5]

By 1823, perhaps influenced by Charles Lamb's essay denouncing textual liberties on stage, actor Charles Kean himself restored the play's original unhappy ending. Regrettably, but to the amusement of his audience, the weight of Mrs. W. West as Cordelia in the final scene was too much for Kean, who nearly dropped her, thus ironically validating the wisdom of Tate's revisions. (Ever since then, young ladies auditioning for the role of Cordelia have been carefully weighed.) Whatever the state of his mind before the opening of the play—and there has been considerable debate about that (see the Kittredge Introduction, p. xi)—the aged monarch's mental capacities deteriorate into pathological incoherence. In 1838, William Charles Macready reintroduced the purged character of the Fool, and a gradual trend began among such famous actors as David Garrick, J.P. Kemble, Edmund Kean and Charles Macready to salvage the original text.

Victorian London theatre was dominated by "big names" who increasingly distracted the audience away from Shakespeare and toward the glamorous actors, like David Garrick, Spranger Barry, Henry Irving, and Ellen Terry. With these stars, who attracted throngs willing to stand in box office lines for hours, came a parallel enthusiasm for elaborate set designs, as well as pleasure in lighting effects. The candlelight of the earlier years gave way by 1831 to hazardous gaslight, then to limelight (produced by running charged hot gas over limestone), then after about 1891 to emerging electricity. The storm scene in *King Lear*, a precursor to Hollywood's Cecil B. DeMille "epic with a cast of thousands", called for "shock-and-awe" heights of lighting and sound effects to supplement Shakespeare's language. The storm scene as symbolic of

---

4   A crux of the play is the question what if anything emerges from King Lear's ordeal? Does the play show that there is really "nothing" to hope for? Or is there hope for redemption? See Kenneth S. Rothwell. "In Search of Nothing: Mapping *King Lear*" in *Shakespeare the Movie*, ed. Lynda Boose and Richard Burt. (London: Routledge, 1999) 135-47.

5   R. W. Ellison, *Shakespeare's Tragedy of King Lear*. 1820, Intro. G.K. Hunter. (London: Cornmarket Press, 1970)

the seismic changes ongoing in the king's shattered consciousness required rolling hunks of wood and banging on sheets of metal to produce the sound of thunder; and of course the changing of ponderous sets created interminable intermissions. Thus, for this and other reasons, William Poel's (1852-1934) bold effort to return Shakespeare productions to the bare boards was a welcome development.

At the Lyceum Theatre, Henry Irving (1838-1905) and Ellen Terry (1847-1928) climbed to the apex of the "star system," but the cataclysmic effects of World War I shattered many theatrical conventions along with other Victorian traditions. The hope and despair in the "waste-land" after World War I offered prime subsoil for the barren world of *King Lear*. It was a new age of melancholy.

What intervened was a revolution in acting styles, and the New York Group Theatre rallied around Konstantin Stanislavsky's new theory of "method" acting. In North America Marlon Brando, who became a pupil of the famous Stella Adler (a student of Stanislavsky) and Lee Strasberg, brought the "method" into the foreground, a style that made overnight sensations of the angry young men in plays like John Osborne's *Look Back in Anger*. Sir John Gielgud, who still fit the Victorian ideal of the gentlemanly and cultivated Shakespearean actor with a voice fit for the gods, suddenly seemed old hat. As Orson Welles allegedly said, Gielgud had "the voice that moved the world." He had a tendency to sing the verses, almost "vibrato-laden,"[6] like an opera star doing recitative, rather than to wrestle, pause, and grunt over their innermost meaning, as method actors did.

Meanwhile, the play that had been thought intractably un-actable grew more and more popular in the age of Pearl Harbor, Dachau, and Hiroshima. A 1968 Broadway production starring Lee J. Cobb, who had immortalized Willy Loman in *Death of a Salesman*, with Stacy Keach as Edmund, ran a record 72 performances. In 1977, a black actor, James Earl Jones, now famous as the sinister voice of Darth Vader in *Star Wars*, undertook the role at the outdoor Delacorte Theater in New York City's Central Park.

Dozens of excellent and sometimes memorable performances of *King Lear* have occurred away from the major cities in the United States, partly as a consequence of widespread support for Shakespeare festivals. The Royall Tyler Theater at the University of Vermont mounted one such production in 2002, when the late Edward Feidner unforgettably wrestled with the king's terrible agony. But the saga never ends. Most recently, in 2004 Christopher Plummer, on Broadway as King Lear directed by Jonathan Miller, was nominated for a Tony Award, and Ian McKellen, directed by Trevor Nunn, came to the United States with his *King Lear* in 2007, with a televised production following in 2009.

---

6   For an elegant comparison of the Gielgud and Brando acting styles, see Claudia Roth Pierpont, "Method Man: How the Greatest American Actor Lost His Way," *The New Yorker*, 27 October 2008: 66.

King Lear in Moving Images

In 1900, the fledgling film industry gobbled up Shakespeare's uncopyrighted plays. At the great 1900 Paris Exhibition, the French superstar Sarah Bernhardt shrewdly sensed the potential of film for immortalizing her image: her brief duel scene with Laertes from *Hamlet* brought instant respectability to the struggling motion picture business. As early as 1909, the Vitagraph company in Brooklyn, New York, headed by J. Stuart Blackton, began churning out a dozen drastically shortened one-reel versions of Shakespeare's plays, averaging ten to fifteen minutes runtime. Shakespeare on silent film was an oxymoron that haunted early film makers, who very rapidly developed desperate gimmicks to fend off the dreadful silence (e.g., planting live speaking actors behind the screen, or experimenting with a tinny phonograph). No real success was achieved with talking pictures, however, until the development in the 1920s of electrical amplification for films like Al Jolson's *The Jazz Singer* (1927).

The best of the *Lear* silent pictures was made in the United States, in 1916, by Thanhouser Films. Ambitiously, the movie includes an epic battle scene, with enough galloping cavalry to rival D. W. Griffith's epic *The Birth of a Nation* (1913). Reaction shots of gloating Goneril and Regan show them ecstatic over the carnage spread out before them. Stalwart infantry hack away with vicious swords or hurl boulders onto the helpless wounded. King Lear is played by a well-known Shakespearean, Frederick B. Warde, an expatriate English actor who toured all over the United States in a variety of roles, often in frontier cities, once going broke in a desolate southwestern town.[7] It remained for the BBC's Royston Morley to produce a pioneering television version of *King Lear* in 1948 that allowed William Devlin in the title role to speak Lear's tumultuous lines aloud.

King Lear entered into full moviedom in the 1970s, with the release almost simultaneously of a Russian version directed by Grigori Kozintsev (1905-1973), and a British version by Peter Brook (b.1925), both achieving a pinnacle in film art. Brook explored the darker side of the play, but Kozintsev was somewhat less funereal. Essentially art-house movies, they were often screened at small theaters, where intellectuals and would-be intellectuals crowded into the lobbies to mingle with the elite, to chatter over avant-garde paintings, and to sip black coffee in tiny cups. In the most searching book by any film director, Kozintsev sets forth in *King Lear, The Space of Tragedy*[8] the profound thought, even *Angst*, that went into his movie. Curiously, a great deal of his inspiration came from a contemplation, on a blazing hot August afternoon, in a Kyoto temple garden of rock, pools, and carp. The film's establishing shot shows a crowd of wretched peasants, some crippled, some in crude wooden carts, some barefooted, some reeling from hunger and thirst, struggling to climb a steep path, strewn with rocks and boulders, to a castle at the peak. High on the stone walls,

---

7   Frederick B. Warde, *Fifty Years of Make-Believe.* (New York: The International Press Syndicate, 1920)

8   Grigori Kozintsev, *King Lear, The Space of Tragedy: The Diary of a Film Director.* (Berkeley: University of California Press, 1977)

staring down at the rude multitude, stands the king (played by Yuri Yarvet) with his entourage, unaware that these people, mere rabble and riffraff, represent the kind of "unaccommodated man" that the king will one day discover himself to be.

Kozintsev once wrote that the secret of filmmaking lies in knowing how and where to point a camera. In the occult rhythms of his *King Lear*, he demonstrates over and over the truth of this superficially banal remark. One need only think how many family snapshots have been ruined because the genial uncle lacked any talent for blocking out the neighbor's flapping laundry. In this Russianized *King Lear* the camera relentlessly closes in on the faces of human beings until their innermost secrets are squeezed out on the screen, like toothpaste from a tube. Bodies are ravaged, askew, and the king himself physically seems unfit for so lofty a role.

A slight man, Yuri Yarvet, a non-Russian speaker from Estonia who originally auditioned for the role of the Fool, sits near the crackling fire in the hearth, studying a huge pseudo-map of Britain, though the warmth of the fire here will later yield to a conflagration that scorches the kingdom. His small stature cannot, however, conceal his raw power and volcanic energy. He struts through the palace, followed by a retinue of sycophants, and selects prize specimens of hound and hawk from a vast stock. The film is suffused in a Slavic sensibility of Boris Pasternak's translations of Shakespeare into the strong cadences of the Russian language, Dmitri Shostakovich's overwhelming musical score, and the serious art of the Russian stage. Since Kozintsev worked in the shadow of Stalinism throughout his career, his film was greeted by the right wing with the suspicion that it would be corrupted with Marxist ideology, though that does not happen. The recurring motif is one of humanitarianism, as the people in the film increasingly resemble "the prisoners of starvation" from the *Internationale*. The swollen, aching feet drag on the rough path to the castle as if the meek will indeed inherit the earth.

The astute editing everywhere visually reinforces the film's emotional drive: for example, after Cordelia departs from her father there is a quick cut to her and the King of France being blessed on the roadside by a priest, before setting off for the continent in a junk heap of creaky wagons and scruffy cavalry. The snapshots include one upsetting vignette of Regan in a white heat, tearing off Edmund's clothing, and shortly after planting an erotic kiss on the lips of her husband Cornwall's corpse. A morbid flash cut shows a lynched Cordelia swinging in the wind high above the castle walls. Lear's Fool does not vanish in the third act, as in the play, but returns again at the end to help with the commentary on the desperate fate of mankind. As the Fool, now transformed into the village idiot, sits amidst the rubble, devastated by the loss of his master, he shares with all of suffering mankind—as well as Shakespeare, Kozintsev, and the audience—Edgar's "image of that horror" (5.3.264).

Peter Brook's 1971 film of *King Lear* was released in London and elsewhere to a generally hostile corps of reviewers, perhaps none more vehement than America's formidable *New Yorker* critic, Pauline Kael, who declared that she "hated" it.[9] Trendy absurdist values, wiry existentialism, grainy texture, out-of-focus frames, flamboyant

---

9   "Peter Brook's Night of the Living Dead," *The New Yorker*, 11 December 1971: 136.

Theatre of Cruelty motifs, and unbridled nihilism recruited squadrons of enemies everywhere, though a sobering estimate came from the distinguished scholar, Frank Kermode, who announced that it was possibly "the best of all Shakespeare movies."[10] A great deal of the hostility stemmed from Brook's goal to make the film thematically and technically a peephole into modern life. Brook was seeking not so much identification with his audience as alienation, and he was engaged not just in making a movie of *King Lear* but also in the "meta-cinematic" task of making a movie about making movies. That is to say, the apparent disarray of the narrative jolts viewers into a greater sensitivity to the way that the film has been edited, rearranged, and put together again.

Even so, many literary critics took the rapid editing for incompetence rather than as a deliberate strategy to capture the elusiveness of human experience. The agony of Edgar disguised as Poor Tom o' Bedlam, though verbally aggressive in Shakespeare's text, in Brook's film becomes a visual rampage. The shadow of an influential book by Jan Kott, *Shakespeare Our Contemporary*,[11] falls everywhere. The "unaccommodated man" morphs into a naked, shivering, quaking excuse for a human being as he stands, streams of icy rainwater splashing on his bare chest, exposed to the howling elements. Edgar's nakedness conjures up images of self-crucifixion, of a Christ-like sacrifice, while battalions of drowned rodents get into the *mise en scène* to make the barrenness, sterility, and utter hopelessness even more depressing. Robust claps of thunder and lightning perpetuate the tradition of creating the perfect storm in *Lear* on stage. All this turmoil has been denounced as excessive, beyond the limits of good taste, but there are few other ways to reify the play's vitality. In *King Lear*, more powerfully than anywhere else, Shakespeare sketched puny man's tempest-tossed universe.

Although Brook's film reflected the major hallmarks of modernism, in 1987 director Jean-Luc Godard took the filming of *King Lear* into the virtual-reality world of post-modernism. The film becomes increasingly not so much a narration as a segmentation, a jigsaw puzzle of bits and pieces awaiting reassembly. It illustrates Courtney Lehmann's clever book "*Shakespeare Remains*" (2002),[12] which shows how Shakespearean fragments still litter the cultural universe. Toward the film's end, a hint from Virginia Woolf's novel *The Waves* shows a phantasmagoric white horse carrying the aura and mystery of the human experience. Iterative title cards hold out cryptic but nevertheless alienating signals: "No-thing," "Power and virtue," "An Approach to Lear." "Fear and Loathing," Many critics, though not always the most open-minded, decided that "not the least of the privations of a nuclear winter would be the threat that its culture might be comprised of films like this,"[13] though the liberal-minded viewed it differently, seeing it as "deft, funny, and intermittently exhilarating."[14]

---

10   "Shakespeare in the Movies," *New York Review of Books* 18, 4 May 1972: 19.

11   Jan Kott, *Shakespeare our Contemporary*. (New York: W. W. Norton & Company, 1974)

12   Courtney Lehmann, *Shakespeare Remains: Theatre to Film, Early Modern to Postmodern*. (Ithaca: Cornell University Press, 2002)

13   "Echoes of Godard," *Times Literary Supplement*, 2 January 1988: 112.

14   *The Village Voice*, 26 January 1988: 53

Richard Eyre's WGBH televising of *King Lear* (1998), originally staged at Britain's National Theatre, features Ian Holm in an energetic and subtle performance. Director Eyre reincarnated the artistic theory of William Poel, the neo-Victorian director who banished pretentious sets in favor of a bare stage and Shakespeare's language. Eyre begins his production with a young man who is blackening a photographic negative in order to stare safely at one of the "late eclipses of the sun" without going blind (like Gloucester). He then peers through a curtain, but instead of the sun he sees a council chamber occupied by Gloucester, Kent, and Edmund, which reprises the opening of *King Lear*. The images of stars and blindness adumbrate the verbal imagery in *King Lear*, as with the ugly mutilation of Gloucester by Cornwall and with Gloucester's declaration that "These late eclipses of the sun and moon portend no good to us" (1.2.112). The way has been set for the unfolding of the play's ghastly events, which may have been determined by the stars as much as by human folly.

Eyre's ingenious prologue relies heavily for its success on imaginative lighting. Despite the bare stage and cramped set, the action nevertheless includes a striking variety of optical effects. The interior shots show the one hundred knights, a disgruntled-looking crowd, carrying on like yahoos in Goneril's palace. Goneril's understandable repugnance for these retainers comes perilously close to stealing sympathy from the king who has orchestrated this boisterous melee. Only in the outcome of the play's events do the authentic, ugly characters of Goneril and Regan appear blatantly enough to demonize them. Throughout these interior scenes, the camera-work goes far to turn the bare stage into the suggestion of a castle, and even the entertainment for the hundred riotous knights is choreographed so slickly that the skimpiness of the props goes unnoticed.

Faux exteriors, actually shot inside the studio with the help of lens filters and over-exposure, take on authenticity. Camera legerdemain bestows an uncanny mystique as Gloucester and Lear confer, in Beckett-like *Waiting for Godot* style, on the moor, looking like survivors of a botched Arctic expedition. The epic dueling scene between Edgar and Edmund, when the two men engage in an ultimate struggle, is accomplished without the drums and spears of the Brook and Kozintsev sets. Eyre manages to enclose the terror of an entire war into one tiny space.

Many other *Lear* productions are attractive and important. There is, for example, the beautiful Japanese *Ran* (1985) directed by Akira Kurosawa (1910-1988) in color. *Ran* translates as "Chaos," which describes *King Lear* quite aptly. The movie "Nipponizes" *King Lear* within the protocols of the formalistic patterns of traditional "Noh" drama. The Japanese code of juxtaposing absolute stillness as prologue to bursts of violent action dictates many editing decisions, a paradigm for this tactic being the Pearl Harbor attack. Just as Brook excels at the close-up, Kurosawa is the master of the long shot, with magnificent horsemen galloping along twilight-tinged skylines, and vistas of pastoral landscapes with rolling hills. The traditional Japanese costumes add even more sparkle and dignity. Anyone looking for a literal representation of the play will be disappointed. Kurosawa moves around the story freely, and great chunks of the movie are really more indebted to *Macbeth* than to *King Lear*.

A survey of *King Lear* in moving images would be incomplete without mention of Laurence Olivier, whose position as the twentieth century's greatest actor is contested only by John Gielgud. Michael Elliott's 1983 television production put the 75-year-old Olivier in a polystyrene mockup of Britain's prehistoric Stonehenge on Salisbury Plain. The decision to tape in color rather than in filmed tragedy's more conventional black-and-white gives the performance an almost light-hearted look, until the king's outburst of choleric rage when Cordelia rebuffs him. Olivier's acting skills remain superb; for example, the way that he manipulates his hands in response to Cordelia's blunt "Nothing," or in a repulsive moment near Dover when he mistakes a live mouse for a piece of cheese.

As with so many of Shakespeare's plays, *King Lear* has generated many modernizations and "spinoffs" from the original text. The filming of Jane Smiley's best-selling novel, *A Thousand Acres* (1997), which starred Jason Robards, Jr., and Jessica Tandy, turns the old king into a mean-spirited Midwestern farmer and child molester, whose daughters rightly despise him. Other modernizations include *The King Is Alive (*2001), a Danish film, directed by a "Dogme" group, an avant-garde filmmaking movement started in 1995, dedicated to abolishing Hollywood's seamless narrative and to shooting entirely with digital video in natural light, in this case on southwest Africa's Namib desert. The Dogme does not, however, interfere with the film's sideways glance at *King Lear*. The Turner Network's *King of Texas* (2002), unlike the Dogme film, looks straight to mainstream America for an audience to appreciate a down-home appropriation of Shakespeare's play. Patrick Stewart (seen as Jean-Luc Picard in *Star Trek*) as the old king is a ranch owner who charmingly begins the movie by hanging one of his daughter's ranch hands. After that display, things can hardly get much worse. At least the movie answers the tiresome question about what happened to the mother of the play's three young women: one of them, Susannah, says unforgettably to her father, "You're nothin' but an old tyrant. You worked our mother to death."

This partial survey of *King Lear* has put the play in the context of the modern entertainment world. Often overwhelming and frequently bewildering, rarely peaceful, difficult to fathom, even thought for decades to be impossible to stage, *King Lear* yet endures on stage and screen.

Editor's Note

In this edition, I have tried to preserve Kittredge's voice as much as possible while updating his notes. The priority for this edition was to promote the reader's understanding of the text itself; therefore I have added explanations for many words and ideas for which Kittredge assumed knowledge among his readers of classical languages, historical and mythical figures that is no longer common. I hope that the updates and additions will enhance the experience of reading and studying the play. All the added notes and amendments are followed by the editor's initials in brackets [K.S.R.] to distinguish them from Kittredge's original work. The editor's new additions to Kittredge's original notes are enclosed within the brackets.

THE TRAGEDY OF
KING LEAR

[**DRAMATIS PERSONÆ.**

Lear, King of Britain.
King of France.
Duke of Burgundy.
Duke of Cornwall.
Duke of Albany.
Earl of Kent.
Earl of Gloucester.
Edgar, son to *Gloucester.*
Edmund, bastard son to *Gloucester.*
Curan, a courtier.
Old Man, tenant to *Gloucester.*
Doctor.
Lear's Fool.
Oswald, Steward to *Goneril.*
A Captain under *Edmund's* command.
Gentleman, attendant on *Cordelia.*
A Herald.
Servants to *Cornwall.*
Goneril,
Regan, } daughters to *Lear.*
Cordelia,

Knights attending on *Lear,* Officers, Messengers, Soldiers, Attendants.

SCENE.—*Britain*

ACT I

SCENE I. [*King Lear's Palace.*]†

Enter Kent, Gloucester, and Edmund.

[Kent and Gloucester converse. Edmund stands back.]

KENT   I thought the King had more affected the Duke of Albany than Cornwall.

GLOUCESTER It did always seem so to us; but now, in the division of the kingdom,
                it appears not which of the Dukes he values most, for equalities are so
                weigh'd that curiosity in neither can make choice of either's moiety.

KENT   Is not this your son, my lord?‡   5

GLOUCESTER His breeding, sir, hath been at my charge. I have so often blush'd to
                acknowledge him that now I am braz'd to't.

KENT   I cannot conceive you.

ACT I. SCENE I. [KING LEAR'S PALACE]
1. **more affected:** inclined to favor.—**Albany:** North Britain, Scotland. 3, 4. **equalities...moiety:** the
equality of their shares is so well balanced that careful scrutiny on the part of neither can choose the
other's share as better than his own. Modern English would require the singular—*equality.* 7. **braz'd:**
hardened—literally, plated with brass. 8. **conceive you:** understand what you mean. Gloucester puns
on the word.

---

†   Directors have invented myriad ways to set up an "establishing shot" for movies of *King Lear.*
     The play's purported setting in pre-historic Britain has made calculations about the appropriate
     costumes and furnishings highly problematical and therefore most productions have erred on the
     side of simplicity for costumes and living quarters. One of the more ambitious is Michael Elliott's
     use of the famous Stonehenge circle of stones s both a framing device and a means to put Laurence
     Olivier as the old monarch in the proper context, though even that may be playing fast and loose
     with accuracy. On the other hand, Peter Brook and Grigori Kozintsev both open their films with
     "extratextual" establishing shots that clearly delineate the directors' opposing views of the social
     and political context of Lear's world. As the King in Kozintsev's production, Yuri Yarvet is im-
     mediately identified with the struggling mass of humanity crawling up the rocky hill toward his
     castle. Peter Brook's film begins with a camera panning over the blank and rather sullen faces of
     Lear's notorious one hundred knights, waiting for the arrival of Paul Scofield as the silent, aloof,
     and obdurate old king. One of the first words he unforgettably utters is "Nothing," the opening
     chord in what becomes the play's key motif. In a 1983 Royal Shakespeare Society live performance,
     Adrian Noble hit on the device of enclosing the entire stage in a blood-red map, with a focus on
     the king's obsession with the geographical division of his kingdom. But perhaps the most original
     was Richard Eyre's televised production, in which a small boy attempts to look at an eclipse (see
     Introduction and 1.3.12 note, below). For the most part the women's costumes in all production
     have been ankle-length gowns richly trimmed with furs.

‡   (*Is this not your son, my Lord?*) An important question for a director to solve is whether or not
     Edmund hears this exchange. If he does not hear what is said about him, he has no motive for hat-
     ing his father. Thus a director must decide where to place Edmund on the set, if he is to overhear
     what many believe is supposed to be a private conversation between Gloucester and Kent. And if
     Edmund stands in the background while Kent and Gloucester are talking, he hears nothing until
     he is called forward ("Do you know this noble gentleman, Edmund?"), to be introduced to "my
     Lord of Kent."

This extra-textual image from the opening of Kozintsev's 1971film version depicts great hoards of poor people anxiously awaiting news of their king's decree, thus suggesting the far reach of its impact.

GLOUCESTER Sir, this young fellow's mother could; whereupon she grew round-
womb'd, and had indeed, sir, a son for her cradle ere she had a hus-
band for her bed. Do you smell a fault?   11

KENT I cannot wish the fault undone, the issue of it being so proper.

GLOUCESTER But I have, sir, a son by order of law, some year elder than this, who
yet is no dearer in my account. Though this knave came something
saucily into the world before he was sent for, yet was his mother fair,
there was good sport at his making, and the whoreson must be ac-
knowledged.—Do you know this noble gentleman, Edmund?   17

EDMUND [comes forward] No, my lord.

GLOUCESTER My Lord of Kent. Remember him hereafter as my honorable friend.

EDMUND My services to your lordship.   20

KENT I must love you, and sue to know you better.

EDMUND Sir, I shall study deserving.

GLOUCESTER He hath been out nine years, and away he shall again. *Sound a sennet.*
The King is coming.

*Enter one bearing a coronet; then Lear; then the Dukes of Albany and Cornwall; next,
Goneril, Regan, Cordelia, with Followers.*

LEAR Attend the lords of France and Burgundy, Gloucester.   25

---

12. **proper:** handsome. 13. **some year:** a year or so; about a year. 14. **knave:** fellow—literally, boy.
Often used in playful affection.—**something:** somewhat, rather. 22. **I shall study deserving:** I shall
make every effort to be worthy of you. 23. **out:** away from Britain—seeking his fortune in a foreign
land, probably in military service. **—a sennet:** a series of notes on a trumpet announcing the approach
of a dignitary.

GLOUCESTER I shall, my liege.   *Exeunt [Gloucester and Edmund].*

LEAR   Meantime we shall express our darker purpose.
             Give me the map there. Know we have divided
             In three our kingdom; and 'tis our fast intent
             To shake all cares and business from our age,   30
             Conferring them on younger strengths while we
             Unburthen'd crawl toward death. Our son of Cornwall,
             And you, our no less loving son of Albany,
             We have this hour a constant will to publish
             Our daughters' several dowers, that future strife   35
             May be prevented now. The princes, France and Burgundy,
             Great rivals in our youngest daughter's love,
             Long in our court have made their amorous sojourn,
             And here are to be answer'd. Tell me, my daughters
             (Since now we will divest us both of rule,   40
             Interest of territory, cares of state),
             Which of you shall we say doth love us most?
             That we our largest bounty may extend
             Where nature doth with merit challenge. Goneril,
             Our eldest-born, speak first.   45

GONERIL   Sir, I love you more than words can wield the matter;
             Dearer than eyesight, space, and liberty;
             Beyond what can be valued, rich or rare;
             No less than life, with grace, health, beauty, honor;
             As much as child e'er lov'd, or father found;   50
             A love that makes breath poor, and speech unable.

---

26. **I shall:** A regular form of obedience to a command. *Shall* was felt to be more respectful than *will*, since it denotes absolute futurity, without any suggestion that obedience is a matter of *will*.—[Note how that most literate of American generals, Douglas MacArthur, used the identical phrasing when he said in WWII of going back to the Philippines, "I shall return." K.S.R.]. **liege:** my liege lord—i.e., the lord to whom I owe allegiance. 27. **we:** The "royal *we*": "I the King."—**our darker purpose:** i.e., the purpose explained in 2.49-54—to give the best share to the daughter who loves him most. This purpose had not been revealed to the Councilors, though they knew that Lear intended to divide his kingdom and had been informed what shares he meant to give [K.S.R.]. 29. **In three:** into three parts. Obviously, however, these parts (though called "thirds" in lines 73 and 121) are not thirds in the exact mathematical sense. This is made clear by lines 40-45 and 78-79. —**fast intent:** fixed purpose. 32. **crawl:** That Lear's old age is not feeble (however he may express himself) is clear from the whole of Act 1. He still goes a-hunting (1.3.7). 34. **a constant will:** Synonymous with "fast intent" (line 29). 36. **prevented:** forestalled; hindered in advance. 36. **France:** the King of France. —**Burgundy:** the Duke of Burgundy. 44. **Where...challenge:** to her whose merit, added to my natural affection, constitutes a claim to the most generous gift. *Nature with merit* means "nature *plus* merit." *With merit* should not be interpreted as "deservedly." 46. **can wield the matter:** can serve to express the fact. Mere words, Goneril says, are not strong enough to *wield*—to handle with full power of expression—the subject of her love. 47-50. **space and liberty:** *Space* expresses the idea of "freedom from confinement"; *liberty* adds the idea of "personal freedom in action." —**what:** whatever; anything that. —**grace:** favor. —**found:** found love from a child.

Beyond all manner of so much I love you.

CORDELIA   [*aside*] What shall Cordelia speak? 3rd person.
Love, and be silent.

LEAR   Of all these bounds, even from this line to this,   55
With shadowy forests and with champains rich'd,
With plenteous rivers and wide-skirted meads,
We make thee lady. To thine and Albany's issue
Be this perpetual.—What says our second daughter,
Our dearest Regan, wife to Cornwall? Speak.   60

REGAN   Sir, I am made , appraise us
Of the selfsame metal that my sister is,
And prize me at her worth. In my true heart
I find she names my very deed of love;
Only she comes too short, that I profess   65
Myself an enemy to all other joys
Which the most precious square of sense possesses,
And find I am alone felicitate
In your dear Highness' love.

CORDELIA   [*aside*]   Then poor Cordelia!
And yet not so; since I am sure my love's   70
More richer than my tongue.

LEAR   To thee and thine hereditary ever
Remain this ample third of our fair kingdom,
No less in space, validity, and pleasure
Than that conferr'd on Goneril.—Now, our joy,   75
Although the last, not least; to whose young love
The vines of France and milk of Burgundy
Strive to be interest; what can you say to draw
A third more opulent than your sisters? Speak.

CORDELIA   Nothing, my lord.   80

52. **Beyond all manner of so much:** beyond every kind of comparison that can be imagined; not "beyond the comparisons that I have just expressed." 55. **these bounds:** Lear indicates the boundaries in the map. Though he seems to give Goneril and Regan a chance to obtain the largest of the three shares, he has already determined their portions, as we learn from 29-44, and he is [somewhat sneakily. K.S.R.] reserving his "largest bounty" for Cordelia, since he is confident that she loves him most. 56. **champains:** fertile plains. —**rich'd:** enriched. 63. **prize me:** Imperative: "value me." This is better than to take *prize me* in the sense of "I appraise myself." 64. **my very deed of love:** my love as it actually *is* in fact. 65. **that:** in that; inasmuch as. 67. **Which...possesses:** which the most delicate test of one's sensibility can claim as joys. *Square* means "criterion." This meaning comes from the use of the carpenter's square for exact measurements. 68. **felicitate:** made happy. 69. **Highness':** "the love that I feel for your Majesty." 71. **More richer than my tongue:** i.e., than I can express in words. 74. **validity:** value. 76-78. **Although the last, not least.** A proverbial phrase, but not so trite in Shakespeare's time as it has since become. The Folios read "last and least," which is strongly defended by some critics, as referring not only to Cordelia's youth, but to her petite figure. —**Strive to be interest:** strive to be a claim; present their claims in rivalry.

Ian McKellen's King Lear, expecting filial obedience, smiles as if in disbelief, when Cordelia refuses to compete with sisters for their father's kingdom. (Nunn, 2008)

LEAR	Nothing?
CORDELIA	Nothing.
LEAR	Nothing can come of nothing. Speak again.
CORDELIA	Unhappy that I am, I cannot heave My heart into my mouth. I love your Majesty 85 According to my bond; no more nor less.
LEAR	How, how, Cordelia? Mend your speech a little, Lest it may mar your fortunes.
CORDELIA	Good my lord, You have begot me, bred me, lov'd me; I Return those duties back as are right fit, 90 Obey you, love you, and most honor you. Why have my sisters husbands, if they say They love you all? Haply, when I shall wed, That lord whose hand must take my plight shall carry Half my love with him, half my care and duty. 95 Sure I shall never marry like my sisters, To love my father all.

---

83. **Nothing can come of nothing:** An old proverb: *Ex nihilo nihil fit.* "Out of nothing, nothing is bred." 86. **my bond:** my bounden duty; as a daughter ought to love a father. 88. **Good my lord:** *My lord* and similar vocative phrases are often treated as single words and preceded by an adjective. 90, 91. **Return...honor you:** In return I give you those duties that are most fitting—obedience, love, and the highest honor. Thus Cordelia explains what she means by "my bond" (line 86). *Duties* are "things that are *due* to one, whether in act or feeling." —**as:** which. 93. **love you all:** bestow all their love on you. 94. **my plight:** my plighted faith in wedlock.

LEAR	But goes thy heart with this?
CORDELIA	Ay, good my lord.
LEAR	So young, and so untender?†
CORDELIA	So young, my lord, and true. 100
LEAR	Let it be so! thy truth then be thy dower!
	For, by the sacred radiance of the sun,
	The mysteries of Hecate and the night,
	By all the operation of the orbs
	From whom we do exist and cease to be; 105
	Here I disclaim all my paternal care,
	Propinquity and property of blood,
	And as a stranger to my heart and me
	Hold thee from this for ever. The barbarous Scythian,
	Or he that makes his generation messes 110
	To gorge his appetite, shall to my bosom
	Be as well neighbour'd, pitied, and reliev'd,
	As thou my sometime daughter.
KENT	Good my liege—
LEAR	Peace, Kent!
	Come not between the dragon and his wrath. 115
	I lov'd her most, and thought to set my rest
	On her kind nursery.—Hence and avoid my sight!—
	So be my grave my peace as here I give
	Her father's heart from her! Call France! Who stirs?

102-4. Lear's oath accords with his pagan religion. —**mysteries:** secret rites to which initiates only are admitted. Hecate, as the goddess of the Lower World, is the patroness of magic. —**orbs:** stars. *Operation* refers to their influence on a man's character and fortunes. 107. **Propinquity:** near relationship. —**property:** identity. Lear disclaims all kinship whatsoever. 109. **The barbarous Scythian.** By literary tradition from classical times the Scythians were regarded as the acme of all barbarians. 119. **generation:** offspring. —**messes:** portions of food. 111, 112. **to...neighbor'd:** as closely hugged to my breast; as dearly lov'd. —**pitied:** i.e., as well (as much) pitied. 113. **thou my sometime daughter:** thou who were once my daughter.—**Good my liege:** Cf. line 88, and note. —**liege:** liege lord. 115. **the dragon:** A dragon was the traditional crest of the ancient British kings. —**his wrath:** the object of his anger. 116, 117. **to set my rest:** to rely with confidence and to the full. An idiom derived from the game of *primero*, meaning literally, to "make one's bet in reliance upon the cards in one's hand." Here the word *rest* has also a suggestion of the repose to which Lear looks forward when he shall have shaken "all cares and business from [his] age" (line 30). —**nursery:** nursing; tender care. —**Hence and avoid my sight!** Addressed to Cordelia. —**avoid:** leave, not "keep out of." 119. **France:** the King of France. Cf. line 46. —**Who stirs?** Merely a form of impatient command: "Call France! and be quick about it, somebody!" Cf. "Who waits there?" and "Who's there?" as calls to an attendant.

---

†   In the televised production directed by Peter Brook, Orson Welles in the role of King Lear presents a roaring, terrifying persona of such dimensions that poor Cordelia seems totally intimidated.

Call Burgundy! Cornwall and Albany,   120
With my two daughters' dowers digest this third;
Let pride, which she calls plainness, marry her.
I do invest you jointly in my power,
Preëminence, and all the large effects
That troop with majesty. Ourself, by monthly course,   125
With reservation of an hundred knights,
By you to be sustain'd, shall our abode
Make with you by due turns. Only we still retain
The name, and all th' additions to a king. The sway,
Revenue, execution of the rest,   130
Belovèd sons, be yours; which to confirm,
This coronet part betwixt you.

KENT   Royal Lear,
Whom I have ever honor'd as my king,
Lov'd as my father, as my master follow'd,
As my great patron thought on in my prayers—   135

LEAR   The bow is bent and drawn; make from the shaft. — *ready
                                                           to snap*

KENT   Let it fall rather, though the fork invade
The region of my heart! Be Kent unmannerly
When Lear is mad. What wouldst thou do, old man?
Think'st thou that duty shall have dread to speak   140
When power to flattery bows? To plainness honor's bound
When majesty falls to folly. Reverse thy doom;
And in thy best consideration check
This hideous rashness. Answer my life my judgment,
Thy youngest daughter does not love thee least,   145
Nor are those empty-hearted whose low sound
Reverbs no hollowness.

LEAR   Kent, on thy life, no more!

---

121. **digest:** combine, incorporate. The word implies such perfect assimilation that no distinction shall hereafter be possible. 122. **Let pride...marry her:** Let her self-confidence be her dowry and (if it can) win a husband for her. —**plainness:** frankness—the quality of being "plain-spoken." 124. **the large effects:** the splendid outward tokens. 125. **Ourself:** I, the King. The royal *we*. 126. Lear reveals for the first time his plan to board with his children and to bring 100 knights with him. It was not unusual in the Elizabethan era for persons of prominence to travel with a large entourage. Queen Elizabeth's visits to the land-owning aristocracy were notorious for their size and painful financial burden on the host. As might be expected, Lear's daughters are less than happy with this plan for invasion of privacy [K.S.R]. 130. **the rest:** everything else that pertains to royalty. 136. **make from the shaft:** avoid the arrow (of my displeasure). 137. **the fork:** an arrowhead that, instead of a barb, has two points like a pitchfork. 139. **What wouldst thou do?** Manifestly a protest against Lear's unwise action in giving his whole kingdom to Goneril and Regan. 142. **Reverse thy doom:** i.e., the judgment that you have pronounced against Cordelia. 144. **rashness:** inconsiderate haste. —**Answer...judgment:** "I will stake my life on my opinion." 147. **Reverbs:** reverberates.

KENT	My life I never held but as a pawn
	To wage against thine enemies; nor fear to lose it,
	Thy safety being the motive.
LEAR	Out of my sight! 150
KENT	See better, Lear, and let me still remain
	The true blank of thine eye.
LEAR	Now by Apollo—
KENT	Now by Apollo, King,
	Thou swear'st thy gods in vain.
LEAR	O vassal! miscreant!
	[*Lays his hand on his sword.*]
ALBANY,	
CORNWALL	Dear sir, forbear! 155
KENT	Do!
	Kill thy physician, and the fee bestow
	Upon the foul disease. Revoke thy gift,
	Or, whilst I can vent clamor from my throat,
	I'll tell thee thou dost evil.
LEAR	Hear me, recreant! 160
	On thine allegiance, hear me!
	Since thou hast sought to make us break our vow—
	Which we durst never yet—and with strain'd pride
	To come between our sentence and our power,—
	Which nor our nature nor our place can bear,— 165
	Our potency made good, take thy reward.
	Five days we do allot thee for provision
	To shield thee from diseases of the world,
	And on the sixth to turn thy hated back
	Upon our kingdom. If, on the tenth day following, 170
	Thy banish'd trunk be found in our dominions,
	The moment is thy death. Away! By Jupiter,
	This shall not be revok'd.
KENT	Fare thee well, King. Since thus thou wilt appear,

---

149. **a pawn**: a pledge (as in a wager). —**To wage**: to stake, to risk. 150. **the motive**: the moving cause.
152. **The true blank of thine eye**: the mark at which thine eye directs itself in accurate sight; the counselor to whom you look for sound advice. The *blank* is the white circle at the centre of the target. 154.
vassal! A term of contempt. —**miscreant**: faithless man. 160. **recreant!** traitor—one who proves false
to his allegiance. 163. **strain'd**: over-strained, excessive. 165. **nor...nor**: neither...nor. 166. **Our potency
made good**: my royal power being in this edict asserted and carried into effect. 167. **for provision**: to
enable thee to provide means. 168. **diseases**: discomforts. 174. **thus**: i.e., as a tyrant.

Freedom lives hence, and banishment is here.   175
[*To Cordelia*] The gods to their dear shelter take thee, maid,
That justly think'st and hast most rightly said!
[*To Regan and Goneril*] And your large speeches may your deeds approve,
That good effects may spring from words of love.
Thus Kent, O princes, bids you all adieu;   180
He'll shape his old course in a country new.   *Exit.*

Flourish. Enter Gloucester, with France and Burgundy; Attendants.

GLOUCESTER Here's France and Burgundy, my noble lord.

LEAR   My Lord of Burgundy,
            We first address toward you, who with this king
            Hath rivall'd for our daughter. What in the least   185
            Will you require in present dower with her,
            Or cease your quest of love?

BURGUNDY   Most royal Majesty.
            I crave no more than hath your Highness offer'd,
            Nor will you tender less.

LEAR   Right noble Burgundy,
            When she was dear to us, we did hold her so;   190
            But now her price is fall'n. Sir, there she stands.
            If aught within that little seeming substance,
            Or all of it, with our displeasure piec'd,
            And nothing more, may fitly like your Grace,
            She's there, and she is yours.

BURGUNDY   I know no answer.   195

LEAR   Will you, with those infirmities she owes,
            Unfriended, new adopted to our hate,
            Dow'r'd with our curse, and stranger'd with our oath,
            Take her, or leave her?

BURGUNDY   Pardon me, royal sir.
            Election makes not up on such conditions.   200

LEAR   Then leave her, sir; for, by the pow'r that made me,

---

178. **approve:** prove true, confirm. 179. **effects:** acts, deeds—in fulfillment of your words. 181. **his old course:** as a faithful and plain-spoken subject. 184. **address toward you:** address myself to you. 186. **require:** ask. Not so imperative as in modern usage: i.e., "dear" in the sense of "at a high valuation," as the next line shows. 192. **that little seeming substance:** that little creature, who seems to be something *real,* but is in fact a mere vain *semblance* of reality. Lear implies that, since the love Cordelia had always shown him was only pretence, there is nothing genuine about her. 194. **like:** please. **—infirmities:** defects of fortune; disabilities. **—owes:** possesses, has. 198. **Dow'r'd...oath:** with my curse as her sole dowry, and disowned by my oath of rejection. 200. **Election...conditions:** Choice is not made—no one can make choice of a thing—when the conditions of the choice are so unfavorable.

I tell you all her wealth. [*To France*] For you, great King.
I would not from your love make such a stray
To match you where I hate; therefore beseech you
T' avert your liking a more worthier way   205
Than on a wretch whom nature is asham'd
Almost t' acknowledge hers.

FRANCE   This is most strange,
That she that even but now was your best object,
The argument of your praise, balm of your age,
Most best, most dearest, should in this trice of time   210
Commit a thing so monstrous to dismantle
So many folds of favor. Sure her offence
Must be of such unnatural degree
That monsters it, or your fore-vouch'd affection
Fall'n into taint; which to believe of her   215
Must be a faith that reason without miracle
Should never plant in me.

CORDELIA   I yet beseech your Majesty,
If for I want that glib and oily art
To speak and purpose not, since what I well intend,
I'll do't before I speak—that you make known   220
It is no vicious blot, murther, or foulness,
No unchaste action or dishonored step,
That hath depriv'd me of your grace and favor;
But even for want of that for which I am richer—
A still-soliciting eye, and such a tongue   225
As I am glad I have not, though not to have it
Hath lost me in your liking.

LEAR   Better thou
Hadst not been born than not t' have pleas'd me better.

FRANCE   Is it but this—a tardiness in nature
Which often leaves the history unspoke   230

202-4. **For:** as for. **—To:** as to. 210. **this trice:** this moment. 214. **monsters it:** makes it a monster.
—forevouch'd: heretofore attested. **—Fall'n into taint:** must have suffered decay. **—her:** Of the two
alternatives France chooses the second, for the first is to him incredible. 216 ff. Cordelia's defense is in
striking contrast with her valediction to Burgundy (lines 241-43). It is manifest which suitor she prefers.
217. **yet:** "in spite of all you have said in denunciation of me." 218. **for:** The sentence is broken—as often
in emotional speech. 221. **no vicious blot:** no fault that leaves a stain on my moral character. **—murder:**
Cordelia is thinking of such "offenses" as would be "unnatural" and "monstrous" (lines 210-11); and, of
these, murder and unchastity ("foulness") are the worst that she can imagine. 222, 223. **dishonored:**
dishonorable. **—grace and favor.** Synonyms. 224. **for which:** for want of which. 225. **still-soliciting:**
always begging favors. 227. **Hath lost me in your liking:** hath ruined me in your regard. Cordelia uses
the cold word *liking* instead of *love*. 229. **a tardiness in nature:** a natural reticence or slowness of speech.

            That it intends to do? My Lord of Burgundy,
            What say you to the lady? Love's not love
            When it is mingled with regards that stands
            Aloof from th' entire point. Will you have her?
            She is herself a dowry.

BURGUNDY   Royal Lear,   235
            Give but that portion which yourself propos'd,
            And here I take Cordelia by the hand,
            Duchess of Burgundy.

LEAR   Nothing! I have sworn; I am firm.

BURGUNDY   I am sorry then you have so lost a father   240
            That you must lose a husband.

CORDELIA   Peace be with Burgundy!
            Since that respects of fortune are his love,
            I shall not be his wife.

FRANCE   Fairest Cordelia, that art most rich, being poor;   245
            Most choice, forsaken; and most lov'd, despis'd!
            Thee and thy virtues here I seize upon.
            Be it lawful I take up what's cast away.
            Gods, gods! 'tis strange that from their cold'st neglect
            My love should kindle to inflam'd respect.
            Thy dow'rless daughter, King, thrown to my chance,   250
            Is queen of us, of ours, and our fair France.
            Not all the dukes in wat'rish Burgundy
            Can buy this unpriz'd precious maid of me.
            Bid them farewell, Cordelia, though unkind.
            Thou losest here, a better where to find.   255

LEAR   Thou hast her, France; let her be thine; for we
            Have no such daughter, nor shall ever see
            That face of hers again. Therefore be gone
            Without our grace, our love, our benison.
            Come, noble Burgundy.   260

Flourish. Exeunt Lear, Burgundy, [Cornwall, Albany, Gloucester, and Attendants].

FRANCE   Bid farewell to your sisters.

CORDELIA   The jewels of our father, with wash'd eyes
            Cordelia leaves you. I know you what you are;

233, 234. **When....point:** when it involves considerations that have nothing to do with the complete and unqualified gist of the matter—i.e., with love that is purely and simply *love*. —**entire:** complete and unqualified. 241. **Peace be with Burgundy!** A formal "good-bye." 242. **respects:** considerations. 249. **inflam'd respect:** passionate regard. 253. **unpriz'd precious.** A strong antithesis: "not prized by her father (2.190-91) but precious in my eyes." 259. **grace:** favor. —**benison:** blessing.

And, like a sister, am most loath to call
Your faults as they are nam'd. Use well our father.   265
To your professed bosoms I commit him;
But yet, alas, stood I within his grace,
I would prefer him to a better place!
So farewell to you both.

GONERIL   Prescribe not us our duties.

REGAN   Let your study   270
Be to content your lord, who hath receiv'd you
At fortune's alms. You have obedience scanted,
And well are worth the want that you have wanted.

CORDELIA   Time shall unfold what plighted cunning hides,
Who cover faults, at last shame them derides.   275
Well may you prosper!

FRANCE   Come, my fair Cordelia.†
                                   Exeunt France and Cordelia.

GONERIL   Sister, it is not little I have to say of what most nearly appertains to us
both. I think our father will hence tonight.

REGAN   That's most certain, and with you; next month with us.

GONERIL   You see how full of changes his age is. The observation we have made
of it hath not been little. He always lov'd our sister most, and with
what poor judgment he hath now cast her off appears too grossly.

REGAN   'Tis the infirmity of his age; yet he hath ever but slenderly known
himself.   284

GONERIL   The best and soundest of his time hath been but rash; then must we
look to receive from his age, not alone the imperfections of long-
ingraffed condition, but therewithal the unruly waywardness that
infirm and choleric years bring with them.

---

265. **as they are nam'd:** by their right names. 266. **professed:** stored with mere professions of love.
268. **prefer:** recommend. 270. **study:** most zealous endeavor. 271, 272. **content:** please. Much stronger
than in modern usage. —**At fortune's alms:** when fortune was doling out petty charities, not bestow-
ing bounteous awards. 273. **the want that you have wanted:** the same lack of affection that you have
shown. Your own lack of affection for your father deserves a similar lack of affection from your husband.
274. **plighted:** enfolded. Their true feelings are covered by many folds of cunning hypocrisy. 278. **will
hence:** will go hence. 281, 282. **with what poor judgment…grossly:** With cynical frankness Goneril
admits that she and Regan have spoken hypocritically and that Lear's love for Cordelia has been well-
deserved. —**grossly:** manifestly. 285-88. **time:** lifetime. —**rash:** hasty. —**long-ingraffed condition:**
a temperament that has been for a long time firmly imbedded in his nature. *Graff* is the old form of
graft. —**therewithal:** therewith; together with them. —**choleric:** irritable.

---

†   In Kozintsev's film, after Cordelia departs from her father there is a quick cut to her and France
being blessed on the roadside by a priest before setting off for the continent in a heap of creaky
wagons and scruffy cavalry.

REGAN	Such unconstant starts are we like to have from him as this of Kent's
	banishment. 290
GONERIL	There is further compliment of leave-taking between France and him.
	Pray you let's hit together. If our father carry authority with such dis-
	positions as he bears, this last surrender of his will but offend us.
REGAN	We shall further think on't.
GONERIL	We must do something, and i' th' heat. *Exeunt.* 295

SCENE II. [The Earl of Gloucester's *Castle.*]

Enter [Edmund the] Bastard solus, [with a letter].

EDMUND	Thou, Nature, art my goddess; to thy law
	My services are bound. Wherefore should I
	Stand in the plague of custom, and permit
	The curiosity of nations to deprive me,
	For that I am some twelve or fourteen moonshines 5
	Lag of a brother? Why bastard? wherefore base?
	When my dimensions are as well compact,
	My mind as generous, and my shape as true,
	As honest madam's issue? Why brand they us
	With base? with baseness? bastardy? base, base? 10
	Who, in the lusty stealth of nature, take
	More composition and fierce quality

[handwritten margin note: why does birth affect me]

289. **unconstant starts:** sudden capricious action [K.S.R.] —**like:** likely. 291-93. **compliment:** cere-mony. —**hit together:** agree in our conduct toward him. —**carry...bears:** show such a mood in wielding his power as he now manifests. —**offend us:** give us trouble instead of being a benefit. 294. **on't:** of it. 295. **do:** in contrast with *think* (line 295). Goneril, throughout the play, shows the more active and domineering spirit. It is difficult to choose between the two sisters; Regan is softer of speech, but prob-ably more venomous than Goneril [K.S.R.].

SCENE II.
This scene takes place on the day after scene 1 for "tonight" in line 24 means "last night." King Lear had left his own palace to accompany Goneril in Scene 1 (see lines 277-78). 1-22. Edmund's soliloquy rings all the changes on the words *natural* and *base* and *legitimate*. He is a "natural son"—i.e., a bastard. The Elizabethans mistakenly thought the word *bastard* to be derived from the adjective *base,* though the resemblance between the words is quite accidental [K.S.R.]. 3. **Stand in the plague of custom:** occupy a position that exposes me to the grievous disabilities that mere [conventional behavior. K.S.R.] inflicts. To *stand in* means "to be in a condition or situation." 4. **deprive me:** deprive me of the right to be my father's heir; disinherit me. Edmund is a younger son, so that even if he were legitimate, he could not inherit his father's lands. 5. **For that:** because. 6. **Lag of:** behind. 6. **Why bastard? wherefore base?** Edmund passes on to discuss the second injustice that custom does him. If *bastard* means "base son," why should he be rated as "base"—i.e., inferior, low, vile—when he is as good in mind and body as any "legitimate" son? 7-9. **my dimensions...compact:** my bodily frame is as well constructed. —**generous:** befitting a gentleman. —**true:** symmetrical. —**honest:** chaste. 10. **base?...base?** Any word, if repeated over and over in a monotone, seems to lose its significance. Edmund plays this trick with *base* and *legiti-mate,* in order to prove that they are meaningless terms. 11-15. **lusty:** vigorous. —**More composition and fierce quality:** more strength of constitution and more energetic quality of body and mind. —**fops:**

Than doth, within a dull, stale, tired bed,

[handwritten margin note: lust sex > marriage sex]

Go to th' creating a whole tribe of fops
Got 'tween asleep and wake? Well then,   15
Legitimate Edgar, I must have your land.
Our father's love is to the bastard Edmund
As to th' legitimate. Fine word—"legitimate"!
Well, my legitimate, if this letter speed,
And my invention thrive, Edmund the base   20
Shall top th' legitimate. I grow; I prosper.
Now, gods, stand up for bastards!

Enter Gloucester.

GLOUCESTER Kent banish'd thus? and France in choler parted?
And the King gone tonight? subscrib'd his pow'r?
Confin'd to exhibition? All this done   25
Upon the gad? Edmund, how now? What news?

EDMUND So please your lordship, none. *[Puts up the letter.]*

GLOUCESTER Why so earnestly seek you to put up that letter?

EDMUND I know no news, my lord.

GLOUCESTER What paper were you reading?   30

EDMUND Nothing, my lord.

GLOUCESTER No? What needed then that terrible dispatch of it into your pocket?
The quality of nothing hath not such need to hide itself. Let's see.
Come, if it be nothing, I shall not need spectacles.

EDMUND I beseech you, sir, pardon me. It is a letter from my brother that I
have not all o'er-read; and for so much as I have perus'd, I find it not
fit for your o'erlooking.   37

GLOUCESTER Give me the letter, sir.

EDMUND I shall offend, either to detain or give it. The contents, as in part I understand them, are to be blame.   40

GLOUCESTER Let's see, let's see!

---

fools, weaklings. **Got:** begotten. 17-18. **Our father's love...legitimate.** Cf. 1.1.19-20.13-17. **speed:**
prosper; succeed in its purpose. —**top.** Edwards's emendation. 23, 24. **choler:** anger. —**parted:** de-
parted, gone. —**tonight:** last night. —**subscrib'd his pow'r:** his royal power having been given up—as
one may "sign away" one's rights by *subscribing* to a document. 25. **exhibition:** an allowance (from his
daughters). 26. **Upon the gad:** on the spur of the moment. A *gad* is, literally, a *goad*. 28 ff. [Gloucester's
insistence on his right to inspect his son's private correspondence shows old-fashioned parental authority
that seems tyrannical today. K.S.R.]—**to put up:** to pocket up; to conceal. 32-33. **that terrible dispatch
of it:** that frantic haste in disposing of it.—**quality:** nature. 35. **pardon me:** excuse me from showing
it. 37. **o'erlooking:** examination, perusal. 39. **to detain:** by withholding. 40. **to blame:** blameworthy,
objectionable.

EDMUND ⁴² I hope, for my brother's justification, he wrote this but as an essay or
⁴³ taste of my virtue.

GLOUCESTER (*reads*) "This policy and reverence of age makes the world bitter to
the best of our times; keeps our fortunes from us till our oldness
cannot relish them. I begin to find an idle and fond bondage in the
oppression of aged tyranny, who sways, not as it hath power, but as it
is suffer'd. Come to me, that of this I may speak more. If our father
would sleep till I wak'd him, you should enjoy half his revenue for
ever, and live the beloved of your brother,   50

                              EDGAR."

Hum! Conspiracy? "Sleep till I wak'd him, you should enjoy half his
revenue." My son Edgar! Had he a hand to write this? a heart and
brain to breed it in? When came this to you? Who brought it?

EDMUND   It was not brought me, my lord: there's the cunning of it. I found it
thrown in at the casement of my closet.   55

GLOUCESTER You know the character to be your brother's?

EDMUND   If the matter were good, my lord, I durst swear it were his; but in respect of that, I would fain think it were not.

GLOUCESTER It is his.

EDMUND   It is his hand, my lord; but I hope his heart is not in the contents.   60

GLOUCESTER Hath he never before sounded you in this business?

EDMUND   Never, my lord. But I have heard him oft maintain it to be fit that,
sons at perfect age, and fathers declining, the father should be as ward
to the son, and the son manage his revenue.

GLOUCESTER O villain, villain! His very opinion in the letter! Abhorred villain!
Unnatural, detested, brutish villain! worse than brutish! Go, sirrah,
seek him. I'll apprehend him. Abominable villain! Where is he?   67

EDMUND   I do not well know, my lord. If it shall please you to suspend your
indignation against my brother till you can derive from him better

---

42, 43. **an essay or taste:** a test. 44-48. **This policy...times:** The established order of society that forces
the young to stand in awe of the aged deprives us of the enjoyment of life when life is at its best. *Policy*
(which often means "cunning" or "strategic art") suggests that this order of society is a clever trick on
the part of the aged. —**an idle and fond bondage:** a servitude to which it is foolish to submit. *Idle* and
fond are synonyms: "silly." —**not...suffer'd:** not by virtue of any power that it has, but merely as the
result of our submission. —**suffer'd:** allowed (to rule); submitted to. 55. **casement:** a window opening on
hinges—what we call a "French window." —**closet:** private room. 56. **character:** handwriting. "though/
thou didst produce My very character (2.1.72-73)." 57. **matter:** subject matter. 57, 58. **in respect of that:**
when I consider *that.*—**would fain think:** should be glad to think. 61. **sounded:** A nautical metaphor.
65-67. **Abhorred...detested:** Synonymous: "destestable." —**sirrah:** A form of *sir;* used in familiar address, as by parents to children or by masters to servants. —**apprehend:** arrest. —**Abominable:** The
usual Elizabethan spelling—*abhominable*—denotes the formerly accepted derivation from *ab homine,*
which suggests the word usually carried the meaning of "unnatural" or "unfit for human society."

testimony of his intent, you should run a certain course; where, if you
violently proceed against him, mistaking his purpose, it would make
a great gap in your own honor and shake in pieces the heart of his
obedience. I dare pawn down my life for him that he hath writ this to
feel my affection to your honor, and to no other pretence of danger.

GLOUCESTER Think you so?   75

EDMUND   If your honor judge it meet, I will place you where you shall hear us
confer of this and by an auricular assurance have your satisfaction,
and that without any further delay than this very evening.

GLOUCESTER He cannot be such a monster.

EDMUND   Nor is not, sure.   80

GLOUCESTER To his father, that so tenderly and entirely loves him. Heaven and
earth! Edmund, seek him out; wind me into him, I pray you; frame
the business after your own wisdom. I would unstate myself to be in a
due resolution.

EDMUND   I will seek him, sir, presently; convey the business as I shall find
means, and acquaint you withal.   86

GLOUCESTER These late eclipses in the sun and moon portend no good to us.[†]
Though the wisdom of nature can reason it thus and thus, yet nature
finds itself scourg'd by the sequent effects. Love cools, friendship
falls off, brothers divide. In cities, mutinies; in countries, discord; in
palaces, treason; and the bond crack'd 'twixt son and father. This villain of mine comes under the prediction; there's son against father:
the King falls from bias of nature; there's father against child. We
have seen the best of our time. Machinations, hollowness, treachery,
and all ruinous disorders follow us disquietly to our graves. Find out
this villain, Edmund; it shall lose thee nothing; do it carefully. And

70-74. **you should run a certain course:** you would be sure to proceed without the risk of making
a mistake. —**where:** whereas. —**to feel my affection:** to test my sentiments. —**pretence of danger:**
dangerous purpose. 76, 77 **meet:** fitting. —**by...satisfaction:** have full information by the certain evidence of hearing the facts. 80-84. **Nor...not:** Double negatives, according to the old idiom, strengthen
the negation. —**wind me into him:** worm your way into his confidence for me. —**I would...resolu-
tion:** I would abandon my rank and fortune to have my doubts cleared up one way or the other. 85-86.
presently: at once; without delay. —**convey:** manage. —**withal:** with it; with the facts of the case.
87. **eclipses.** See Introduction on the date of the play. 88, 89. **Though the wisdom...effects:** Though
scientific reasoning as to natural causes can explain the matter of eclipses in one way or another, yet the
natural world of man finds itself scourged in the results that follow. 90. **mutinies:** insurrections, riots.
93. **bias of nature:** natural course or tendency. A figure from bowling. The *bias* is the curve that the
bowl makes in its course. 94-96. **machinations:** plottings. —**lose thee nothing:** cause thee no loss. A
backhanded promise to reward his detective work.

†   (*These late eclipses of the sun and moon...*) Eyre's televised production begins with a young boy
blackening a photographic negative in order to stare safely at "one of the late eclipses of the sun"
without being blinded, as Gloucester is later. (See Introduction, p. xxii)

the noble and true-hearted Kent banish'd! his offence, honesty! 'Tis strange.   *Exit.*   98

EDMUND   This is the excellent foppery of the world, that, when we are sick in fortune, often the surfeit of our own behaviour, we make guilty of our disasters the sun, the moon, and the stars; as if we were villains on necessity; fools by heavenly compulsion, knaves, thieves, and treachers by spherical predominance; drunkards, liars, and adulterers by an enforc'd obedience of planetary influence; and all that we are evil in, by a divine thrusting on. An admirable evasion, of whoremaster man, to lay his goatish disposition to the charge of a star! My father compounded with my mother under the Dragon's Tail, and my nativity was under Ursa Major, so that it follows I am rough and lecherous. Fut! I should have been that I am, had the maidenliest star in the firmament twinkled on my bastardizing. Edgar—   110

Enter Edgar.

and pat! he comes, like the catastrophe of the old comedy. My cue is villanous melancholy, with a sigh like Tom o' Bedlam. O, these eclipses do portend these divisions! Fa, sol, la, mi.

EDGAR   How now, brother Edmund? What serious contemplation are you in?

EDMUND   I am thinking, brother, of a prediction I read this other day, what should follow these eclipses.   116

EDGAR   Do you busy yourself with that?

EDMUND   I promise you, the effects he writes of succeed unhappily: as of unnaturalness between the child and the parent; death, dearth, dissolutions of ancient amities; divisions in state, menaces and maledictions against king and nobles; needless diffidences, banishment of friends, dissipation of cohorts, nuptial breaches, and I know not what.   122

99-107. **foppery:** foolishness. —**often the surfeit of our own behavior:** Our fortune has had too much of our own foolish conduct—more than it can digest—and the result is misfortune. *Surfeit* means "overeating" and "indigestion." —**treachers:** traitors. —**by spherical predominance:** as the result of the predominance of some planet; i.e., of its being the most powerful of all the planets at the moment of our birth. —**influence:** An astrological term for the effect of a planet on one's nature and fortunes. It means literally *on-flowing,* as if a mysterious force came streaming down upon us. —**goatish:** lustful. —**nativity:** birth. 109. **Fut!** Pooh! Nonsense! [recent scholarship suggests that *fut* may be a garbled censorship of *fuck.* K.S.R.] —. **that I am:** what I am. 111. **pat:** on the dot; just when he is needed. Edmund will not be obliged to "seek him out" (line 105). —**the catastrophe:** the event which brings the plot to an end. 112. **villanous:** miserable. —**Tom o' Bedlam:** a common phrase for a vagabond maniac. Compare Edgar's description of a "Bedlam beggar" (2.3.9 ff.). *Bedlam* (i.e., Bethlehem Hospital) was the London madhouse. 113. **Fa, sol, la, mi.** Edmund sings to himself in order to seem to be in a brown study and unaware of his brother's approach. 118-22. **the effects:** the several fulfillments of the prediction.—**succeed:** follow. —**dearth:** famine. —**diffidences:** cases of mutual distrust. —**dissipation of cohorts:** the breaking up armed troops. The word *cohorts* fits the era of the play as Shakespeare seems to have imagined that era—the time of more or less Romanized Britain—though the fabled Lear's reign was long before that time.

EDGAR	How long have you been a sectary astronomical?	
EDMUND	Come, come! When saw you my father last?	
EDGAR	The night gone by.	125
EDMUND	Spake you with him?	
EDGAR	Ay, two hours together.	
EDMUND	Parted you in good terms? Found you no displeasure in him by word or countenance?	
EDGAR	None at all.	130
EDMUND	Bethink yourself wherein you may have offended him; and at my entreaty forbear his presence until some little time hath qualified the heat of his displeasure, which at this instant so rageth in him that with the mischief of your person it would scarcely allay.	
EDGAR	Some villain hath done me wrong.†	135
EDMUND	That's my fear. I pray you have a continent forbearance till the speed of his rage goes slower; and, as I say, retire with me to my lodging, from whence I will fitly bring you to hear my lord speak. Pray ye, go! There's my key. If you do stir abroad, go arm'd.	
EDGAR	Arm'd, brother?	140
EDMUND	Brother, I advise you to the best. Go arm'd. I am no honest man if there be any good meaning toward you. I have told you what I have seen and heard; but faintly, nothing like the image and horror of it. Pray you, away!	
EDGAR	Shall I hear from you anon?	145
EDMUND	I do serve you in this business. *Exit Edgar.*	
	A credulous father and a brother noble	
	Whose nature is so far from doing harms	
	That he suspects none; on whose foolish honesty	
	My practices ride easy! I see the business.	150

---

123. **a sectary astronomical:** a devotee of the astrological sect; a believer in astrology. We may note that both Edmund and Edgar have no respect for astrology. 124. **Come, come!** A smiling protest against being regarded as "a sectary astronomical." Then Edmund becomes serious, as his question shows. 129-34. **countenance:** behavior, manner. —**qualified:** modified, lessened. —**with...allay:** He would do you some bodily harm, and even then his anger would hardly be satisfied. 136. **have a continent forbearance:** restrain yourself and keep out of his presence. 143. **the image and horror:** the horrible reality. Hendiadys. [a Greek rhetorical figure in which two words do the work of one; for example, "he is nice and warm" instead of "he is nicely warm." K.S.R.] 150. **practices:** plots.

---

† In Olivier's film the wicked Edmund quickly persuades Edgar that he is in peril of being accused as a lethal enemy What is astonishing is the jumbo size of the swords wielded by the two men. Edmund's self-inflicted wound is anything but a pinprick. The effect creates a clear impression of serious trouble in the Gloucester family.

Let me, if not by birth, have lands by wit;
All with me's meet that I can fashion fit.   *Exit.*

SCENE III. [The Duke of Albany's *Palace*.]

Enter Goneril and [her] Steward [Oswald].

GONERIL   Did my father strike my gentleman for chiding of his fool?

OSWALD   Ay, madam.

GONERIL   By day and night, he wrongs me! Every hour
He flashes into one gross crime or other
That sets us all at odds. I'll not endure it.   5
His knights grow riotous, and himself upbraids us
On every trifle. When he returns from hunting,
I will not speak with him. Say I am sick.
If you come slack of former services,
You shall do well; the fault of it I'll answer. [*Horns within.*]   10

OSWALD   He's coming, madam; I hear him.

GONERIL   Put on what weary negligence you please,
You and your fellows. I'd have it come to question.
If he distaste it, let him to our sister,
Whose mind and mine I know in that are one,   15
Not to be overrul'd. Idle old man,
That still would manage those authorities
That he hath given away! Now, by my life,
Old fools are babes again, and must be us'd
With checks as flatteries, when they are seen abus'd.   20
Remember what I have said.

OSWALD   Very well, madam.

---

152. **All…fit:** Everything, in my opinion, is proper for me that I can shape to fit my designs. —**fashion fit:** literally, make fitting by manipulation.
SCENE III.
Between this scene and scene I, there is an interval of less than a fortnight (1.4.266-67), during which King Lear has resided with Goneril. Shakespeare allows the audience first to see the old king living with his relatively mild Goneril before plunging him into the nightmare world of Cornwall and Regan, though Goneril turns out to be the more effectively aggressive of the two sisters [K.S.R.].
2. Coleridge calls Oswald "the only character of utter unredeemable *baseness* in Shakespeare." Note however Oswald's fidelity at the point of death (4.6.238-43). 3, 4. **By day and night:** An oath. King Lear also swears by day and night in 1.1.102-3. —**crime:** offense. The word was less specialized than in modern usage. 6. **His knights grow riotous.** See 1.4.47, note. 10. **answer:** be answerable for. 14. **distaste:** dislike. 16. **Idle:** foolish, silly. Cf. 1.2.46. 19. **us'd:** treated. 20. **With checks…abus'd:** not merely with *soothing words,* but, when they are seen to be deluded as to their position in life, with *rebukes* as well. Children are sometimes coaxed, sometimes scolded: the same treatment must be applied to childish old men. —**they:** The antecedent is *old fools,* not *flatteries.*

GONERIL   And let his knights have colder looks among you.
What grows of it, no matter. Advise your fellows so.
I would breed from hence occasions, and I shall,
That I may speak. I'll write straight to my sister   25
To hold my very course. Prepare for dinner.   *Exeunt.*

SCENE IV. [The Duke of Albany's *Palace*.]

Enter Kent, [disguised].

KENT   If but as well I other accents borrow,
That can my speech defuse, my good intent
May carry through itself to that full issue
For which I raz'd my likeness. Now, banish'd Kent,
If thou canst serve where thou dost stand condemn'd,   5
So may it come, thy master, whom thou lov'st,
Shall find thee full of labors.

Horns within. Enter Lear, [Knights,] and Attendants.

LEAR   Let me not stay a jot for dinner; go get it ready. [*Exit an Attendant.*]
How now? What art thou?

KENT   A man, sir.   10

LEAR   What dost thou profess? What wouldst thou with us?

KENT   I do profess to be no less than I seem, to serve him truly that will put
me in trust, to love him that is honest, to converse with him that is
wise and says little, to fear judgment, to fight when I cannot choose,
and to eat no fish.   15

LEAR   What art thou?

KENT   A very honest-hearted fellow, and as poor as the King.

23-25. **Advise...so:** Give your fellow servants similar instructions. Goneril takes the lead in the plot against her father, but Regan is quite ready to fall in with her plans. —**occasions:** opportunities. —**straight:** straightway, immediately.

SCENE IV.
This scene is practically continuous with scene 3.
2. **defuse:** disguise—literally, disorder. 4. **raz'd my likeness:** made my appearance unrecognizable. 5. **canst serve:** canst manage to be engaged as a servant. Thus Kent explains why he has "raz'd his likeness." 7. **Horns within.** Lear "returns from hunting"(1.3.7). This is significant. He is hale and hearty, though eighty years of age (4.7.61). 11-14. **What dost thou profess?** Lear means, "What is thy profession (i.e., trade or calling)?" Kent, in his reply, twists the sense of *profess.* —**honest:** honorable. —**converse:** associate. —**judgment:** i.e., God's final judgment, which will call all men to account. 14. **cannot choose:** cannot help it. —**to eat no fish.** Since many of the Roman Catholics of Shakespeare's time were hostile to the government, this phrase became proverbial in the sense of "to be a sound Protestant and loyal to the state."

LEAR	If thou be'st as poor for a subject as he's for a king, thou art poor enough. What wouldst thou?
KENT	Service. 20
LEAR	Who wouldst thou serve?
KENT	You.
LEAR	Dost thou know me, fellow?
KENT	No, sir; but you have that in your countenance which I would fain call master. 25
LEAR	What's that?
KENT	Authority.
LEAR	What services canst thou do?
KENT	I can keep honest counsel, ride, run, mar a curious tale in telling it and deliver a plain message bluntly. That which ordinary men are fit for I am qualified in, and the best of me is diligence. 31
LEAR	How old art thou?
KENT	Not so young, sir, to love a woman for singing, nor so old to dote on her for anything. I have years on my back forty-eight.
LEAR	Follow me; thou shalt serve me. If I like thee no worse after dinner, I will not part from thee yet. Dinner, ho, dinner! Where's my knave? my fool? Go you and call my fool hither. *[Exit an Attendant.]* 37

Enter [Oswald the] Steward.

	You, you, sirrah, where's my daughter?
OSWALD	So please you— *Exit.*
LEAR	What says the fellow there? Call the clotpoll back.*[Exit a Knight.]* Where's my fool, ho? I think the world's asleep. 41

[Enter Knight.]

	How now? Where's that mongrel?
KNIGHT	He says, my lord, your daughter is not well.
LEAR	Why came not the slave back to me when I call'd him?
KNIGHT	Sir, he answered me in the roundest manner, he would not. 45

---

24. **countenance:** bearing—not merely "face." 29. **can keep honest counsel:** can keep a secret when it is an honorable one. —**curious:** elaborate; complicated. Kent implies that he is too outspoken to be a skillful talker. 33. **to love:** as to love. 36. **knave:** boy. Often used as a term of familiarity—sometimes in affection, sometimes in contempt. 38. **sirrah.** See 1.2.66, note. 39. **So please you:** if you please—literally, may it be pleasing to you. Oswald obeys Goneril and "puts on weary negligence" in his treatment of the King (1.3). 40. **clotpoll:** stupid creature, literally, "one who has a clod of earth for a head." 45. **roundest:** plainest; most outspoken.

LEAR	He would not?
KNIGHT	My lord, I know not what the matter is; but to my judgment your Highness is not entertain'd with that ceremonious affection as you were wont. There's a great abatement of kindness appears as well in the general dependants as in the Duke himself also and your daughter. 51
LEAR	Ha! say'st thou so?
KNIGHT	I beseech you pardon me, my lord, if I be mistaken; for my duty cannot be silent when I think your Highness wrong'd.
LEAR	Thou but rememb'rest me of mine own conception. I have perceived a most faint neglect of late, which I have rather blamed as mine own jealous curiosity than as a very pretence and purpose of unkindness. I will look further into't. But where's my fool? I have not seen him this two days. 59
KNIGHT	Since my young lady's going into France, sir, the fool hath much pined away.
LEAR	No more of that; I have noted it well. Go you and tell my daughter I would speak with her. [*Exit Knight.*] Go you, call hither my fool. *[Exit an Attendant.]*

Enter [Oswald the] Steward.

	O, you, sir, you! Come you hither, sir. Who am I, sir?
OSWALD	My lady's father. 65
LEAR	"My lady's father"? My lord's knave! You whoreson dog! you slave! you cur!
OSWALD	I am none of these, my lord; I beseech your pardon.
LEAR	Do you bandy looks with me, you rascal? [*Strikes him.*]
OSWALD	I'll not be strucken, my lord. 70
KENT	Nor tripp'd neither, you base football player? [*Trips up his heels.*]
LEAR	I thank thee, fellow. Thou serv'st me, and I'll love thee.

---

47 ff. We observe that Lear's Knights never show riotous or quarrelsome behavior. They justify the King's favorable testimony (lines 235-38), Goneril's assertions to the contrary are mere falsehood. 48. **entertain'd:** treated. 49. **appears:** that appears. 55. **remembr'st:** remindest. —**conception:** idea. 56. **a most faint neglect:** a very languid and neglectful manner. Lear's phrase repeats the Knight's "a great abatement of kindness" (line 49). It is synonymous with Goneril's phrase, "weary negligence" (1.3.12). 57. **jealous curiosity:** suspicious watchfulness about trifles. 69. **bandy:** literally, to "bat to and fro," as a ball in tennis. 71. **football player:** Football was regarded as a low game in Shakespeare's day.

| KENT | Come, sir, arise, away! I'll teach you differences. Away, away! If you will measure your lubber's length again, tarry; but away! Go to! Have you wisdom? So.   75 |

[Pushes him out.]

| LEAR | Now, my friendly knave, I thank thee. There's earnest of thy service.   *[Gives money.]* |

Enter Fool.

| FOOL | Let me hire him too. Here's my coxcomb.   *[Offers Kent his cap.]* |

| LEAR | How now, my pretty knave? How dost thou? |

| FOOL | Sirrah, you were best take my coxcomb.   80 |

| KENT | Why, fool? |

| FOOL | Why? For taking one's part that's out of favor. Nay, an thou canst not smile as the wind sits, thou'lt catch cold shortly. There, take my coxcomb! Why, this fellow hath banish'd two on's daughters, and did the third a blessing against his will. If thou follow him, thou must needs wear my coxcomb—How now, nuncle? Would I had two coxcombs and two daughters!   87 |

| LEAR | Why, my boy? |

| FOOL | If I gave them all my living, I'ld keep my coxcombs myself. There's mine! beg another of thy daughters.   90 |

| LEAR | Take heed, sirrah—the whip. |

| FOOL | Truth's a dog must to kennel; he must be whipp'd out, when Lady the brach may stand by th' fire and stink.† |

---

73. **I'll teach you differences:** I'll teach you to observe the proper distinctions of rank. 74. **Go to!** A mere interjection of impatience or protest, like "Come, come!" The phrase literally means "Go away!" 75. **So:** There, that's right! Off you go! 77. **earnest:** a small sum paid in advance to bind a bargain. 78. **coxcomb:** The professional fool (the jester), whether in real life or on the stage, wore a hood or cap crested with a piece of red flannel, patterned after the comb of a cock. 83. **an:** if. —**smile as the wind sits:** take sides with the party that's in power. 84, 85. **banish'd:** By dividing his kingdom between Goneril and Regan Lear has made his daughters independent, and so he has lost them. —**on's:** of his. —**did the third a blessing:** His banishment of Cordelia has made her Queen of France. 86. **needs:** Emphatic: "None but a fool would be Lear's follower now." —. **How now, nuncle?** Hullo, uncle. How d'you do? —**nuncle:** contracted from *mine uncle.* 89, 90. Thus he calls Lear a double-dyed fool. 91. **the whip:** Whipping was the punishment for fools who took too great liberties, as it was for naughty children. Lear's fool has apparently escaped whipping for many a day. He is a privileged character—"all-licens'd," as Goneril calls him (line 170); but Lear uses the customary warning. 92, 93. **Truth...stink:** Truth is whipped out of the hall; but Flattery is allowed to keep a comfortable place by the fire, no matter how ill she behaves. —**Lady:** a common name for a *brach,* i.e., a bitch hound. "Lady, my brach."

---

† (*Stand by the fire and stink*) In Trevor Nunn's televised production the Fool crouches and passes wind, much to the delight of everyone on stage. Scatological humor was popular in early-modern England (See note 1.4.207 below).

LEAR	A pestilent gall to me!

FOOL   Sirrah, I'll teach thee a speech.   95

LEAR   Do.

FOOL   Mark it, nuncle.
>   Have more than thou showest,
>   Speak less than thou knowest,
>   Lend less than thou owest,   100
>   Ride more than thou goest,
>   Learn more than thou trowest,
>   Set less than thou throwest;
>   Leave thy drink and thy whore,
>   And keep in-a-door,   105
>   And thou shalt have more
>   Than two tens to a score.

KENT   This is nothing, fool.

FOOL   Then 'tis like the breath of an unfeed lawyer—you gave me nothing
for't. Can you make no use of nothing, nuncle?   110

LEAR   Why, no, boy. Nothing can be made out of nothing.

FOOL   [*to Kent*] Prithee tell him, so much the rent of his land comes to. He
will not believe a fool.

LEAR   A bitter fool!

FOOL   Dost thou know the difference, my boy, between a bitter fool and a
sweet fool?   116

LEAR   No, lad; teach me.

FOOL   That lord that counsell'd thee
>   To give away thy land,
>   Come place him here by me—   120
>   Do thou for him stand.
>   The sweet and bitter fool

---

94. **A pestilent gall to me!** This fellow is always making me wince by his satirical gibes! So, in line 115,
Lear exclaims, "A bitter fool!" —**pestilent:** plaguey. —**gall:** an irritation; an irritating creature. To *gall*
is, literally, to "rub the skin off, so as to make a sore spot." To *gall at* is to "taunt." 98-107. A string of
prudential maxims: "Don't show all the money you have. Don't tell everything you know. Don't lend
your last penny. Don't tire yourself out with walking when you have a horse to ride. Don't believe everything you hear. Don't stake at the next throw of the dice all the money that you have just won. Give up
drinking and licentiousness and remain quietly at home instead of gadding about. Follow these precepts
and your savings will increase." 100. **owest:** ownest; dost possess. 105. **in-a-door:** indoors. 118-25. As
he speaks these verses the Fool places himself opposite Lear and at some little distance. He accompanies
the recitation with gestures. 118, 119. **That lord...land:** The Fool implies that nobody gave Lear such
idiotic advice: Lear was his own foolish counselor. 121. **Do thou for him stand:** Stand where you are
and impersonate that lord.

	Will presently appear;	
	The one in motley here,	
	The other found out there.	125

LEAR   Dost thou call me fool, boy?

FOOL   All thy other titles thou hast given away; that thou wast born with.†

KENT   This is not altogether fool, my lord.

FOOL   No, faith; lords and great men will not let me. If I had a monopoly
          out, they would have part on't. And ladies too, they will not let me
          have all the fool to myself; they'll be snatching. Give me an egg,
          nuncle, and I'll give thee two crowns.   132

LEAR   What two crowns shall they be?

FOOL   Why, after I have cut the egg i' th' middle and eat up the meat, the
          two crowns of the egg. When thou clovest thy crown i' th' middle and
          gav'st away both parts, thou bor'st thine ass on thy back o'er the dirt.
          Thou hadst little wit in thy bald crown when thou gav'st thy golden
          one away. If I speak like myself in this, let him be whipp'd that first
          finds it so.
          [Sings] Fools had ne'er less grace in a year,   140
                  For wise men are grown foppish;
              They know not how their wits to wear,
              Their manners are so apish.

LEAR   When were you wont to be so full of songs, sirrah?

FOOL   I have us'd it, nuncle, ever since thou mad'st thy daughters thy
          mother; for when thou gav'st them the rod, and put'st down thine
          own breeches,   147

---

123. **presently:** instantly. 124, 125. **The one:** i.e., the sweet fool. He points at himself. *Motley* is the
regular word for a fool's ludicrously variegated costume. See note on line 80. —**The other...there:** i.e.,
yourself, "the bitter fool." He points at Lear. 127. **that thou wast born with:** Thus he calls Lear "a born
fool"—an idiot. 129-32. The Fool picks up Kent's phrase ("altogether fool") and plays with it as if it
meant "one who has all the folly that there is." —**a monopoly:** a royal patent entitling me to be the
sole dealer in foolishness. —**out:** granted me. —**they would have part on't...snatching:** the courtiers
who had helped me to secure the monopoly would insist on having their share—and so would the court
ladies. Monopolies, and the bribery or corrupt influence by means of which they were often obtained,
were constant subjects of satire in Shakespeare's time. 133-34. The answer to the Fool's conundrum is
obvious, since *crowns* was a common term for the two parts of the eggshell; but Lear wishes to let him
make his joke. Conundrums are not meant to be guessed. 136. **thou...dirt:** You acted as foolishly as a
man who carries his ass instead of letting it carry him. The Fool remembers a well-known fable. 138,
139. **If I speak...so:** If I am a fool to be so outspoken, do not have me whipped for my foolish frankness; let *him* be whipped who first discovers that I have told you the truth. The implication is that Lear
has already made this discovery and that *he*, if anybody, should be whipped for folly. 141-43. **foppish:**
silly. —**apish:** ridiculous, grotesque.

---

†   (*All those other titles thou has given away*)In Nunn's production, Ian McKellen's King Lear laughs
     uproariously here, as if the Fool is making a great joke.

[*Sings*] Then they for sudden joy did weep,
  And I for sorrow sung,
  That such a king should play bo-peep   150
  And go the fools among.

Prithee, nuncle, keep a schoolmaster that can teach thy fool to lie. I
would fain learn to lie.

LEAR An you lie, sirrah, we'll have you whipp'd.

FOOL I marvel what kin thou and thy daughters are. They'll have me
whipp'd for speaking true; thou'lt have me whipp'd for lying; and
sometimes I am whipp'd for holding my peace. I had rather be any
kind o' thing than a fool! And yet I would not be thee, nuncle. Thou
hast pared thy wit o' both sides and left nothing i' th' middle. Here
comes one o' the parings.   160

     Enter Goneril.

LEAR How now, daughter? What makes that frontlet on? Methinks you are
too much o' late i' th' frown.

FOOL Thou wast a pretty fellow when thou hadst no need to care for her
frowning. Now thou art an O without a figure. I am better than thou
art now: I am a fool, thou art nothing. [*To Goneril*] Yes, forsooth, I
will hold my tongue. So your face bids me, though you say nothing.
Mum, mum!   167
  He that keeps nor crust nor crum,
  Weary of all, shall want some.
[*Points at Lear*] That's a sheal'd peascod.   170

GONERIL Not only, sir, this your all-licens'd fool,
But other of your insolent retinue
Do hourly carp and quarrel, breaking forth
In rank and not-to-be-endured riots. Sir,
I had thought, by making this well known unto you, 175
To have found a safe redress, but now grow fearful,
By what yourself, too, late have spoke and done,
That you protect this course, and put it on
By your allowance; which if you should, the fault
Would not scape censure, nor the redresses sleep, 180

148, 149. **Then they...sung:** The Fool adapts an old song. 150. **should play bo-peep:** should be so
childish as to hide himself—i.e., renounce his royalty. 160. **one o' the parings:** Goneril, he argues,
must have half of the King's wits, since he parted with all his wits when he gave away his kingdom. 161.
makes: is doing. —**frontlet:** a forehead cloth; a band worn on the forehead by ladies. Lear uses the term
figuratively. 164. **an O:** a cipher, a zero. 168. **crum:** the soft part of the loaf. 170. **a shell'd peascod:** a
shelled peapod. 171-73. **all-licens'd:** privileged to say and do anything and everything. —**carp:** find
fault. 176. **safe:** sure. 178, 179. **put it on:** encourage it. —**allowance:** approval.

Which, in the tender of a wholesome weal,
Might in their working do you that offence
Which else were shame, that then necessity
Must call discreet proceeding.

FOOL   For you know, nuncle,   185
                The hedge-sparrow fed the cuckoo so long
                That it had it head bit off by it young.
            So out went the candle, and we were left darkling.

LEAR   Are you our daughter?

GONERIL   Come, sir,   190
            I would you would make use of that good wisdom
            Whereof I know you are fraught, and put away
            These dispositions that of late transform you
            From what you rightly are.

FOOL   May not an ass know when the cart draws the horse?   195
            Whoop, Jug, I love thee!

LEAR   Doth any here know me? This is not Lear.
            Doth Lear walk thus? speak thus? Where are his eyes?
            Either his notion weakens, his discernings
            Are lethargied—Ha! waking? 'Tis not so!   200
            Who is it that can tell me who I am?

FOOL   Lear's shadow.

LEAR   I would learn that; for, by the marks of sovereignty,
            Knowledge, and reason, I should be false persuaded
            I had daughters.   205

FOOL   Which they will make an obedient father.

LEAR   Your name, fair gentlewoman?†

181-84. **Which...proceeding:** [Goneril's warning to her father is couched in elaborate syntactical tangles. K.S.R.] And the acts of redress that we should find necessary in our care for a sound condition of the state might, in their operation, annoy you to an extent which, under other circumstances, would be shameful, but which the necessities of the case would at this juncture force one to style discreet procedure on our part. 186, 187. The cuckoo lays its eggs in other birds' nests. **—it...it:** its...its. **—by it young:** by its ungrateful nestling—the young cuckoo. 188. **So...darkling:** It was not unusual for a fool, after making some rather outrageous jest which might call for censure, to cap it with a bit of pure nonsense in order to raise a laugh and thus avoid trouble. Lear's Fool seems to resort to this professional trick here, as he certainly does in line 196 and in 3.2.33. **—darkling:** in the dark. 192. **Whereof:** with which. **— fraught:** well furnished—literally, freighted. 193. **dispositions:** states of mind; fits of capricious temper. 195. **an ass:** even a fool like me. 193. **Whoop, Jug, I love thee!** Doubtless accompanied by a grimace and a caper. See note on line 188. **—Jug:** a nickname for *Joan.* 199. **his notion:** his understanding. 200. **waking?** Am I awake? 203-5. **that:** i.e., who I am. Lear pays no attention to the Fool's speech. **—the marks of sovereignty...daughters:** the outward signs of sovereignty, which would persuade me that I

---

†   (*fair gentlewoman*) In Nunn's production, McKellen's King Lear crouches to pass wind here and
     is hailed with laughter by his hundred knights.

GONERIL   This admiration, sir, is much o' th' savor
             Of other your new pranks. I do beseech you
             To understand my purposes aright.   210
             As you are old and reverend, you should be wise.
             Here do you keep a hundred knights and squires;
             Men so disorder'd, so debosh'd, and bold
             That this our court, infected with their manners,
             Shows like a riotous inn. Epicurism and lust   215
             Make it more like a tavern or a brothel
             Than a grac'd palace. The shame itself doth speak
             For instant remedy. Be then desir'd
             By her that else will take the thing she begs
             A little to disquantity your train,   220
             And the remainder that shall still depend
             To be such men as may besort your age,
             Which know themselves, and you.

LEAR   Darkness and devils!
             Saddle my horses! Call my train together!
             Degenerate bastard, I'll not trouble thee;   225
             Yet have I left a daughter.

GONERIL   You strike my people, and your disorder'd rabble
             Make servants of their betters.

                      Enter Albany.

LEAR   Woe that too late repents!—O, sir, are you come?
             Is it your will? Speak, sir!—Prepare my horses.   230
             Ingratitude, thou marble-hearted fiend,
             More hideous when thou show'st thee in a child
             Than the sea-monster!

ALBANY   Pray, sir, be patient.

LEAR   [*to Goneril*] Detested kite, thou liest!
             My train are men of choice and rarest parts,   235

---

am King Lear—and *he*, I know, had daughters. *Knowledge* and *reason* are not to be taken as in apposition
with "the marks of sovereignty." 206. **Which…father:** Yes, you have daughters; and they will make you
an obedient father. **—Which:** whom. 208. **This admiration:** this pretending to wonder who you are.
212. **keep:** support, maintain. 213. **disorder'd:** disorderly. **—debosh'd:** debauched. 214. **manners:**
conduct and character. Cf. Latin *mores.* 215. **Shows:** appears. **—Epicurism:** riotous living. 217. **grac'd:**
honorable. 220. **disquantity your train:** reduce the size of your retinue. 221, 222. **depend:** attend you
as dependents; remain in your service. **—besort:** befit. 229. **Woe that:** Woe to him that. 233. **Than the
sea-monster:** than any monster of the deep. **—patient:** calm. 234. **Detested:** detestable. Cf. 1.2.65.
235. **choice and rarest:** choicest and rarest. **—parts:** qualities. Those critics who regard Goneril's com-
plaints about the behavior of Lear's attendants as more or less justified fail to note the manifest purpose
of Lear's words here. That his Knights were well-behaved is indicated also by the moderation of speech
and manner shown by one of them in lines 43 ff.

That all particulars of duty know
And in the most exact regard support
The worships of their name.—O most small fault,
How ugly didst thou in Cordelia show!
Which, like an engine, wrench'd my frame of nature   240
From the fix'd place; drew from my heart all love
And added to the gall. O Lear, Lear, Lear!
Beat at this gate that let thy folly in

[Strikes his head.]

And thy dear judgment out! Go, go, my people.

ALBANY   My lord, I am guiltless, as I am ignorant   245
Of what hath mov'd you.

LEAR   It may be so, my lord.
Hear, Nature, hear! dear goddess, hear!
Suspend thy purpose, if thou didst intend
To make this creature fruitful.
Into her womb convey sterility;   250
Dry up in her the organs of increase;
And from her derogate body never spring
A babe to honor her! If she must teem,
Create her child of spleen, that it may live
And be a thwart disnatur'd torment to her.   255
Let it stamp wrinkles in her brow of youth,
With cadent tears fret channels in her cheeks,
Turn all her mother's pains and benefits
To laughter and contempt, that she may feel
How sharper than a serpent's tooth it is   260
To have a thankless child! Away, away!†   *Exit.*

ALBANY   Now, gods that we adore, whereof comes this?

GONERIL   Never afflict yourself to know the cause;
But let his disposition have that scope
That dotage gives it.   265

---

238. **worships:** honor. 239. **show:** appear. 240. **my frame of nature:** the whole structure of my nature. The figure is that of a building that is thrown off its foundation ("the fix'd place") by a powerful mechanical contrivance. *Engine* was a general word for a machine of any kind. 242. **gall:** bitterness. 244. **dear:** precious. 251, 252. **increase:** fertility. —**derogate:** blighted (by barrenness)—literally, deteriorated. 253. **teem:** bear children. 255. **thwart:** perverse—always feeling and acting in opposition. —**disnatur'd:** unnatural. 256-58. **brow of youth:** youthful brow. —**cadent:** falling. —**fret:** wear. —**pains:** care. 264. **disposition:** mood. Cf. line 193.

---

† (*Hear, Nature...thankless child*) In Nunn's production Goneril begins slowly breaking down during her father's curse. A few lines later ("I'll tell thee," lines 268 ff.), at these words she begins weeping.

Enter Lear.

LEAR   What, fifty of my followers at a clap?
        Within a fortnight?

ALBANY   What's the matter, sir?

LEAR   I'll tell thee. [*To Goneril*] Life and death! I am asham'd
        That thou hast power to shake my manhood thus;
        That these hot tears, which break from me perforce,   270
        Should make thee worth them. Blasts and fogs upon thee!
        Th' untented woundings of a father's curse
        Pierce every sense about thee!—Old fond eyes,
        Beweep this cause again, I'll pluck ye out,
        And cast you, with the waters that you lose,   275
        To temper clay. Yea, is it come to this?
        Let it be so. Yet have I left a daughter,
        Who I am sure is kind and comfortable.
        When she shall hear this of thee, with her nails
        She'll flay thy wolvish visage. Thou shalt find   280
        That I'll resume the shape which thou dost think
        I have cast off for ever; thou shalt, I warrant thee.
                        Exeunt [Lear, Kent, and Attendants].

GONERIL Do you mark that, my lord?

ALBANY   I cannot be so partial, Goneril,
         To the great love I bear you—   285

GONERIL Pray you, content.—What, Oswald, ho!
         [*To the Fool*] You, sir, more knave than fool, after your master!

FOOL   Nuncle Lear, nuncle Lear, tarry! Take the fool with thee.
             A fox, when one has caught her,
             And such a daughter,   290
             Should sure to the slaughter,
             If my cap would buy a halter.
             So the fool follows after.

GONERIL This man hath had good counsel! A hundred knights?
         'Tis politic and safe to let him keep   295

---

267. **Within a fortnight.** Less than a fortnight, then, has elapsed since the end of scene 1. 271. **Blasts and fogs upon thee!** Fog and mist were thought to contain the seeds of pestilence. —**Blasts:** blighting strokes of pestilence. 272. **untented:** that are too deep to be probed; or, more exactly, to be searched with a *tent*—a slender roll of lint with which wounds are cleansed. 273-6. **fond:** foolish. —**lose:** waste, since these tears are of no avail. —**temper:** moisten, soften. — 277. **Yet:** The emphatic *yet:* "after all"; "in spite of everything." 278. **comfortable:** ready to give me aid and comfort. 289. **content:** be satisfied; don't worry. 288. **Take the fool with thee:** An absolutely perfect pun. The literal sense is obvious; but the phrase was a regular farewell gibe: "Take the epithet 'fool' with you as you go!" "Good-bye, fool as you are!". 291, 292. **Should sure to:** should certainly be sent to. —**a halter:** a hangman's rope.

At point a hundred knights; yes, that on every dream,
Each buzz, each fancy, each complaint, dislike,
He may enguard his dotage with their pow'rs,
And hold our lives in mercy.—Oswald, I say!

ALBANY   Well, you may fear too far.

GONERIL   Safer than trust too far.   300
Let me still take away the harms I fear,
Not fear still to be taken. I know his heart.
What he hath utter'd I have writ my sister.
If she sustain him and his hundred knights,
When I have show'd th' unfitness—

Enter [Oswald the] Steward.

                    How now, Oswald?   305
What, have you writ that letter to my sister?

OSWALD   Yes, madam.

GONERIL   Take you some company, and away to horse!
Inform her full of my particular fear,
And thereto add such reasons of your own   310
As may compact it more. Get you gone,
And hasten your return. [*Exit Oswald.*] No, no, my lord!
This milky gentleness and course of yours,
Though I condemn it not, yet, under pardon,
You are much more at task for want of wisdom   315
Than prais'd for harmful mildness.

ALBANY   How far your eyes may pierce I cannot tell.
Striving to better, oft we mar what's well.

GONERIL   Nay then—

ALBANY   Well, well; th' event.   *Exeunt.*   320

---

296. **At point:** fully equipped. 297. **buzz:** whisper; idle rumor. 301. **still:** ever, always. 302. **Not...taken:** rather than always live in fear to be attacked by some harm. 309. **particular:** own. 311. **compact it more:** make what I fear seem more solid, more substantial. 314. **under pardon:** if you will pardon me for saying so. 315. **at task:** taken to task; blameworthy. 316. **for harmful mildness:** for lenity that may prove injurious. 320. **th' event:** Let us wait for the outcome. That will show which of us is right. [If Albany seems "hen-pecked," he also shows physical courage and moral awareness. K.S.R.].

SCENE V. [*Court before the* Duke of Albany's *Palace.*]

Enter Lear, Kent, and Fool.

LEAR   Go you before to Gloucester with these letters. Acquaint my daughter no further with anything you know than comes from her demand out of the letter. If your diligence be not speedy, I shall be there afore you.

KENT   I will not sleep, my lord, till I have delivered your letter.   *Exit.*

FOOL   If a man's brains were in's heels, were't not in danger of kibes?   5

LEAR   Ay, boy.

FOOL   Then I prithee be merry. Thy wit shall ne'er go slipshod.

LEAR   Ha, ha, ha!

FOOL   Shalt see thy other daughter will use thee kindly; for though she's as like this as a crab's like an apple, yet I can tell what I can tell.   10

LEAR   What canst tell, boy?

FOOL   She'll taste as like this as a crab does to a crab. Thou canst tell why one's nose stands i' th' middle on's face?

LEAR   No.

FOOL   Why, to keep one's eyes of either side's nose, that what a man cannot smell out, 'a may spy into.   16

LEAR   I did her wrong.

FOOL   Canst tell how an oyster makes his shell?

LEAR   No.

FOOL   Nor I neither; but I can tell why a snail has a house.   20

LEAR   Why?

FOOL   Why, to put's head in; not to give it away to his daughters, and leave his horns without a case.

LEAR   I will forget my nature. So kind a father!—Be my horses ready?

SCENE V.
This scene occurs on the same day as scenes 3 and 4.

1-3. **these letters:** this letter. —**demand:** question, enquiry. —**out of:** suggested by. 5. **in's:** in his. —**'t:** it—i.e., his brain. —**kibes:** heel sores, chilblains. [a swelling caused by the cold. K.S.R.] 7. **slipshod:** in slippers, because of heel sores; for you have no wits and therefore will have no kibes on them. 9, 10. **Shalt:** Thou shalt. —**kindly:** The Fool puns on *kindly* in the ordinary sense and in the sense of "according to her nature." —**a crab:** a wild apple, a crabapple—notoriously sour. 11. **canst:** can you. 13-16. **on's:** of his. —**of:** on. —**side's:** side [of] his. —**'a:** he. 22-23. **put's:** put his. —**horns.** Shakespeare's audience immediately recognized the cliche "horns" joke, for which they were on the alert. [For some reason "horns" were always identified with cuckoldry and their identification with married men was thought to be hilarious. K.S.R.]

FOOL   Thy asses are gone about 'em. The reason why the seven stars are no
            moe than seven is a pretty reason.   26

LEAR   Because they are not eight?

FOOL   Yes indeed. Thou wouldst make a good fool.

LEAR   To take't again perforce! Monster ingratitude!

FOOL   If thou wert my fool, nuncle, I'ld have thee beaten for being old be-
            fore thy time.   31

LEAR   How's that?

FOOL   Thou shouldst not have been old till thou hadst been wise.

LEAR   O, let me not be mad, not mad, sweet heaven!
            Keep me in temper; I would not be mad!   35

                        [Enter a Gentleman.]

            How now? Are the horses ready?

GENTLEMAN   Ready, my lord.

LEAR   Come, boy.

FOOL   She that's a maid now, and laughs at my departure,
            Shall not be a maid long, unless things be cut shorter.   *Exeunt.* 40

25-27. **the seven stars:** the Pleiades. —**moe:** more. Not a contraction of *more* but an independent forma-
tion from the same root. —**not eight?** The Fool has intentionally prepared a conundrum so obvious that
the answer is inevitable. Then he can make the point that he wishes: "Thou wouldst make a good fool";
"You're good at this kind of foolery." 29. **To tak't again perforce:** He is meditating on his resumption
of his royalty. 35. **in temper:** in a normal condition of mind. *Temper* is literally one's natural "temperament" or "disposition." 39, 40. This bit of buffoonery is addressed to the audience. The Fool holds the
stage for a moment before he follows his master.

ACT II

SCENE I. [*A court within the Castle of the* Earl of Gloucester.]

Enter [Edmund the] Bastard and Curan, meeting.

EDMUND   Save thee, Curan.

CURAN   And you, sir. I have been with your father, and given him notice that the Duke of Cornwall and Regan his Duchess will be here with him this night.

EDMUND   How comes that?   5

CURAN   Nay, I know not. You have heard of the news abroad—I mean the whisper'd ones, for they are yet but ear-kissing arguments?

EDMUND   Not I. Pray you, what are they?   *gossip -*

CURAN   Have you heard of no likely wars toward 'twixt the two Dukes of Cornwall and Albany?   10

EDMUND   Not a word.

CURAN   You may do, then, in time. Fare you well, sir.   *Exit.*

EDMUND   The Duke be here tonight? The better! best!
This weaves itself perforce into my business.
My father hath set guard to take my brother;   15
And I have one thing, of a queasy question,
Which I must act. Briefness and fortune, work!
Brother, a word! Descend! Brother, I say!

Enter Edgar.

My father watches. O sir, fly this place!
Intelligence is given where you are hid.   20
You have now the good advantage of the night.

ACT II. SCENE I.

Many readers have found the sequence of events confusing to follow as Lear moves around among his daughters' castles. This scene opens in the night that follows Lear's departure for the Duke of Cornwall's castle at the end of 1.5, and closes just before dawn on the next day.

1. **Save thee:** God save thee. A common greeting, to which Curan makes the conventional answer. The introduction of Curan as a messenger gives yet another example of the way that Shakespeare employs minor characters as messengers to implement the plot. 7. **ones:** *News* was originally a plural—"new things." —**ear-kissing:** whispered. —**arguments:** subjects of speech; remarks. 9. **toward:** coming; in the near future. 16. **of a queasy question:** *Queasy* is, literally, "qualmish" and applies to an uneasy condition of the stomach. 18. **Descend!** Edgar is hiding in Edmund's chamber.

Have you not spoken 'gainst the Duke of Cornwall?
He's coming hither; now, i' th' night, i' th' haste,
And Regan with him. Have you nothing said
Upon his party 'gainst the Duke of Albany?   25
Advise yourself.

EDGAR   I am sure on't, not a word.

EDMUND   I hear my father coming. Pardon me!
In cunning I must draw my sword upon you.
Draw, seem to defend yourself; now quit you well.—
Yield! Come before my father. Light, ho, here!   30
Fly, brother.—Torches, torches!—So farewell.   *Exit Edgar.*
Some blood drawn on me would beget opinion
Of my more fierce endeavour. [*Stabs his arm.*]
I have seen drunkards
Do more than this in sport.—Father, father!—   35
Stop, stop! No help?

                Enter Gloucester, and Servants with torches.

GLOUCESTER Now, Edmund, where's the villain?

EDMUND   Here stood he in the dark, his sharp sword out,
Mumbling of wicked charms, conjuring the moon
To stand's auspicious mistress.

GLOUCESTER   But where is he?   40

EDMUND   Look, sir, I bleed.

GLOUCESTER   Where is the villain, Edmund?

EDMUND   Fled this way, sir. When by no means he could—

GLOUCESTER Pursue him, ho! Go after.   [*Exeunt some Servants.*]
By no means what?

EDMUND   Persuade me to the murther of your lordship;   45
But that I told him the revenging gods
'Gainst parricides did all their thunders bend;
Spoke with how manifold and strong a bond
The child was bound to th' father—sir, in fine,

22-26. **Have you not spoken,** etc.: Have you not committed yourself, on one side or the other, in the quarrel between the two Dukes? See lines 9-25.—**Upon his party:** on *his* side. —**Advise yourself:** Bethink yourself; consider. 28. **In cunning:** as a trick—in order that I may not seem to be in collusion with you. 29. **quit you well:** put up a vigorous defense. 34, 35. **I have seen...sport.** A wild gallant would sometimes stab his arm and mix the blood with the wine when he drank his lady's health. 39, 40. **Mumbling of wicked charms,** etc. Edmund adapts his story to his father's superstition. —**stand's:** stand his. 46, 47. **that:** when that, when. —**revenging:** avenging. —**bend:** direct, aim.

Seeing how loathly opposite I stood   50
To his unnatural purpose, in fell motion
With his prepared sword he charges home
My unprovided body, lanch'd mine arm;
But when he saw my best alarum'd spirits,
Bold in the quarrel's right, rous'd to th' encounter,   55
Or whether gasted by the noise I made,
Full suddenly he fled.

GLOUCESTER   Let him fly far.
Not in this land shall he remain uncaught;
And found—dispatch. The noble Duke my master,
My worthy arch and patron, comes tonight.   60
By his authority I will proclaim it,
That he which finds him shall deserve our thanks,
Bringing the murderous caitiff to the stake;
He that conceals him, death.

EDMUND   When I dissuaded him from his intent   65
And found him pight to do it, with curst speech
I threaten'd to discover him. He replied,
"Thou unpossessing bastard, dost thou think,
If I would stand against thee, would the reposal
Of any trust, virtue, or worth in thee   70
Make thy words faith'd? No. What I should deny
(As this I would; ay, though thou didst produce
My very character), I'd turn it all
To thy suggestion, plot, and damned practice;
And thou must make a dullard of the world,   75
If they not thought the profits of my death
Were very pregnant and potential spurs
To make thee seek it."

GLOUCESTER   Strong and fast'ned villain!
Would he deny his letter? I never got him.

                                        Tucket within.

---

50. **loathly opposite:** bitterly opposed. 51-53. **fell:** fierce. —**home:** with an attempt at a home thrust. —**unprovided:** undefended—since I was not on my guard. —**lanch'd:** lanced, pierced. 54. **my best alarum'd spirits:** all my best powers (energies) called to arms (*all' arme*). 56. **gasted.** A strong word—"panic-stricken." 59. **dispatch:** finish him. 60. **worthy:** honorable. —**arch and patron:** chief patron. 63. **caitiff:** wretch, rascal. —**to the stake:** to the place of execution; to his death. A figure derived from the stake to which one was fastened for execution by fire. Not to be taken literally. 66, 67. **pight:** determined. *Pight* is the past participle of *pitch,* "to fix firmly" (as in "pitch a tent"). —**curst:** angry. —**discover him:** reveal his purpose. 71-74. **faith'd:** believed, trusted.—**character:** handwriting. —**suggestion:** evil suggestion. —**practice.** Synonymous with *plot.* 77. **pregnant and potential:** ready and powerful. 78. **fast'ned:** confirmed (in his villainy). 79. **his letter?** See 1.2.35 ff. —**got:** begot. —**Tucket:** A succession of notes on a trumpet. Gloucester recognizes this particular tucket as the Duke's special signal. —**within:** behind the scenes.

Hark, the Duke's trumpets! I know not why he comes.   80
All ports I'll bar; the villain shall not scape;
The Duke must grant me that. Besides, his picture
I will send far and near, that all the kingdom
May have due note of him, and of my land,
Loyal and natural boy, I'll work the means   85
To make thee capable.

Enter Cornwall, Regan, and Attendants.

CORNWALL   How now, my noble friend? Since I came hither
(Which I can call but now) I have heard strange news.

REGAN   If it be true, all vengeance comes too short
Which can pursue th' offender. How dost, my lord?   90

GLOUCESTER   O madam, my old heart is crack'd, it's crack'd!

REGAN   What, did my father's godson seek your life?
He whom my father nam'd? your Edgar?

GLOUCESTER   O lady, lady, shame would have it hid!

REGAN   Was he not companion with the riotous knights   95
That tend upon my father?†

GLOUCESTER   I know not, madam. 'Tis too bad, too bad!

EDMUND   Yes, madam, he was of that consort.

REGAN   No marvel then though he were ill affected.
'Tis they have put him on the old man's death,   100
To have th' expense and waste of his revenues.
I have this present evening from my sister
Been well inform'd of them, and with such cautions
That, if they come to sojourn at my house,
I'll not be there.

CORNWALL   Nor I, assure thee, Regan.   105
Edmund, I hear that you have shown your father

---

81. **ports:** seaports. See 2.3.3. 85. **natural:** Gloucester has both senses of the word in mind. Edmund is his "natural son" and (he thinks) feels for him the "natural affection" of a son for a father. 86. **capable:** *Capable of* means "legally capable of inheriting." Gloucester promises to legitimatize the bastard by due process of law. 90. **dost?** dost thou? 92, 93. Thus Regan venomously suggests a subtle association between her father's character and Edgar's plot of parricide. She is more outspoken in lines 100-101. 98. **consort:** Often used in contempt or reprobation—as if it were a "gang." 99. **though:** if. —**were ill affected:** had disloyal sentiments toward you. 100. **put him on:** incited him to. 101. **expense:** spending. 105. **assure thee:** assure thyself; be assured.

---

†   (*Was he not companion with the riotous knights*) At this point, in Trevor Nunn's production, Regan and Cornwall are introduced as steady drinkers, sipping continuously throughout the play.

A childlike office.

EDMUND   'Twas my duty, sir.

GLOUCESTER He did bewray his practice, and receiv'd
             This hurt you see, striving to apprehend him.

CORNWALL   Is he pursued?

GLOUCESTER   Ay, my good lord.   110

CORNWALL   If he be taken, he shall never more
             Be fear'd of doing harm. Make your own purpose,
             How in my strength you please. For you, Edmund,
             Whose virtue and obedience doth this instant
             So much commend itself, you shall be ours.   115
             Natures of such deep trust we shall much need;
             You we first seize on.

EDMUND   I shall serve you, sir,
             Truly, however else.

GLOUCESTER   For him I thank your Grace.

CORNWALL   You know not why we came to visit you—

REGAN   Thus out of season, threading dark-ey'd night.   120
             Occasions, noble Gloucester, of some poise,
             Wherein we must have use of your advice.
             Our father he hath writ, so hath our sister,
             Of differences, which I best thought it fit
             To answer from our home. The several messengers 125
             From hence attend dispatch. Our good old friend,
             Lay comforts to your bosom, and bestow
             Your needful counsel to our business,
             Which craves the instant use.

GLOUCESTER   I serve you, madam.
             Your Graces are right welcome.†   *Exeunt. Flourish.*   130

---

107. **A childlike office:** dutiful service befitting a son. 108, 109. **bewray:** reveal; make known. —**prac-tice:** plot. —**apprehend:** arrest. 112, 113. **of:** with reference to. —**Make...please:** Form your own plan for his capture and punishment, using my authority in any way that may seem good to you. —**For:** as for. 115. **ours:** The "royal *we.*" 120. **threading:** making our way through. 121. **poise:** weight, impor-tance. 124, 125. **differences:** disputes. —**which:** which letters. —**from our home:** when away from home. 126. **attend dispatch:** are waiting to be sent. 129. **craves the instant use:** requires to be carried out without delay.

---

† *(Your graces are right welcome)* As everyone exits in Trevor Nunn's televised production, Regan (Monica Dolan) and Edmund (Philip Winchester) leave together, with Regan smiling flirtatiously.

SCENE II. [*Before* Gloucester's *Castle.*]

Enter Kent and [Oswald the] Steward, severally.

OSWALD   Good dawning to thee, friend. Art of this house?

KENT   Ay.

OSWALD   Where may we set our horses?

KENT   I' th' mire.

OSWALD   Prithee, if thou lov'st me, tell me.   5

KENT   I love thee not.

OSWALD   Why then, I care not for thee.

KENT   If I had thee in Lipsbury Pinfold, I would make thee care for me.

OSWALD   Why dost thou use me thus? I know thee not.

KENT   Fellow, I know thee.   10

OSWALD   What dost thou know me for?

KENT   A knave; a rascal; an eater of broken meats; a base, proud, shallow, beggarly, three-suited, hundred-pound, filthy, worsted-stocking knave; a lily-liver'd, action-taking, whoreson, glass-gazing, superserviceable, finical rogue; one-trunk-inheriting slave; one that wouldst be a bawd in way of good service, and art nothing but the composition of a knave, beggar, coward, pander, and the son and heir of a mongrel bitch; one whom I will beat into clamorous whining, if thou deny the least syllable of thy addition.   19

SCENE II.
This scene begins and closes about sunrise on the same day on which scene 1 ends (2.2.170).
1. **Art of:** Art thou of; Do you belong to? 8. **in Lipsbury Pinfold.** A *pinfold* is a cattle pound—a pen in which stray cattle are confined. *Lipsbury* means "Lipsburgh" "Liptown." "In the Liptown pen,' then, is "in the enclosure adjacent to the lips," i.e., "'between my teeth,'" "in my jaws"; and so, "in my clutches." 12-19. Kent upbraids Oswald as a cowardly menial who parades as a gentleman. —**three-suited:** Edgar, in the guise of Poor Tom, when he describes himself as formerly a serving-man, declares that he then "had three suits to his back" (3.4.113). This seems to have been the regular allowance for a manservant. —**hundred pound:** a hundred-pound gentleman, i.e., one of very small property. —**worsted-stocking:** Gentlemen wore silk stockings. —**lily-liver'd:** white-livered; i.e., having no blood in your liver, and therefore cowardly. —**action-taking:** going to law instead of meeting one's enemy in combat. —**glass-gazing:** always preening himself in a mirror. —**superserviceable:** ready to serve one's master in ways that are beyond the limits of honorable service. —**finical:** fussy about trifles. —**one-trunk-inheriting:** all of whose possessions are contained in a single box or trunk. To *inherit* means to "possess" (cf. 4.6.123). —**bawd:** pander, procurer. —**in way of good service:** if it comes in your day's work as a devoted servant. —**the composition:** a compound. —**and heir.** A fine touch!—not merely the *son*, but the *heir*, inheriting all the mongrel's qualities. —**thy addition:** the titles I have just given thee.

OSWALD	Why, what a monstrous fellow art thou, thus to rail on one that's neither known of thee nor knows thee!
KENT	What a brazen-fac'd varlet art thou, to deny thou knowest me! Is it two days ago since I beat thee and tripp'd up thy heels before the King? [*Draws his sword.*] Draw, you rogue! for, though it be night, yet the moon shines. I'll make a sop o' th' moonshine o' you. Draw, you whoreson cullionly barbermonger! draw! 26
OSWALD	Away! I have nothing to do with thee.
KENT	Draw, you rascal! You come with letters against the King, and take Vanity the puppet's part against the royalty of her father. Draw, you rogue, or I'll so carbonado your shanks! Draw, you rascal! Come your ways! 31
OSWALD	Help, ho! murther! help!
KENT	Strike, you slave! Stand, rogue! Stand, you neat slave! Strike! [*Beats him.*]
OSWALD	Help, ho! murther! murther! 35

Enter Edmund, with his rapier drawn, Gloucester, Cornwall, Regan, Servants.

EDMUND	How now? What's the matter?	*Parts [them].*
KENT	With you, goodman boy, an you please! Come, I'll flesh ye! Come on, young master!	
GLOUCESTER	Weapons? arms? What's the matter here?	
CORNWALL	Keep peace, upon your lives! 40 He dies that strikes again. What is the matter?	
REGAN	The messengers from our sister and the King.	
CORNWALL	What is your difference? Speak.	
OSWALD	I am scarce in breath, my lord.	
KENT	No marvel, you have so bestirr'd your valor. You cowardly rascal, nature disclaims in thee; a tailor made thee. 46	
CORNWALL	Thou art a strange fellow. A tailor make a man?	

---

21. **of thee:** by thee. 25-26. **I'll make…o' you:** I'll drill you full of holes, so that the moonlight can soak into you until you are a mere sop, steeped in moonshine. —**Draw:** draw your sword. —**cullionly:** vile.—**barbermonger:** constant dealer with barbers for the care of your hair and beard. 29-34. **Vanity the puppet.** Puppet shows were popular in Shakespeare's time. They frequently produced morality plays with allegorical *dramatis personæ*. —**carbonado:** slash (as a piece of meat for broiling). —**Come your ways!** Come on! On your way! —**you neat slave:** you foppish fellow. See line 46: "a tailor made thee." 36. **What's the matter?** What's the quarrel about? 37. **With you:** A challenge: "My quarrel is with *you*, if you like!" "I am ready to fight with *you*!" —**goodman boy.** A form of address to a presumptuous youngster. —**flesh ye!** initiate you; give you your first taste of fighting. 43. **your difference:** your dispute.

KENT	Ay, a tailor, sir. A stonecutter or a painter could not have made him so ill, though he had been but two hours at the trade.	
CORNWALL	Speak yet, how grew your quarrel?	50
OSWALD	This ancient ruffian, sir, whose life I have spar'd At suit of his grey beard—	
KENT	Thou whoreson zed! thou unnecessary letter! My lord, if you'll give me leave, I will tread this unbolted villain into mortar and daub the walls of a jakes with him. "Spare my grey beard," you wagtail?	55
CORNWALL	Peace, sirrah! You beastly knave, know you no reverence?	
KENT	Yes, sir, but anger hath a privilege.	
CORNWALL	Why art thou angry?	
KENT	That such a slave as this should wear a sword. Who wears no honesty. Such smiling rogues as these, Like rats, oft bite the holy cords atwain Which are too intrinse t' unloose; smooth every passion That in the natures of their lords rebel, Bring oil to fire, snow to their colder moods; Renege, affirm, and turn their halcyon beaks With every gale and vary of their masters, Knowing naught (like dogs) but following. A plague upon your epileptic visage! Smile you my speeches, as I were a fool? Goose, an I had you upon Sarum Plain, I'd drive ye cackling home to Camelot.	60 65 70
CORNWALL	What, art thou mad, old fellow?	
GLOUCESTER	How fell you out? Say that.	

53-55. **zed!...unnecessary letter!** The letter z is unnecessary because its sound is usually expressed by *s*. —**this unbolted villain:** this unsifted rascal; this fellow who is rascal through-and-through. — **daub:** plaster. —**a jakes:** a privy. —**wagtail?** A comically uneasy bird, so called from the spasmodic up-and-down jerking of its tail. Oswald is too scared to stand still. 61. **honesty:** honorable character. 62, 63. **the holy cords:** the sacred bonds of family affection.—**too intrinse:** tied in too close and intricate a knot. —**smooth:** aid and abet by their flattery. *Smooth* for "flatter" is common. 66. **Renege, affirm:** say "no" or "yes" to suit their masters' varying moods. —**renege:** deny. The g is pronounced like g in *get*. —**turn their halcyon beaks:** It was believed that the halcyon (kingfisher), if hung up, would serve as a weathervane, turning about so that its beak would always point in the direction from which the wind comes. 67. **gale and vary:** Hendiadys (see note on 1.2.143): "varying gale," "turn of the wind." 68. **following:** always *following* their master, though they do not know whether he is right or wrong. 69. **epileptic:** Oswald is trying to smile, but he is so frightened that his face looks as if he were in a fit. 70. **Smile:** smile at. —**as...fool:** as if I were a jester trying to make you laugh. 71, 72. **Sarum Plain:** Salisbury Plain. —**Camelot:** the site of King Arthur's court. Tradition identified it with an anciently fortified hill near Cadbury. In the moors in that vicinity there were flocks of geese.

KENT	No contraries hold more antipathy	75
	Than I and such a knave.	
CORNWALL	Why dost thou call him knave? What is his fault?	
KENT	His countenance likes me not.	
CORNWALL	No more perchance does mine, or his, or hers.	
KENT	Sir, 'tis my occupation to be plain.	80
	I have seen better faces in my time	
	Than stands on any shoulder that I see	
	Before me at this instant.	
CORNWALL	This is some fellow	
	Who, having been prais'd for bluntness, doth affect	
	A saucy roughness, and constrains the garb	85
	Quite from his nature. He cannot flatter, he!	
	An honest mind and plain—he must speak truth!	
	An they will take it, so; if not, he's plain.	
	These kind of knaves I know which in this plainness	
	Harbor more craft and more corrupter ends	90
	Than twenty silly-ducking observants	
	That stretch their duties nicely.	
KENT	Sir, in good faith, in sincere verity,	
	Under th' allowance of your great aspect,	
	Whose influence, like the wreath of radiant fire	95
	On flickering Phœbus' front—	
CORNWALL	What mean'st by this?	
KENT	To go out of my dialect, which you discommend so much. I know,	
	sir, I am no flatterer. He that beguil'd you in a plain accent was a plain	
	knave, which, for my part, I will not be, though I should win your	
	displeasure to entreat me to't.	100

75. **antipathy:** The phenomena which more recent science has explained by the doctrine of "attraction and repulsion" were ascribed to "sympathy and antipathy" in the nature of objects. 78. **likes:** pleases. 80. **plain:** plain-spoken. 85, 86. **constrains the garb…nature:** puts on by force the style of blunt sauciness in speech, quite contrary to his real nature. —**from:** literally "away from," and so, "contrary to." 88-90. **so:** well and good! —**These kind:** A common old idiom. —**ends:** purposes. 91-96. **silly-ducking observants:** obsequious parasites, who are always making low bows after their ridiculous fashion. —**stretch their duties nicely:** exert themselves to be as precise and accurate as possible in performing their duties. —**nicely:** punctiliously. Kent parodies the style and manner of a "silly-ducking observant." —**in sincere verity:** an affected synonym for "in good faith." —**Under…influence:** with humble submission to the sovereign sway of your Highness, whose influence, etc. —**aspect:** An astrological term denoting the way in which a planet *looks upon* a man, i.e., with good or bad effect. —**influence:** Another astrological term. Cf. 1.2.100-101. —**Phœbus' front:** the forehead of the sun. —**mean'st:** meanest thou. 98-100. **He that beguil'd you…to't:** I infer from what you have said that, in the past, some such rascal as you describe has deceived you. If so, he was an out-and-out knave—and *that* I will never be, even if I could induce you to lay aside your displeasure so far as to beg me to be one.

CORNWALL   What was th' offence you gave him?

OSWALD   I never gave him any.
            It pleas'd the King his master very late
            To strike at me, upon his misconstruction;
            When he, conjunct, and flattering his displeasure,   105
            Tripp'd me behind; being down, insulted, rail'd
            And put upon him such a deal of man
            That worthied him, got praises of the King
            For him attempting who was self-subdu'd;
            And, in the fleshment of this dread exploit,   110
            Drew on me here again.

KENT   None of these rogues and cowards
            But Ajax is their fool.

CORNWALL   Fetch forth the stocks!†
            You stubborn ancient knave, you reverent braggart,
            We'll teach you—

KENT   Sir, I am too old to learn.   115
            Call not your stocks for me. I serve the King;
            On whose employment I was sent to you.
            You shall do small respect, show too bold malice
            Against the grace and person of my master,
            Stocking his messenger.   120

CORNWALL   Fetch forth the stocks! As I have life and honor,
            There shall he sit till noon.

104, 105. **upon his misconstruction:** as the result of misinterpreting something he said. —**conjunct:** taking the King's part; taking sides with him. 108-10. **That worthied him:** as won honor for himself. —**For…self-subdu'd:** for attacking one who submitted without a struggle. —**in the fleshment:** while still in the ferocious mood that this dread exploit produced. To *flesh* a dog was to "make him fierce by feeding him on raw meat." 113. **Ajax is their fool:** the great hero Ajax is (by their own account) a fool in comparison with *them*—i.e., vastly their inferior. 114. **stubborn:** fierce, ferocious. —**reverent:** reverend. 118. **shall:** will assuredly. —**malice:** ill will. Not here used in the limited modern sense. 119. **grace and person.** As the King's messenger, Kent is to be treated with respect. 121. **Fetch the stocks.** [Cornwall's directive here brings the play's language to new depths of cruelty, as Regan joins in by volunteering ideas for even more painful punishments, such as putting Kent outside all night. K.S.R.]. Such a punishment would be not only an outrage on the King's *grace* (i.e., his royal honor) but a *personal* insult to him.

---

†   The scenes in front of Gloucester's palace are enormously enhanced by the clever back lighting in Richard Eyre's version, where Kent and Oswald ("Draw, you rascal") struggle until the "fiery" Duke himself intervenes to investigate the cause of the quarrel. When the Duke cries out "Fetch forth the stocks," an absolutely terrifying machine is dragged out for Kent's pinioning so that he will suffer horribly, with a tight collar around his neck. Meanwhile, in the background while this sadistic tableau takes place, Edmund flirts erotically with a seductive and attractive Regan. The Duke himself delivers a memorable scolding to Kent on the hypocrisy of posing as blunt and plain-spoken, when one is exactly the opposite. The combination of erotic and sadistic elements brings the play close to the twentieth century's fashionable Theater of Cruelty.

REGAN   Till noon? Till night, my lord, and all night too!

KENT   Why, madam, if I were your father's dog,
             You should not use me so.

REGAN   Sir, being his knave, I will.   125

CORNWALL   This is a fellow of the selfsame color
             Our sister speaks of. Come, bring away the stocks!

                                     Stocks brought out.

GLOUCESTER   Let me beseech your Grace not to do so.
             His fault is much, and the good King his master
             Will check him for't. Your purpos'd low correction   130
             Is such as basest and contemn'dest wretches
             For pilf'rings and most common trespasses
             Are punish'd with. The King must take it ill
             That he, so slightly valued in his messenger,
             Should have him thus restrain'd.

CORNWALL   I'll answer that.   135

REGAN   My sister may receive it much more worse,
             To have her gentleman abus'd, assaulted,
             For following her affairs. Put in his legs.—
             [*Kent is put in the stocks.*]
             Come, my good lord, away.

                          Exeunt [all but Gloucester and Kent].

GLOUCESTER   I am sorry for thee, friend. 'Tis the Duke's pleasure,   140
             Whose disposition, all the world well knows,
             Will not be rubb'd nor stopp'd. I'll entreat for thee.

KENT   Pray do not, sir. I have watch'd and travell'd hard.
             Some time I shall sleep out, the rest I'll whistle.
             A good man's fortune may grow out at heels.   145
             Give you good morrow!

GLOUCESTER   The Duke's to blame in this; 'twill be ill taken.   *Exit.*

KENT   Good King, that must approve the common saw,
             Thou out of heaven's benediction com'st
             To the warm sun!   150

---

125. **should:** would certainly. 127. **bring away:** bring along; bring hither. 130. **check:** rebuke. 132.
pilf'rings: petty thefts. 135. **answer:** be accountable for. 142. **Will not be:** will not allow itself to be.
—**rubb'd:** impeded; interfered with. This sense comes from bowling. A *rub* is anything that hinders or
deflects the course of the bowl. 143. **watch'd:** gone without sleep. 145. **A good man's:** even a *good* man's.
146. **Give...morrow!** God give you good morning! 147. **to blame:** blameworthy, censurable. 148. **must
approve the common saw:** art fated, it seems, to exemplify the familiar saying. 149, 150. **Thou...sun!**
The proverb describes bad judgment by the figure of one who, on a hot day, leaves a comfortable seat in
the shade for a place in the sun.

Approach, thou beacon to this under globe,
That by thy comfortable beams I may
Peruse this letter. Nothing almost sees miracles
But misery. I know 'tis from Cordelia,
Who hath most fortunately been inform'd   155
Of my obscured course—and [*reads*] "shall find time
From this enormous state, seeking to give
Losses their remedies"—All weary and o'er-watch'd,
Take vantage, heavy eyes, not to behold
This shameful lodging.   160
Fortune, good night; smile once more, turn thy wheel.   *Sleeps.*

[SCENE III. *The open country.*]

Enter Edgar.

EDGAR   I heard myself proclaim'd,
And by the happy hollow of a tree
Escap'd the hunt. No port is free, no place
That guard and most unusual vigilance
Does not attend my taking. Whiles I may scape,   5
I will preserve myself; and am bethought
To take the basest and most poorest shape
That ever penury, in contempt of man,
Brought near to beast. My face I'll grime with filth,†
Blanket my loins, elf all my hair in knots,   10
And with presented nakedness outface
The winds and persecutions of the sky.
The country gives me proof and precedent

153-54. **Nothing...misery:** for, when we are in despair, any relief seems miraculous. 156. **my obscured course:** my course of action in this disguise. **—shall find time.** Kent is reading from Cordelia's letter. 157. **this enormous state:** the present anomalous condition of the realm. 158, 159. **o'er-watch'd:** worn out by lack of sleep. To *watch* often means to "be awake." **—Take vantage:** Take advantage of drowsiness. 161. **turn thy wheel.** On Fortune's wheel, see the note on 5.3.174.

SCENE III.
This scene takes place on the same day as scene 2.
1. **proclaim'd:** Cf. 2.1.80-84. 2. **happy:** opportune. 3. **No port is free.** Cf. 2.1.81.
6. **am bethought:** it occurs to me; it comes to my mind. 8. **in contempt of man:** as if to show how contemptible a creature a man may be. 10. **elf...knots:** Matted and tangled locks of hair—due to neglect and filthy habits—were ascribed to the action of mischievous elves and hence called "elflocks". 11. **presented:** meeting them boldly. **—outface:** defy. 13. **proof:** example.

---

†   (*My face I'll grime*) In Trevor Nunn's production, Edgar (Ben Meyjes) strips off his shirt and rubs filth into his face and hair, disguising himself as an escapee from St. Mary's of Bethleham (Bedlam) Hospital.

Of Bedlam beggars, who, with roaring voices,
Strike in their numb'd and mortified bare arms   15
Pins, wooden pricks, nails, sprigs of rosemary;
And with this horrible object, from low farms,
Poor pelting villages, sheepcotes, and mills,
Sometime with lunatic bans, sometime with prayers,
Enforce their charity. "Poor Turlygod! poor Tom!"   20
That's something yet! Edgar I nothing am.   *Exit.*

[SCENE IV. *Before* Gloucester's *Castle*; Kent *in the stocks.*]

Enter Lear, Fool, and Gentleman.

LEAR   'Tis strange that they should so depart from home,
            And not send back my messenger.

GENTLEMAN   As I learn'd,
            The night before there was no purpose in them
            Of this remove.

KENT   Hail to thee, noble master!

LEAR   Ha!   5
            Mak'st thou this shame thy pastime?

KENT   No, my lord.

FOOL   Ha, ha! look! he wears cruel garters.

            Horses are tied by the head, dogs and bears by th' neck, monkeys by
            th' loins, and men by th' legs. When a man 's over-lusty at legs, then
            he wears wooden nether-stocks.   10

---

14. **Bedlam beggars.** [Escaped patients. K.S.R.]. *Bedlam* is merely a shortened form of *Bethlehem,* the London hospital for the mentally ill, which was originally a priory of the religious order of the Star of Bethlehem. 15. **mortified:** deadened by hardship and exposure. A stronger synonym of *numbed.* 17, 18. **object:** sight, spectacle. 238. **low:** lowly, humble. —**pelting:** paltry, insignificant. —**sheepcotes, and mills:** both of which were often distant from any village. 19. **Sometime:** sometimes. —**bans:** curses. 20. **"Poor Turlygod! poor Tom!"** Edgar practices the Bedlam beggar's whine. For *Tom* cf. "Tom o' Bedlam" (1.2.147). *Turlygod* seems to have been a name by which such a beggar sometimes called himself, but it occurs nowhere else. 21. **There's something yet! Edgar I nothing am:** As Poor Tom there is, after all, some hope for me. In my real character as Edgar, I am as good as dead—i.e., I have no chance of preserving my life.

SCENE IV.
This scene takes place on the day that was dawning at the end of scene 2—on the same day, therefore, as Scene 3.
2. **my messenger:** i.e., Kent. See 1.5.1. 7-10. **cruel:** with a pun on *crewel,* "worsted" [wool. K.S.R.]. —**monkeys by th' loins.** Monkeys were kept as pets by the Elizabethan ladies. —**over-lusty at legs:** too vigorous in using his legs; too much of a vagabond. —**nether-stocks:** stockings. Overstocks (upper stocks) were breeches.

LEAR   What's he that hath so much thy place mistook
             To set thee here?

KENT   It is both he and she—
             Your son and daughter.

LEAR   No.

KENT   Yes.   15

LEAR   No, I say.

KENT   I say yea.

LEAR   No, no, they would not!

KENT   Yes, they have.

LEAR   By Jupiter I swear no!   20

KENT   By Juno I swear ay!

LEAR   They durst not do't;
             They would not, could not do't. 'Tis worse than murther
             To do upon respect such violent outrage.
             Resolve me with all modest haste which way
             Thou mightst deserve or they impose this usage,   25
             Coming from us.

KENT   My lord, when at their home
             I did commend your Highness' letters to them,
             Ere I was risen from the place that show'd
             My duty kneeling, came there a reeking post,   30
             Stew'd in his haste, half breathless, panting forth
             From Goneril his mistress salutations;
             Deliver'd letters, spite of intermission,
             Which presently they read; on whose contents,
             They summon'd up their meiny, straight took horse,   35
             Commanded me to follow and attend
             The leisure of their answer, gave me cold looks,
             And meeting here the other messenger,
             Whose welcome I perceiv'd had poison'd mine—
             Being the very fellow which of late   40
             Display'd so saucily against your Highness—
             Having more man than wit about me, drew.

11, 12. **thy place:** thy position as a king's messenger. **—To:** as to. 23. **upon respect:** against the respect due to the King. 24-26. **Resolve me:** Explain to me. **—modest:** moderate. **—mightst:** could. **—from us:** from me, the King. 28. **commend:** hand over, deliver. 33-35. **letters:** a letter. **—spite of intermission:** in spite of the fact that it interrupted the audience they had granted me. **—on:** as the result of. **—meiny:** household attendants. **—straight:** straightway. 41, 42. **Display'd so saucily:** made such an impudent exhibition of himself. **—your Highness:** your Majesty. **—more man than wit:** more courage than common sense. **—drew:** I drew my sword.

He rais'd the house with loud and coward cries.
Your son and daughter found this trespass worth
The shame which here it suffers.   45

FOOL   Winter's not gone yet, if the wild geese fly that way.
            Fathers that wear rags
            Do make their children blind;
            But fathers that bear bags
            Shall see their children kind.   50
            Fortune, that arrant whore,
            Ne'er turns the key to th' poor.

        But for all this, thou shalt have as many dolours for thy daughters as
        thou canst tell in a year.

LEAR   O, how this mother swells up toward my heart!   55
        Hysterica passio! Down, thou climbing sorrow!
        Thy element's below! Where is this daughter?

KENT   With the Earl, sir, here within.

LEAR   Follow me not;
        Stay here.   *Exit.*

GENTLEMAN Made you no more offence but what you speak of?   60

KENT   None.
        How chance the King comes with so small a number?

FOOL   An thou hadst been set i' th' stocks for that question, thou'dst well
        deserv'd it.

KENT   Why, fool?   65

FOOL   We'll set thee to school to an ant, to teach thee there's no laboring i'
        th' winter. All that follow their noses are led by their eyes but blind
        men, and there's not a nose among twenty but can smell him that's
        stinking. Let go thy hold when a great wheel runs down a hill, lest it
        break thy neck with following it; but the great one that goes upward,
        let him draw thee after. When a wise man gives thee better counsel,
        give me mine again. I would have none but knaves follow it, since a
        fool gives it.   73

51-54. Fortune is often called a harlot because she shows favor to every man and is constant to none. —**turns the key:** opens the door. —**dolours:** sorrows—with a pun on *dollars.* —**for:** because of.—**tell:** relate—with a pun on *tell* in the sense of "count." 55-57. **this mother.** The *mother* was the popular name for *hysterica passio*—"hysterical suffering," "hysteria". Lear describes the symptoms: a feeling of distress rising from below toward the heart. Thence it often ascends into the throat with the sensation of choking, called "the hysteric ball." —**thy element:** thy proper place. 62. **How chance:** How chances it. 63, 64. **thou'dst well deserv'd it:** because it's a foolish question, since the answer is so obvious. 66 ff. In a series of brief parables the Fool explains that Lear's fortunes are in a bad way, and that it is therefore not strange that he comes with so small a retinue. —**All that follow their noses:** To "follow one's nose" is an old idiom (still in use) for to "go straight ahead in the direction in which one's nose points."

That sir which serves and seeks for gain,
　　And follows but for form,   75
Will pack when it begins to rain
　　And leave thee in the storm.
But I will tarry; the fool will stay,
　　And let the wise man fly.
The knave turns fool that runs away;   80
　　The fool no knave, perdy.

KENT　　　Where learn'd you this, fool?

FOOL　　　Not i' th' stocks, fool.

Enter Lear and Gloucester.

LEAR　　　Deny to speak with me? They are sick? they are weary?
　　　　　They have travell'd all the night? Mere fetches—   85
　　　　　The images of revolt and flying off!
　　　　　Fetch me a better answer.

GLOUCESTER　　　　　　　　　　　　My dear lord,
　　　　　You know the fiery quality of the Duke,
　　　　　How unremovable and fix'd he is
　　　　　In his own course.   90

LEAR　　　Vengeance! plague! death! confusion!
　　　　　Fiery? What quality? Why, Gloucester, Gloucester,
　　　　　I'ld speak with the Duke of Cornwall and his wife.

GLOUCESTER　Well, my good lord, I have inform'd them so.

LEAR　　　Inform'd them? Dost thou understand me, man?   95

GLOUCESTER　Ay, my good lord.

LEAR　　　The King would speak with Cornwall; the dear father
　　　　　Would with his daughter speak, commands her service.
　　　　　Are they inform'd of this? My breath and blood!
　　　　　Fiery? the fiery Duke? Tell the hot Duke that—   100
　　　　　No, but not yet! May be he is not well.
　　　　　Infirmity doth still neglect all office
　　　　　Whereto our health is bound. We are not ourselves
　　　　　When nature, being oppress'd, commands the mind

---

76. **pack:** be off, run away. 80, 81. **The knave...no knave:** The fellow that forsakes his master is (from the point of view of the higher wisdom) a fool, since true wisdom implies fidelity; and the fool who, like me, remains faithful is, at all events, no knave. —**perdy:** assuredly (from the French *par dieu*). 84-86. **Deny:** refuse. —**fetches:** pretences, pretexts. —**The images:** the plainest possible signs. *Image* means, literally, "the exact figure or likeness." 88. **quality:** character. 91. A string of curses. —**confusion!** ruin, destruction. 92. **What quality?** What has his character to do with the matter? 99. **My breath and blood!** Upon my life! Another oath, used merely as a passionate exclamation. 102. **neglect:** omit, leave undone. —**office:** service, duty.

	To suffer with the body. I'll forbear;	105
	And am fallen out with my more headier will,	
	To take the indispos'd and sickly fit	
	For the sound man.—Death on my state! Wherefore	
	Should he sit here? This act persuades me	
	That this remotion of the Duke and her	110
	Is practice only. Give me my servant forth.	
	Go tell the Duke and 's wife I'd speak with them—	
	Now, presently. Bid them come forth and hear me,	
	Or at their chamber door I'll beat the drum	
	Till it cry sleep to death.	115
GLOUCESTER	I would have all well betwixt you. *Exit.*	
LEAR	O me, my heart, my rising heart! But down!	
FOOL	Cry to it, nuncle, as the cockney did to the eels when she put 'em i' th' paste alive. She knapp'd 'em o' th' coxcombs with a stick and cried "Down, wantons, down!" 'Twas her brother that, in pure kindness to his horse, buttered his hay.	121

Enter Cornwall, Regan, Gloucester, Servants.

LEAR	Good morrow to you both.	
CORNWALL	Hail to your Grace!	

Kent here set at liberty.

REGAN	I am glad to see your Highness.	
LEAR	Regan, I think you are; I know what reason	
	I have to think so. If thou shouldst not be glad,	125
	I would divorce me from thy mother's tomb,	
	Sepulchring an adultress. [*To Kent*] O, are you free?	
	Some other time for that.—Beloved Regan,	
	Thy sister's naught. O Regan, she hath tied	
	Sharp-tooth'd unkindness, like a vulture, here!	130
	[*Lays his hand on his heart.*]	

106, 107. **am fallen out with:** am angry with. **—more headier:** too impulsive. **—will:** impulse. **—To take:** for taking. 108. **Death on my state!** Another curse. **—my state:** my royal power. 110-13. **this remotion:** this keeping away from me; this avoidance of an interview. **—practice:** trickery. See 1.2.150, note. **—Give...forth:** Release (from the stocks). **—and 's:** and his. **—presently:** instantly. 115. **cry sleep to death:** make sleep impossible by its noise. 118-20. *Cockney* has various meanings: "spoiled child," "pampered darling"; "cook"; "Londoner." Here it seems to denote a city woman, unfamiliar with such vulgar things as the making of eel pies. She has had no experience with live eels and does not even know that they must be killed before baking. When they tried to squirm out of the dish, she *knapped* (rapped) them on their silly heads and cried, "Down, you playful creatures, down!" **—her brother:** a member of the same family of fools; another fool of the same breed. 122. **your Grace!** your Majesty. 127. **Sepulchring:** as being the tomb of. 129. **naught:** wicked. 130. **like a vulture:** An allusion, from Greek mythology, to the vulture sent by the gods that gnawed daily on Prometheus's liver [K.S.R.].

I can scarce speak to thee. Thou'lt not believe
With how deprav'd a quality—O Regan!

REGAN   I pray you, sir, take patience. I have hope
You less know how to value her desert
Than she to scant her duty.

LEAR   Say, how is that?   135

REGAN   I cannot think my sister in the least
Would fail her obligation. If, sir, perchance
She have restrain'd the riots of your followers,
'Tis on such ground, and to such wholesome end,
As clears her from all blame.   140

LEAR   My curses on her!

REGAN   O, sir, you are old!
Nature in you stands on the very verge
Of her confine. You should be rul'd, and led
By some discretion that discerns your state
Better than you yourself. Therefore I pray you   145
That to our sister you do make return;
Say you have wrong'd her, sir.

LEAR   Ask her forgiveness?
Do you but mark how this becomes the house:
"Dear daughter, I confess that I am old   [Kneels.]
Age is unnecessary. On my knees I beg   150
That you'll vouchsafe me raiment, bed, and food."

REGAN   Good sir, no more! These are unsightly tricks.
Return you to my sister.

LEAR   [rises] Never, Regan!
She hath abated me of half my train;
Look'd black upon me; struck me with her tongue,   155
Most serpent-like, upon the very heart.
All the stor'd vengeances of heaven fall
On her ingrateful top! Strike her young bones,
You taking airs, with lameness!

CORNWALL   Fie, sir, fie!

---

133. **take patience:** be calm. 134, 135. **You less…duty:** She does not come short in doing her duty to
you. The trouble is that you cannot appreciate her merits. 144. **your state:** your condition of mind. 146
make return: go back again. 148. **becomes the house:** befits family relations. Spoken with bitter irony:
fathers would not kneel to their children in any normal family. 150. **Age is unnecessary:** Old folk are
of no use in the world. 158-63. Lear prays that Goneril may be smitten with lameness and blindness
and that her beauty may be blasted with ugliness. 158. **her young bones:** Goneril's own youthful frame.
159. **taking:** infectious.

LEAR	You nimble lightnings, dart your blinding flames 160
	Into her scornful eyes! Infect her beauty,
	You fen-suck'd fogs, drawn by the pow'rful sun,
	To fall and blast her pride!
REGAN	O the blest gods! so will you wish on me
	When the rash mood is on. 165
LEAR	No, Regan, thou shalt never have my curse.
	Thy tender-hefted nature shall not give
	Thee o'er to harshness. Her eyes are fierce; but thine
	Do comfort, and not burn. 'Tis not in thee
	To grudge my pleasures, to cut off my train, 170
	To bandy hasty words, to scant my sizes,
	And, in conclusion, to oppose the bolt
	Against my coming in. Thou better know'st
	The offices of nature, bond of childhood,
	Effects of courtesy, dues of gratitude. 175
	Thy half o' th' kingdom hast thou not forgot,
	Wherein I thee endow'd.
REGAN	Good sir, to th' purpose. *Tucket within.*
LEAR	Who put my man i' th' stocks?
CORNWALL	What trumpet's that?
REGAN	I know't—my sister's. This approves her letter,
	That she would soon be here.

Enter [Oswald the] Steward.

	Is your lady come? 180
LEAR	This is a slave, whose easy-borrowed pride
	Dwells in the fickle grace of her he follows.
	Out, varlet, from my sight!
CORNWALL	What means your Grace?

Enter Goneril.

LEAR	Who stock'd my servant? Regan, I have good hope
	Thou didst not know on't.—Who comes here? 185

161-63. **Infect...pride!** Cf. 1.4.271: "Blasts and fogs upon thee!" —**To fall:** to fall upon her—not (as some editors think), to cause to fall, to humble. 165. **rash:** hasty. 167. **tender-hefted:** If the reading (which is that of the Folios) is correct, this must mean "heaved (i.e., moved, swayed, governed) by tender emotions only"; it is the tenderness of Regan's nature, not of her bodily frame, that Lear has in mind. 171. **sizes:** allowances. 174, 175. **offices:** duties. —**bond of childhood:** a child's duty toward a parent. —**effects:** actions. 177. **S.D.** *within:* behind the scenes. 179. **approves:** confirms. 181. **easy-borrowed pride:** easily borrowed because it does not take much to make him proud. 183. **varlet:** fellow. A common term of contempt.

O heavens!
If you do love old men, if your sweet sway
Allow obedience—if yourselves are old,
Make it your cause! Send down, and take my part!
[*To Goneril*] Art not asham'd to look upon this beard?—   190
O Regan, wilt thou take her by the hand?

GONERIL   Why not by th' hand, sir? How have I offended?
All's not offence that indiscretion finds
And dotage terms so.

LEAR   O sides, you are too tough!
Will you yet hold? How came my man i' th' stocks?   195

CORNWALL   I set him there, sir; but his own disorders
Deserv'd much less advancement.

LEAR   You? Did you?

REGAN   I pray you, father, being weak, seem so.
If, till the expiration of your month,
You will return and sojourn with my sister,   200
Dismissing half your train, come then to me.
I am now from home, and out of that provision
Which shall be needful for your entertainment.

LEAR   Return to her, and fifty men dismiss'd?
No, rather I abjure all roofs, and choose   205
To wage against the enmity o' th' air,
To be a comrade with the wolf and owl—
Necessity's sharp pinch! Return with her?
Why, the hot-blooded France, that dowerless took
Our youngest born, I could as well be brought   210
To knee his throne, and, squire-like, pension beg
To keep base life afoot. Return with her?
Persuade me rather to be slave and sumpter
To this detested groom.   [*Points at Oswald.*]

GONERIL   At your choice, sir.

LEAR   I prithee, daughter, do not make me mad.   215
I will not trouble thee, my child; farewell.

---

188. **Allow:** approve. **—are old:** so that you may well sympathize with old men in their troubles. 190.
Art: art thou. 196. **disorders:** misconduct. 197. **much less advancement:** far less honor than that. 198.
seem so: i.e., be content to speak and act like a feeble old man, and submit without protest to those who
have you in charge. 203. **shall be:** will certainly be. **—entertainment:** proper maintenance; care and
attention. 206. **To wage against:** to wage war with; to meet in a contest of strength. 208. **Necessity's
sharp pinch!** It is the hard lot of poverty to be homeless and exposed to cold and storm. 211-14. **knee:**
kneel before. **—squire-like:** as if I were one of his attendants. **—sumpter:** packhorse; beast of burden.
—detested groom: detestable underling.

We'll no more meet, no more see one another.
But yet thou art my flesh, my blood, my daughter;
Or rather a disease that's in my flesh
Which I must needs call mine. Thou art a boil, 220
A plague sore, an embossed carbuncle
In my corrupted blood. But I'll not chide thee.
Let shame come when it will, I do not call it.
I do not bid the Thunder-bearer shoot
Nor tell tales of thee to high-judging Jove. 225
Mend when thou canst; be better at thy leisure;
I can be patient, I can stay with Regan,
I and my hundred knights.

REGAN   Not altogether so.
I look'd not for you yet, nor am provided
For your fit welcome. Give ear, sir, to my sister; 230
For those that mingle reason with your passion
Must be content to think you old, and so—
But she knows what she does.

LEAR   Is this well spoken?

REGAN   I dare avouch it, sir. What, fifty followers?
Is it not well? What should you need of more? 235
Yea, or so many, sith that both charge and danger
Speak 'gainst so great a number? How in one house
Should many people, under two commands,
Hold amity? 'Tis hard, almost impossible.

GONERIL   Why might not you, my lord, receive attendance 240
From those that she calls servants, or from mine?

REGAN   Why not, my lord? If then they chanc'd to slack ye,
We could control them. If you will come to me
(For now I spy a danger), I entreat you
To bring but five-and-twenty. To no more 245
Will I give place or notice.

LEAR   I gave you all—

REGAN   And in good time you gave it!

---

221. **embossed:** headed; rising in a round knob (like the boss of a shield). 224, 225. **the Thunder-bearer:** Jupiter. —**shoot:** dart his thunderbolts at thee. —**high-judging Jove:** Jove, the almighty judge. 231, 232. **that mingle reason with your passion:** who consider your violent words and actions in the light of reason and can tell you what such conduct means. —**old.** She breaks off abruptly, with a gesture: "You are *old*—and no further explanation is necessary!" 234. **avouch it:** stand by it; affirm it as sound doctrine. 236. **sith that:** since. —**charge:** expense. 242, 243. **slack:** neglect. —**control:** regulate. 246. **notice:** recognition. 247. **And in good time you gave it!** A characteristic interruption by the soft-spoken but venomous Regan.

LEAR   Made you my guardians, my depositaries;
            But kept a reservation to be followed
            With such a number. What, must I come to you   250
            With five-and-twenty, Regan? Said you so?

REGAN   And speak't again, my lord. No more with me.

LEAR   Those wicked creatures yet do look well-favor'd
            When others are more wicked; not being the worst
            Stands in some rank of praise. [*To Goneril*] I'll go with thee.   255
            Thy fifty yet doth double five-and-twenty,
            And thou art twice her love.

GONERIL   Hear me, my lord.
            What need you five-and-twenty, ten, or five,
            To follow in a house where twice so many
            Have a command to tend you?

REGAN   What need one?   260

LEAR   O, reason not the need! Our basest beggars
            Are in the poorest thing superfluous.
            Allow not nature more than nature needs,
            Man's life is cheap as beast's. Thou art a lady:
            If only to go warm were gorgeous,   265
            Why, nature needs not what thou gorgeous wear'st,
            Which scarcely keeps thee warm. But, for true need—
            You heavens, give me that patience, patience I need!
            You see me here, you gods, a poor old man,
            As full of grief as age; wretched in both.   270
            If it be you that stirs these daughters' hearts
            Against their father, fool me not so much
            To bear it tamely; touch me with noble anger,
            And let not women's weapons, water drops,

---

248. **Made you my guardians:** entrusted all my possessions to your care. —**depositaries.** Synonymous with *guardians*. 253. **Those wicked creatures.** Lear's remark is a general truth: "Such creatures as are wicked always have a good appearance in contrast with others that are more wicked." —**well-favor'd:** fair, handsome. 259. **To follow:** to be your followers, your attendants. 261-68. Lear distinguishes between absolute necessity (in which sense his daughters have used the word *need*) and that which may be properly regarded as necessary for comfort and dignity. But he breaks off abruptly when about to define "true need" (line 267); for the thought forces itself upon him that the one thing he really *needs* is the gift of *patience* (i.e. fortitude), which may keep him from the shame of tears. 261, 262. **Our basest beggars…superfluous:** The most miserable beggars have some things among their poorest possessions that they do not actually need—that they could get along without. —**superfluous:** possessing more than merely enough. 265, 266. **If…wear'st:** If mere warmth were all the gorgeousness that a lady required of her apparel, then the gorgeousness of your attire would not be needed, for gorgeousness is certainly not—like warmth—a *natural* necessity. 268. **that patience…need!** that degree of fortitude (strength to endure suffering) that my case requires—it is fortitude that I need! 272, 273. **fool me not so much:** Do not make me so much of a weakling. —**To:** as to. 274. **women's weapons, water drops:** That tears are womanish is an idea often repeated in Shakespeare.

In Edwin Sherwin's 1973 film, thunder sounds as James Earl Jones' Lear rebukes of his daughters (2.4.275ff.), threatening "The terrors of the earth!"

      Stain my man's cheeks! No, you unnatural hags! 275
      I will have such revenges on you both
      That all the world shall—I will do such things—
      What they are yet, I know not; but they shall be
      The terrors of the earth! You think I'll weep.
      No, I'll not weep, 280
      I have full cause of weeping, but this heart
      Shall break into a hundred thousand flaws
      Or ere I'll weep. O fool, I shall go mad!

weeping while saying, not to weep

              Exeunt Lear, Gloucester, Kent, and Fool.
                       Storm and tempest.

CORNWALL   Let us withdraw; 'twill be a storm.

REGAN   This house is little; the old man and 's people 285
           Cannot be well bestow'd.

GONERIL   'Tis his own blame; hath put himself from rest
           And must needs taste his folly.

REGAN   For his particular, I'll receive him gladly,
           But not one follower.

GONERIL   So am I purpos'd. 290

---

279. **The terrors of the earth:** things so terrible as to frighten the whole world. 282, 283. **flaws:** fragments. **—Or ere.** *Or* and *ere* both mean "before." **—I shall go mad!** Cf. line 221. [There is ironic foreshadowing here. K.S.R.] 285, 286. **and 's:** and his. **—bestow'd:** lodged, accommodated. 287, 288. **hath:** he hath. **—taste his folly:** suffer the consequences of his folly. 289. **For his particular:** as for him in particular; so far as concerns him personally—not, for his own sake.

Where is my Lord of Gloucester?

CORNWALL   Followed the old man forth.

Enter Gloucester.

He is return'd.

GLOUCESTER   The King is in high rage.

CORNWALL   Whither is he going?

GLOUCESTER   He calls to horse, but will I know not whither.

CORNWALL   'Tis best to give him way; he leads himself   295

GONERIL   My lord, entreat him by no means to stay.

GLOUCESTER   Alack, the night comes on, and the bleak winds
Do sorely ruffle. For many miles about
There's scarce a bush.

REGAN   O, sir, to wilful men
The injuries that they themselves procure   300
Must be their schoolmasters. Shut up your doors.
He is attended with a desperate train,
And what they may incense him to, being apt
To have his ear abus'd, wisdom bids fear.

CORNWALL   Shut up your doors, my lord; 'tis a wild night.   305
My Regan counsels well. Come out o' th' storm.   *Exeunt.*

Act III

Scene I. [*A heath.*]

Storm still. Enter Kent and a Gentleman at several doors.

KENT   Who's there, besides foul weather?[†]

---

295. **to give him way:** not to hinder his departure. —**he leads himself:** he submits to no guidance; he insists on having his own way. 298. **ruffle:** rage. A strong word. A *ruffler* is a brawling ruffian. 302-4. **with:** by. —**a desperate train:** Regan, like Goneril, shamelessly misrepresents the character of Lear's Knights. See 1.4.47, note. —**incense:** instigate. —**apt:** ready. —**abus'd:** deceived.
Act III. Scene I.
This scene takes place on the same day as 2.4, with which it is practically continuous. Gloucester "follows" Lear "forth" at 2.4.292, returns (2.4.293), and then goes out to rejoin Lear, pretending that he is "ill and gone to bed" (3.3.12). Meanwhile Kent has been separated from Lear in the storm but means to search for him. He finds him at 3.2.38.

---

†   (*Who's there?*) This opening question suggests a storm so strong that vision is obscured.

GENTLEMAN   One minded like the weather, most unquietly.

KENT   I know you. Where's the King?

GENTLEMAN   Contending with the fretful elements;
Bids the wind blow the earth into the sea,   5
Or swell the curled waters 'bove the main,
That things might change or cease; tears his white hair,
Which the impetuous blasts, with eyeless rage,
Catch in their fury and make nothing of;
Strives in his little world of man to outscorn   10
The to-and-fro-conflicting wind and rain.
This night, wherein the cub-drawn bear would couch,
The lion and the belly-pinched wolf
Keep their fur dry, unbonneted he runs,
And bids what will take all.

KENT   But who is with him?   15

GENTLEMAN   None but the fool, who labors to outjest
His heart-struck injuries.

KENT   Sir, I do know you,
And dare upon the warrant of my note
Commend a dear thing to you. There is division
(Although as yet the face of it be cover'd   20
With mutual cunning) 'twixt Albany and Cornwall;
Who have (as who have not, that their great stars
Thron'd and set high?) servants, who seem no less,
Which are to France the spies and speculations
Intelligent of our state. What hath been seen,   25
Either in snuffs and packings of the Dukes,
Or the hard rein which both of them have borne

6-9. **the main:** the land. —**things:** the world; the whole order of nature. —**eyeless:** blind—since they rage at everything without discrimination or definite object. —**make nothing of:** show no respect for. 10. **his little world of man:** A man is a microcosm ("a little cosmos" "a universe in miniature") compared to the *macrocosm,* "the great cosmos." 12. **cub-drawn:** "with udders all drawn dry" by her cubs and therefore wild with hunger. —**couch:** lie hidden from the storm. 15. **bids...take all:** "Take all!" is the cry of the gambler when he stakes, at a final cast of the dice, all the money that he has left. Hence it is used figuratively as a cry of despair or desperate defiance. 16. **to outjest:** to relieve by his jests. It is the Fool's tragedy that his efforts to cheer up his master serve only to emphasize Lear's folly and its dreadful results; for the Fool's mind instinctively concentrates on that one idea and he calls Lear "fool" over and over again. 18, 19. **note:** knowledge of you. —**Commend:** intrust. —**a dear thing:** an important matter. 23. **no less:** nothing more or less than servants. 24-26. **speculations:** Synonymous with *spies.* —**Intelligent of our state:** giving information about our government. —**What hath been seen:** what has been already discernible. —**snuffs:** cases in which they have openly taken offense at each other's actions. To *take* anything *in snuff* is to "resent it strongly." The phrase comes from the way in which some persons show anger—by drawing in the breath audibly through the nostrils. —**packings:** plots, secret machinations. "Here's packing...to deceive us all!"

Against the old kind King, or something deeper,
Whereof, perchance, these are but furnishings—
But, true it is, from France there comes a power   30
Into this scattered kingdom, who already,
Wise in our negligence, have secret feet
In some of our best ports and are at point
To show their open banner. Now to you:
If on my credit you dare build so far   35
To make your speed to Dover, you shall find
Some that will thank you, making just report
Of how unnatural and bemadding sorrow
The King hath cause to plain.
I am a gentleman of blood and breeding,   40
And from some knowledge and assurance offer
This office to you.

GENTLEMAN   I will talk further with you.

KENT   No, do not.
For confirmation that I am much more
Than my out-wall, open this purse and take   45
What it contains. If you shall see Cordelia
(As fear not but you shall), show her this ring,
And she will tell you who your fellow is
That yet you do not know. Fie on this storm!
I will go seek the King.   50

GENTLEMAN   Give me your hand. Have you no more to say?

KENT   Few words, but, to effect, more than all yet:
That, when we have found the King (in which your pain
That way, I'll this), he that first lights on him
Holla the other.   *Exeunt [severally].* 55

29-31. **furnishings:** pretexts that conceal the real purpose of the French invasion. Kent does not finish his sentence. He means: "For some reason, the French are invading Britain—whether because of what spies have informed them about the quarrels and plots of the Dukes or about their harsh treatment of the King, or, perhaps, for some purpose that the invaders conceal, using these things as pretexts. What the facts are, I do not know; but, at all events, it is certain that the French have actually landed." —**a power:** an armed troop.—**scattered:** broken up, divided. 33. **at point:** fully prepared; all ready. 35, 36. **my credit:** your trust in me. —**To:** as to. 37-39. **making:** if you make. —**just:** true and accurate. —**plain:** complain. 41, 42. **assurance:** trustworthy information. —**office:** duty. 45. **out-wall:** Kent wears the garb of a serving-man. 48. **your fellow:** your companion; your associate in the King's service. Thus Kent confirms the suggestion that he is a more important person than his present position would indicate. 52. **to effect:** in effect; in importance. 53, 54. **in which your pain That way:** With a gesture: "Use your best efforts to find him in that direction." —**I'll this:** I'll seek him in *this* direction.

SCENE II. [*Another part of the heath.*]

Storm still. Enter Lear and Fool.

LEAR	Blow, winds, and crack your cheeks! rage! blow!
	You cataracts and hurricanoes, spout
	Till you have drench'd our steeples, drown'd the cocks!
	You sulph'rous and thought-executing fires,
	Vaunt-couriers to oak-cleaving thunderbolts, 5
	Singe my white head! And thou, all-shaking thunder,
	Strike flat the thick rotundity o' th' world, — *pregnant*
	Crack Nature's moulds, all germains spill at once,†
	That make ingrateful man!
FOOL	O nuncle, court holy water in a dry house is better than this rain
	water out o'door. Good nuncle, in, and ask thy daughters' blessing!
	Here's a night pities neither wise men nor fools. 12
LEAR	Rumble thy bellyful! Spit, fire! spout, rain!
	Nor rain, wind, thunder, fire are my daughters.
	I tax not you, you elements, with unkindness. 15
	I never gave you kingdom, call'd you children,
	You owe me no subscription. Then let fall
	Your horrible pleasure. Here I stand your slave,
	A poor, infirm, weak, and despis'd old man.
	But yet I call you servile ministers, 20
	That will with two pernicious daughters join
	Your high-engender'd battles 'gainst a head
	So old and white as this! O! O! 'tis foul!‡

SCENE II.
This scene takes place in the stormy night mentioned at the end of 2.4. Kent, who has been seeking Lear (3.1.53-55), finds him and conducts him toward a hovel that is "hard by" (line 57).
2, 3. cataracts and hurricanoes: "water-spouts." —**cocks:** weathercocks, weathervanes. **4, 5. thought-executing:** executing with rapidity equal to thought. —**thunderbolts:** Fiery bolts, or stone missiles, were supposed to be discharged from the clouds by the thunder. **8. Nature's moulds:** the moulds which Nature uses in forming men. —**germains:** seeds. —**spill:** destroy. **10-11. court holy water:** complements, fair words, flattering speeches. —**ask thy daughters' blessing!** ask a blessing from your daughters. **15-17. tax not you...with:** do not accuse you of. —**subscription:** submission, obedience. **20. ministers:** agents. **22. high-engender'd:** engendered high in the heavens. There is also a suggestion of the meaning "sublime." —**battles:** battalions, armies.

---

† (*Crack nature's moulds...ungrateful man*) In Trevor Nunn's production this line summons loud and repeated thunder, as noted below.

‡ (*So old and white as this*) Thunder sounds again, in Nunn's production.

FOOL   He that has a house to put 's head in has a good headpiece.
                The codpiece that will house   25
                    Before the head has any,
                The head and he shall louse:
                    So beggars marry many.
                The man that makes his toe
                    What he his heart should make   30
                Shall of a corn cry woe,
                    And turn his sleep to wake.
            For there was never yet fair woman but she made mouths in a glass.

                            Enter Kent.

LEAR   No, I will be the pattern of all patience;
            I will say nothing.   35

KENT   Who's there?

FOOL   Marry, here's grace and a codpiece; that's a wise man and a fool.

KENT   Alas, sir, are you here? Things that love night
            Love not such nights as these. The wrathful skies
            Gallow the very wanderers of the dark   40
            And make them keep their caves. Since I was man,
            Such sheets of fire, such bursts of horrid thunder,
            Such groans of roaring wind and rain, I never
            Remember to have heard. Man's nature cannot carry
            Th' affliction nor the fear.

LEAR   Let the great gods,   45
            That keep this dreadful pudder o'er our heads,
            Find out their enemies now. Tremble, thou wretch,
            That hast within thee undivulged crimes
            Unwhipp'd of justice. Hide thee, thou bloody hand;

---

24. **put's:** put his. —**a good headpiece:** The Fool puns on two senses of the phrase: (1) a good helmet, covering for the head, and (2) a good head—i.e., a wise brain. 25-28. **The...many:** The man who begets children before he has a house will surely become a lousy vagabond. Thus it is that many beggars get married. 29-32. **The man...wake:** The man who exchanges the places of his toe and his heart will get a corn on his heart instead of on his foot, and that will give him such a heartache as will keep him awake nights. The Fool alludes to Lear's folly in showing favor to Goneril and Regan and disowning Cordelia. 33. A mere bit of Fool's nonsense, such as was often used to distract attention from too keen a piece of satire. The Fool instinctively plays the tricks of his profession. —**made...glass:** practiced making pretty faces in a mirror. 37. **Marry:** Originally an oath by the Virgin Mary, but used as a mere exclamation. —**grace:** an honorable person. —**that's a wise man and a fool:** He leaves it to Kent to decide which is which. 40. **Gallow:** terrify. A very strong word. Whalemen still use *gallied* to describe a whale that is panic-stricken. 44, 45. **cannot carry...fear:** cannot bear up under the actual bodily affliction (the buffeting by the storm) and the terror that accompanies it. 46. **pudder:** hubbub, turmoil; din. 47. **Find out:** i.e., by the terror which such offenders must show. 49. **of:** by.

Thou perjur'd, and thou simular man of virtue   50
That art incestuous. Caitiff, in pieces shake
That under covert and convenient seeming
Hast practis'd on man's life. Close pent-up guilts,
Rive your concealing continents, and cry
These dreadful summoners grace. I am a man   55
More sinn'd against than sinning.†

KENT   Alack, bareheaded?
Gracious my lord, hard by here is a hovel;
Some friendship will it lend you 'gainst the tempest.
Repose you there, whilst I to this hard house
(More harder than the stones whereof 'tis rais'd,   60
Which even but now, demanding after you,
Denied me to come in) return, and force
Their scanted courtesy.

LEAR   My wits begin to turn.
Come on, my boy. How dost, my boy? Art cold?
I am cold myself. Where is this straw, my fellow?   65
The art of our necessities is strange,   *alchemy.*
That can make vile things precious. Come, your hovel.
Poor fool and knave, I have one part in my heart
That's sorry yet for thee.

FOOL   [*sings*]
            He that has and a little tiny wit—   70
               With hey, ho, the wind and the rain—
            Must make content with his fortunes fit,
               For the rain it raineth every day.

LEAR   True, my good boy. Come, bring us to this hovel.
                              Exeunt [Lear and Kent].

50, 51. **thou simular man of virtue:** thou man that wearest the guise of virtue. —**Caitiff:** wretch. Cf. 2.1.63. 52, 53. **under covert....seeming:** under such an appearance of conventional virtue as masked thy purpose. —**practis'd on:** plotted against. See 1.2.150, note. 54, 55. **Rive...grace:** Break open the concealments that hide you, and appeal to these dreadful summoners for mercy. A *summoner* is an officer who summons offenders to an ecclesiastical court. —**I:** Emphatic. Thus Lear points out his reason for not fearing the storm. 58. **lend:** afford. 61, 62. **demanding after you:** asking for you. —**Denied:** prohibited, forbade. 63. **My wits begin to turn.** The first intimation of Lear's delirium. 66, 67. **art:** The figure alludes to alchemy, which professed to turn base metals into gold and silver. —**vile:** worthless. 72. **Must...fit:** must make his happiness fit his fortunes; must be contented and happy, even when his fortunes are bad. 74. **True:** Lear accepts the Fool's saying as applicable to himself.

---

†   (*I am a man more sinned against than sinning*) In Trevor Nunn's production, a medium shot here frames King Lear between Kent and the Fool, with the King's suffering reflected in Kent's anguished face. The framing of these characters conveys a sense of community among the outcasts.

FOOL   This is a brave night to cool a courtesan. I'll speak a prophecy ere I go:
            When priests are more in word than matter;   76
            When brewers mar their malt with water;
            When nobles are their tailors' tutors,
            No heretics burn'd, but wenches' suitors;
            When every case in law is right,   80
            No squire in debt nor no poor knight;
            When slanders do not live in tongues,
            Nor cutpurses come not to throngs;
            When usurers tell their gold i' th' field,
            And bawds and whores do churches build: 85
            Then shall the realm of Albion
            Come to great confusion.
            Then comes the time, who lives to see't,
            That going shall be us'd with feet.
            This prophecy Merlin shall make, for I live before his time.   *Exit.*

SCENE III. [Gloucester's *Castle.*]

Enter Gloucester and Edmund.

GLOUCESTER Alack, alack, Edmund, I like not this unnatural dealing! When I
            desir'd their leave that I might pity him, they took from me the use of
            mine own house, charg'd me on pain of perpetual displeasure neither
            to speak of him, entreat for him, nor any way sustain him.

EDMUND   Most savage and unnatural!   5

GLOUCESTER Go to; say you nothing. There is division betwixt the Dukes, and a
            worse matter than that. I have received a letter this night—'tis danger-
            ous to be spoken—I have lock'd the letter in my closet. These injuries
            the King now bears will be revenged home; there's part of a power al-
            ready footed; we must incline to the King. I will seek him and privily

75. **brave:** fine, splendid. 76. **more in word than matter:** better in talk than in substance; or better in
preaching than in practice. 78. **their tailors' tutors:** even greater experts in clothing than the tailors
they employ. 83. **cut-purses:** literally, thieves who slash purses (worn as a pouch at the belt) and steal
the contents; then, in general, pickpockets. 84. **tell:** count. 86. **Albion:** An old name for Britain. 87.
confusion: a ruinous condition. 88. **who:** if anybody. 89. **That going...feet:** when feet shall be used for
walking. An intentionally absurd truism—such as fools frequently pronounced with a solemn air as a
burlesque on the philosophers' profound adages. The audience is at liberty to make it mean: "The world
shall once more be in a normal condition." 90. **This...time.** This line makes the Fool a real prophet, for
Merlin's date was centuries later than Lear's. Merlin is the seer of the Arthurian legend.
SCENE III.
The same stormy night as in scene 2. Gloucester means to find Lear and relieve him. He finds him in the
next scene (3.4.107). 4. **nor any way sustain him:** nor do anything whatever to relieve him. 6. **Go to:**
Enough! 9-14. **home:** to the utmost. The figure comes from a "home thrust" [that wounds in a vital part.
K.S.R.] —**a power:** an army. —**footed:** landed. —**incline to:** take part with; take the side of. —**privily:**
secretly. —**of him:** by him. —**toward:** in preparation; coming.

relieve him. Go you and maintain talk with the Duke, that my charity be not of him perceived. If he ask for me, I am ill and gone to bed. Though I die for't, as no less is threat'ned me, the King my old master must be relieved. There is some strange thing toward, Edmund. Pray you be careful.   *Exit.*   15

EDMUND   This courtesy, forbid thee, shall the Duke
Instantly know, and of that letter too.
This seems a fair deserving, and must draw me
That which my father loses—no less than all.
The younger rises when the old doth fall.   *Exit.*   20

SCENE IV. [*The heath. Before a hovel.*]

Storm still. Enter Lear, Kent, and Fool.

KENT   Here is the place, my lord. Good my lord, enter.
The tyranny of the open night's too rough
For nature to endure.

LEAR   Let me alone.

KENT   Good my lord, enter here.

LEAR   Wilt break my heart?

KENT   I had rather break mine own. Good my lord, enter.   5

LEAR   Thou think'st 'tis much that this contentious storm
Invades us to the skin. So 'tis to thee;
But where the greater malady is fix'd,
The lesser is scarce felt. Thou'dst shun a bear;
But if thy flight lay toward the raging sea,   10
Thou'dst meet the bear i' th' mouth. When the mind's free,
The body's delicate. The tempest in my mind
Doth from my senses take all feeling else
Save what beats there. Filial ingratitude!
Is it not as this mouth should tear this hand   15
For lifting food to't? But I will punish home!
No, I will weep no more. In such a night

---

18. **This seems...deserving:** My giving the Duke this information will seem to him a good piece of service.
SCENE IV.
The same stormy night as in scene 3. Gloucester finds Lear (line 107) and leads him to a farmhouse for shelter (lines 129 ff.).
1. **Good my lord:** See 1.1.88, note. 2. **The tyranny of the open night:** the boisterous roughness of such a night in the open air. 3. **nature:** a man's natural strength. 11. **free:** untroubled; at peace. 14. **beats there:** throbs in my mind and heart. 15. **as:** as if.

To shut me out! Pour on; I will endure.
In such a night as this! O Regan, Goneril!
Your old kind father, whose frank heart gave all!   20
O, that way madness lies; let me shun that!
No more of that.

KENT   Good my lord, enter here.

LEAR   Prithee go in thyself; seek thine own ease.
This tempest will not give me leave to ponder
On things would hurt me more. But I'll go in.   25
[*To the Fool*] In, boy; go first.—You houseless poverty—
Nay, get thee in. I'll pray, and then I'll sleep.   *Exit [Fool]*.
Poor naked wretches, wheresoe'er you are,
That bide the pelting of this pitiless storm,
How shall your houseless heads and unfed sides,   30
Your loop'd and window'd raggedness, defend you
From seasons such as these? O, I have ta'en
Too little care of this! Take physic, pomp;
Expose thyself to feel what wretches feel,
That thou mayst shake the superflux to them   35
And show the heavens more just.

EDGAR   [*within*] Fathom and half, fathom and half! Poor Tom!

Enter Fool [from the hovel].

FOOL   Come not in here, nuncle, here's a spirit. Help me, help me!

KENT   Give me thy hand. Who's there?

FOOL   A spirit, a spirit! He says his name's poor Tom.   40

KENT   What art thou that dost grumble there i' th' straw? Come forth.

Enter Edgar [disguised as a madman].

EDGAR   Away! the foul fiend follows me! Through the sharp hawthorn blows
the cold wind. Humh! go to thy cold bed, and warm thee.

LEAR   Hast thou given all to thy two daughters, and art thou come to this?

---

20. **frank:** free, generous. 25. **would:** that would. 26. **You houseless poverty:** Synonymous with "Poor naked wretches" (line 28). 29. **bide:** suffer, endure. 31. **loop'd and window'd.** Synonymous: "full of holes." A *loop* is, literally, a "loophole." 33. **Take physic, pomp:** O ye great and mighty ones of the earth, take this remedy to cure your unfeeling hearts. 35, 36. **That...just:** That you may cast off what you do not need ("the superflux," superfluity) and bestow it on them, and so may make God's treatment of humanity more impartial than it now seems to be. 37. **Fathom and half!** Edgar speaks as if he were a sailor sounding the depth of the water in the hold of a leaking ship. He is almost "swamped" by the storm. 43. **Humh!** The interjection expresses his shivering with cold. —**go to thy cold bed, and warm thee:** Edgar, taking his cue from Lear's word "given," repeats the kind of petition expected of Bedlam beggars, who "enforce charity" with "prayers" as well as "with lunatic bans" (2.3.19 ff.).

EDGAR	Who gives anything to poor Tom? whom the foul fiend hath led through fire and through flame, through ford and whirlpool, o'er bog and quagmire; that hath laid knives under his pillow and halters in his pew, set ratsbane by his porridge, made him proud of heart, to ride on a bay trotting horse over four-inch'd bridges, to course his own shadow for a traitor. Bless thy five wits! Tom's acold. O, do de, do de, do de. Bless thee from whirlwinds, star-blasting, and taking! Do poor Tom some charity, whom the foul fiend vexes. There could I have him now—and there—and there again—and there! *Storm still.* 53
LEAR	What, have his daughters brought him to this pass? Couldst thou save nothing? Didst thou give 'em all? 55
FOOL	Nay, he reserv'd a blanket, else we had been all sham'd.
LEAR	Now all the plagues that in the pendulous air Hang fated o'er men's faults light on thy daughters!
KENT	He hath no daughters, sir.
LEAR	Death, traitor! nothing could have subdu'd nature 60 To such a lowness but his unkind daughters. Is it the fashion that discarded fathers Should have thus little mercy on their flesh? Judicious punishment! 'Twas this flesh begot Those pelican daughters. 65
EDGAR	Pillicock sat on Pillicock's Hill. 'Allow, 'allow, loo, loo!
FOOL	This cold night will turn us all to fools and madmen.
EDGAR	Take heed o' th' foul fiend; obey thy parents; keep thy word justly; swear not; commit not with man's sworn spouse; set not thy sweet heart on proud array. Tom's acold. 70
LEAR	What hast thou been?

47-49. **that:** who. The antecedent is *fiend.*—**hath laid knives,** etc.: i.e., to tempt him to kill himself. For the idea that a demon may prompt or aid a man to commit suicide see 4.6.69-72. —**pew:** a gallery in a house or outside a chamber window—not a pew in church. —**course:** chase. 50, 51. **Bless:** God bless. —**thy five wits:** thy five mental powers: common wit, imagination, fantasy, estimation, and memory. —**O, do de, do de, do de.** He is shuddering with cold. —**taking!** infection; the stroke of disease. 52, 53. **There could I have him now,** etc. Edgar makes grabs at different parts of his body as if to catch vermin—or devils. Cf. 3.6.14: "The foul fiend bites my back." 54. **this pass:** this desperate condition. 57. **pendulous:** overhanging. In the context the word suggests "low-hanging," "brooding over us." 60. **subdu'd:** reduced. —**nature:** a man's natural powers. 63. **thus little mercy on their flesh?** Edgar has gone so far in his impersonation of a Bedlam beggar as to pierce his arms with splinters or thorns. See 2.3.15, 16. 64. **Judicious:** well-judged; just and fitting; condign. 65. **pelican:** Young pelicans were supposed to pluck feathers from their mother's breast and drink her blood [K.S.R.]. 66. **Pillicock:** Edgar, in pretended madness, echoes Lear's word "pelican," distorting it to "Pillicock" (a term of comic endearment) and reciting part of a nursery rhyme. —**Allow...loo!** A wild "halloo," as if he were calling a hawk. 68, 69. **obey thy parents,** etc. Edgar speaks solemnly as if he were trying to recite the Ten Commandments. —**justly:** exactly, scrupulously. —**commit:** commit adultery.

EDGAR   A servingman, proud in heart and mind; that curl'd my hair, wore
gloves in my cap; serv'd the lust of my mistress' heart and did the
act of darkness with her; swore as many oaths as I spake words, and
broke them in the sweet face of heaven; one that slept in the contriv-
ing of lust, and wak'd to do it. Wine lov'd I deeply, dice dearly; and in
woman out-paramour'd the Turk. False of heart, light of ear, bloody
of hand; hog in sloth, fox in stealth, wolf in greediness, dog in madness, lion in prey. Let not the creaking of shoes nor the rustling of
silks betray thy poor heart to woman. Keep thy foot out of brothel,
thy hand out of placket, thy pen from lender's book, and defy the foul
fiend. Still through the hawthorn blows the cold wind; says suum,
mun, hey, no, nonny. Dolphin my boy, my boy, sessa! let him
trot by.   *Storm still.*   84

LEAR   Why, thou wert better in thy grave than to answer with thy uncover'd
body this extremity of the skies. Is man no more than this? Consider
him well. Thou ow'st the worm no silk, the beast no hide, the sheep
no wool, the cat no perfume. Ha! Here's three on's are sophisticated!
Thou art the thing itself; unaccommodated man is no more but such
a poor, bare, forked animal as thou art. Off, off, you lendings! Come,
unbutton here. [*Tears at his clothes.*]   91

FOOL   Prithee, nuncle, be contented! 'Tis a naughty night to swim in. Now a
little fire in a wild field were like an old lecher's heart—a small spark,
all the rest on's body cold. Look, here comes a walking fire.

                    Enter Gloucester with a torch.

EDGAR   This is the foul fiend Flibbertigibbet. He begins at curfew, and walks
till the first cock. He gives the web and the pin, squints the eye, and

---

72, 73. **wore gloves in my cap:** To wear a lady's glove in the cap was a common attention on the part
of a gallant. 77. **out-paramour'd:** surpassed in the number of my mistresses. —**the Turk:** the Great
Turk, the Sultan.—**light of ear:** ready to listen to malicious gossip [K.S.R]. 78, 79. **hog in sloth...lion
in prey:** The Seven Deadly Sins were figured in the shape of seven animals. 79, 80. **Let not...woman:**
Give your heart to a woman as soon as you hear her shoes creak and her silk gown rustle. —**the creaking of shoes:** Shoes that creaked were fashionable. 81. **placket:** the slit in a petticoat. —**lender's book.**
The borrower was expected to sign an acknowledgment of receipt in the moneylender's book of record.
82, 83. **Still...wind:** This sounds like a line from some old song. — **suum...nonny:** He imitates the
whistling of the wind. — **Dolphin...trot by:** Probably words from an old song. 88. **the cat:** the civet
cat [which produced musk used in perfume. K.S.R.]. Cf. 4.6.127. —**on's:** of us. 89. **unaccommodated
man:** man pure and simple, without any artificial furnishings to which he is accustomed. 90. **Off:** To
tear off one's clothes is a common symptom of delirium. —**lendings:** Clothes are not given by nature:
they are *lent* by art. 91. **unbutton:** Lear instinctively uses the imperative, for he has never before taken
off his clothes without a valet's services. 92. **naughty:** very bad, wicked. Not a trivial or childish word,
as in modern usage. 95-97. *Fliberdigibbet* is one of the dancing devils in Harsnet's *Declaration.* [Samuel
Harsnet (1561-1631) was an Anglican prelate and author of *A Declaration of Egregious Popish Impostures*
(1603), an influential work condemning the form of exorcism practiced by the Jesuits. Shakespeare shows
indebtedness to this work in both *Pericles* and *The Tempest*, as well as *King Lear*. K.S.R.] —**at curfew:**

makes the harelip; mildews the white wheat, and hurts the poor creature of earth.

    Saint Withold footed thrice the 'old;
    He met the nightmare, and her nine fold;   100
        Bid her alight
        And her troth plight,
    And aroint thee, witch, aroint thee!

KENT   How fares your Grace?

LEAR   What's he?   105

KENT   Who's there? What is't you seek?

GLOUCESTER What are you there? Your names?

EDGAR   Poor Tom, that eats the swimming frog, the toad, the todpole, the
wall-newt and the water; that in the fury of his heart, when the
foul fiend rages, eats cow-dung for sallets, swallows the old rat and
the ditch-dog, drinks the green mantle of the standing pool; who is
whipp'd from tithing to tithing, and stock-punish'd and imprison'd;
who hath had three suits to his back, six shirts to his body, horse to
ride, and weapon to wear;   114

    But mice and rats, and such small deer,
    Have been Tom's food for seven long year.
Beware my follower. Peace, Smulkin! peace, thou fiend!

GLOUCESTER What, hath your Grace no better company?

EDGAR   The prince of darkness is a gentleman!
Modo he's call'd, and Mahu.   120

GLOUCESTER Our flesh and blood is grown so vile, my lord,
That it doth hate what gets it.

---

at nine o'clock at night. —**first cock:** The hours of cockcrow, were conventionally fixed as follows: first cock, midnight; second cock, 3 A.M. —**the web and the pin:** An old name for the disease of the eye known as "cataract."—**harelip:** cleft upper lip. 100-103. The nightmare was, in ancient belief, a demon. The word comes from the Anglo-Saxon *mare,* "incubus." This charm has the so-called "epic" (narrative) form in the first four lines. To recite how St. Withold encountered the demon and her "nine fold" (her nine offspring) and subdued her served as a charm against her power. —**footed:** traversed. —**the 'old:** the wold—an upland plain. —**her troth plight:** pledge her solemn word (not to do any harm). —**And aroint thee:** Addressed by the reciter directly to the demon: "Away with thee"; "be gone." 108-12. **todpole:** A form of *tadpole,* "young frog." —**wall-newt:** wall-lizard. —**the water:** the water-newt. —**sallets:** salads. —**mantle:** scum. —**standing:** stagnant. —**from tithing to tithing:** from district to district—practically, from parish to parish. —**stock-punish'd:** set in the stocks. 115. **deer:** game 117. **my follower:** the fiend that always attends me. Then Edgar speaks to the fiend as if it were his dog. —**Smulkin.** The name of another fiend in Harsnet's *Declaration.* 119: **The prince of darkness is a gentleman!** and therefore good enough company even for a king. 120. **Modo...Mahu:** another fiend in Harsnet's *Declaration.* 122. **gets:** begets.

EDGAR   Poor Tom's acold.

GLOUCESTER   Go in with me. My duty cannot suffer
             T' obey in all your daughters' hard commands.   125
             Though their injunction be to bar my doors
             And let this tyrannous night take hold upon you,
             Yet have I ventur'd to come seek you out
             And bring you where both fire and food is ready.

LEAR   First let me talk with this philosopher.   130
             What is the cause of thunder?

KENT   Good my lord, take his offer; go into th' house.

LEAR   I'll talk a word with this same learned Theban.
             What is your study?

EDGAR   How to prevent the fiend and to kill vermin.   135

LEAR   Let me ask you one word in private.

KENT   Importune him once more to go, my lord.
             His wits begin t' unsettle.

GLOUCESTER   Canst thou blame him?   *Storm still.*
             His daughters seek his death. Ah, that good Kent!
             He said it would be thus—poor banish'd man!   140
             Thou say'st the King grows mad: I'll tell thee, friend,
             I am almost mad myself. I had a son,
             Now outlaw'd from my blood. He sought my life
             But lately, very late. I lov'd him, friend—
             No father his son dearer. True to tell thee,   145
             The grief hath craz'd my wits. What a night's this!
             I do beseech your Grace—

LEAR   O, cry you mercy, sir.
             Noble philosopher, your company.

EDGAR   Tom's acold.

GLOUCESTER   In, fellow, there, into th' hovel; keep thee warm.   150

124-25. **cannot suffer:** cannot allow me. —**all:** Emphatic. 130. **philosopher:** man of science. 131. **What is the cause of thunder?** A much-discussed scientific problem in old times. 134-36: **What is your study?** What is your special department of scientific research? Edgar picks up the word *study* and applies it in another sense: "That to which I give all my attention is—how to forestall the assaults of the fiend and kill the vermin that torment me." —**in private:** Lear speaks as if the learned philosopher had answered him sensibly, and as if, therefore, a private conference with him might be useful in the present crisis. 138. **His wits begin t' unsettle:** Significant to the history of Lear's madness. This remark alone is enough to disprove the theory of those who contend that Lear suffers from "senile dementia" at the beginning of the play. 139. **seek his death:** See 2.4.295 ff. 140. **He said it would be thus:** Cf 1.1.139-60. 146. **craz'd:** The literal meaning is "cracked." 147. **cry you mercy:** I beg your pardon for not attending to you. Lear is a little impatient at being interrupted in his conference with the "noble philosopher."

LEAR	Come, let's in all.
KENT	This way, my lord.
LEAR	With him!
	I will keep still with my philosopher.
KENT	Good my lord, soothe him; let him take the fellow.
GLOUCESTER	Take him you on.
KENT	Sirrah, come on; go along with us. 155
LEAR	Come, good Athenian.
GLOUCESTER	No words, no words! hush.
EDGAR	Child Rowland to the dark tower came;
	His word was still
	Fie, foh, and fum! 160
	I smell the blood of a British man. *Exeunt.*

SCENE V. [Gloucester's *Castle.*]

Enter Cornwall and Edmund.

CORNWALL	I will have my revenge ere I depart his house.
EDMUND	How, my lord, I may be censured, that nature thus gives way to loyalty, something fears me to think of.
CORNWALL	I now perceive it was not altogether your brother's evil disposition made him seek his death; but a provoking merit, set awork by a reproveable badness in himself. 6

152. **still:** ever, always. "I will not part company with this learned man." 153. **soothe him:** indulge him; let him have his own way. To *soothe* is literally to "reply 'Sooth!'" (i.e., "True!") to whatever a person says. 154. **Take him you on:** Gloucester assents: "Very well. *You* take the fellow along to the farmhouse, and I will follow with the King." 158-59. **Child Rowland...came:** This may or may not be a line from some ballad—now lost beyond recovery. *Child* was the old title for a candidate for knighthood, not yet dubbed *Sir Knight.* —**Rowland:** Roland, Charlemagne's nephew and the chief Knight in the Charlemagne epic cycle. —**His word was still:** Not a part of any ballad. It is merely Edgar's remark: "His motto or watchword was always—," and then he completes the sentence with something that had nothing to do with Child Rowland and would be instantly recognized by the audience as the Giant's speech in *Jack the Giant-Killer,* and as therefore absurdly inappropriate for a knightly hero: "Fie, foh, and fum! I smell the blood of an English-man."

SCENE V.
The same stormy night as in 3.2-4. Edmund is sent by Cornwall to seek Gloucester in order that he may be arrested.
1. **I will have my revenge:** Edmund has informed Cornwall of Gloucester's intention to relieve Lear and to join the invading party in the King's interest (3.3.6 ff.). 2, 3. **censured:** judged—not blamed. Cf. 5.3.3. —**something fears:** gives me some concern. 4-6. **I now perceive...in himself:** I had supposed that it was merely your brother's evil disposition that made him seek your father's death. I now perceive that there was something else that impelled him—namely, the fact that your father deserved to die. That

EDMUND   How malicious is my fortune that I must repent to be just! This is
              the letter he spoke of, which approves him an intelligent party to the
              advantages of France. O heavens! that this treason were not—or not I
              the detector!   10

CORNWALL   Go with me to the Duchess.

EDMUND   If the matter of this paper be certain, you have mighty business in
              hand.

CORNWALL   True or false, it hath made thee Earl of Gloucester. Seek out where
              thy father is, that he may be ready for our apprehension.   15

EDMUND   [aside] If I find him comforting the King, it will stuff his suspicion
              more fully.—I will persever in my course of loyalty, though the con-
              flict be sore between that and my blood.

CORNWALL   I will lay trust upon thee, and thou shalt find a dearer father in my
              love.   Exeunt.   20

SCENE VI. [A farmhouse near Gloucester's Castle.]

Enter Gloucester, Lear, Kent, Fool, and Edgar.

GLOUCESTER   Here is better than the open air; take it thankfully. I will piece out the
              comfort with what addition I can. I will not be long from you.

KENT   All the power of his wits have given way to his impatience. The gods
              reward your kindness!   Exit [Gloucester].

EDGAR   Fraretetto calls me, and tells me Nero is an angler in the lake of dark-
              ness. Pray, innocent, and beware the foul fiend.   6

---

fact, however, needed your brother's evil nature to make it operate as a cause for his murderous plot.
—**made him seek his death.** Such was the false information that Cornwall and Regan had received on
arriving at Gloucester's castle (2.1.88 ff.). —**a provoking merit:** i.e., on Edmund's part. *Merit* means
"deserts"—a deserving (of death). Cornwall regards Gloucester as a traitor, and therefore as a complete
villain. His character, he suggests, might tempt anyone to kill him. *Provoking* means "inciting." —**in
himself:** in Edgar. 7-9. **just:** righteous, upright. Loyalty, Edmund implies, has forced him to reveal his
father's treason. —**the letter:** Edmund has stolen the letter of which his father told him (3.3.7). —**approves:** proves. —**an intelligent…France:** a person engaged in giving information that will aid the
invading King of France. *Intelligent* has the active sense: "giving information."
15. **apprehension:** arrest. 16. **comforting:** giving aid and comfort to; assisting. 17, 18. **persever:** perse-
vere, remain steadfast. —**my blood:** my natural feelings toward my kindred.
SCENE VI.
The same stormy night as in scenes 1-5. Gloucester leaves Lear in the farmhouse (3.4.150 ff.), returns to
his own castle, and, learning of "a plot of death" against the King (line 82), comes back to the farmhouse
and arranges for Lear to be taken to Dover.
5, 6. **Fraretetto:** Another Harsnet devil. See note on 3.4.94. —**innocent:** fool.

FOOL	Prithee, nuncle, tell me whether a madman be a gentleman or a yeoman?
LEAR	A king, a king!
FOOL	No, he's a yeoman that has a gentleman to his son; for he's a mad yeoman that sees his son a gentleman before him. 11
LEAR	To have a thousand with red burning spits Come hizzing in upon 'em—
EDGAR	The foul fiend bites my back.
FOOL	He's mad that trusts in the tameness of a wolf, a horse's health, a boy's love, or a whore's oath. 16
LEAR	It shall be done; I will arraign them straight. [*To Edgar*] Come, sit thou here, most learned justicer. [*To the Fool*] Thou, sapient sir, sit here. Now, you she-foxes!
EDGAR	Look, where he stands and glares! 20 Want'st thou eyes at trial, madam? Come o'er the bourn, Bessy, to me.
FOOL	Her boat hath a leak, And she must not speak Why she dares not come over to thee. 25
EDGAR	The foul fiend haunts poor Tom in the voice of a nightingale. Hoppedance cries in Tom's belly for two white herring. Croak not, black angel; I have no food for thee.
KENT	How do you, sir? Stand you not so amaz'd. Will you lie down and rest upon the cushions? 30

7-16. The fool expects no answer to his conundrum and of course rejects Lear's passionate solution and furnishes the "correct" answer, which involves a wittily illogical inference from a bit of more or less proverbial worldly wisdom. Then he continues his discourse on madmen with a further definition: "He's mad that trusts," etc. 10, 11. **yeoman:** one who holds property but is not a gentleman in rank. —**before him:** before he has attained that rank himself. 13. **hizzing:** A form of *hissing*. It suggests the whizzing sound of the red-hot weapons as they are to be brandished by the thousand assailants. 14. **bites my back:** Cf. 3.4.135. 15. **a horse's health:** A horse was believed above all other animals to be subject to diseases. 17, 18. **arraign them:** In his delirium Lear abandons the idea of attacking his daughters with an armed force and decides to bring them to trial. —**straight:** straightway, immediately. —**justicer:** judge. 21. **Want'st thou eyes at trial, madam?** Edgar addresses the imaginary Goneril or Regan whom Lear is arraigning: "Do you wish for spectators at your trial, madam? If so, there's a fiend to glare at you." 22. **Come…to me:** Edgar, with a beckoning gesture, addresses the imaginary Goneril or Regan in the words of an old song in which a lover calls upon his sweetheart to come to him "across the brook." 25-28. **in the voice of a nightingale:** The Fool has sung the three lines that precede, which are his improvisation, not a part of the old song. —**Hoppedance:** "Hobberdidance" or "Haberdidance" is a fiend's name in Harsnet's *Declaration.* —**cries in Tom's belly:** He refers to the rumbling sound that indicates an empty stomach. —**white herring:** unsmoked herring. —**Croak not:** a rumbling stomach suggesting hunger. 28. **amaz'd:** in a maze, a strong word indicating a state of confusion.

LEAR	I'll see their trial first. Bring in their evidence.	
	[*To Edgar*] Thou, robed man of justice, take thy place.	
	[*To the Fool*] And thou, his yokefellow of equity,	
	Bench by his side. [*To Kent*] You are o' th' commission,	
	Sit you too.	35
EDGAR	Let us deal justly.	
	Sleepest or wakest thou, jolly shepherd?	
	Thy sheep be in the corn;	
	And for one blast of thy minikin mouth	
	Thy sheep shall take no harm.	40
	Purr! the cat is gray.	
LEAR	Arraign her first. 'Tis Goneril. I here take my oath before this honor-	
	able assembly, she kick'd the poor King her father.	
FOOL	Come hither, mistress. Is your name Goneril?	
LEAR	She cannot deny it.	45
FOOL	Cry you mercy, I took you for a jointstool.	
LEAR	And here's another, whose warp'd looks proclaim	
	What store her heart is made on. Stop her there!	
	Arms, arms! sword! fire! Corruption in the place!	
	False justicer, why hast thou let her scape?	50
EDGAR	Bless thy five wits!	
KENT	O pity! Sir, where is the patience now	
	That you so oft have boasted to retain?	
EDGAR	[*aside*] My tears begin to take his part so much	
	They'll mar my counterfeiting.	55
LEAR	The little dogs and all,	
	Tray, Blanch, and Sweetheart, see, they bark at me.	

---

31. **their evidence:** the witnesses who are to testify against them. 32. **robed:** Edgar wears a blanket which Lear takes for a justice's robe of office. See 3.4.56. 34. **Bench:** Take thy seat on the bench as a judge. —**You are o' th' commission:** You are commissioned as a justice of the peace. 36. **Let us deal justly:** Edgar assumes the air and manner of a dignified judge, but instantly breaks into song and follows his song with a mad exclamation, as if he saw a demon in the shape of a grey cat. 38-41. Apparently a stanza of some old song. —**in the corn:** in the wheatfield. —**for one blast:** for the time it takes to play one strain on your shepherd's pipe. —**minikin:** pretty; fine little. 44. **Come hither…Goneril?** The Fool plays his part as if this were the good old time when he acted in plays at court. —**mistress:** madam. 46. **Cry…stool:** A conventional jocose apology for over-looking a person: "I beg your pardon. I didn't notice that it was you. I thought it was a stool." The Fool takes professional delight in this opportunity to give the worn-out phrase a point; for, in this case, the stool is there and Goneril is not. A *joint-stool* is a stool fitted together by a joiner (a furniture-maker) in distinction from one of ruder manufacture. 47, 48. **warp'd:** distorted by evil passions. —**store:** material. —**on:** of. —**Stop her there!** In his delirium Lear sees Regan escaping from the courtroom. 49. **Corruption in the place!** Bribery in the seat of justice! 51. **Bless thy five wits!** Cf. 3.4.57, note. 52. **patience:** self-control.

EDGAR   Tom will throw his head at them.
                 Avaunt, you curs!
                         Be thy mouth or black or white,   60
                         Tooth that poisons if it bite;
                         Mastiff, greyhound, mongrel grim,
                         Hound or spaniel, brach or lym,
                         Bobtail tyke or trundle-tail—
                         Tom will make them weep and wail;   65
                         For, with throwing thus my head,
                         Dogs leap the hatch, and all are fled.
                 Do de, de, de. Sessa! Come, march to wakes and fairs and market
                 towns. Poor Tom, thy horn is dry.

LEAR   Then let them anatomize Regan. See what breeds about her heart. Is
                 there any cause in nature that makes these hard hearts? [*To Edgar*]
                 You, sir—I entertain you for one of my hundred; only I do not like
                 the fashion of your garments. You'll say they are Persian attire; but let
                 them be chang'd.   74

KENT   Now, good my lord, lie here and rest awhile.

LEAR   Make no noise, make no noise; draw the curtains. So, so, so. We'll go
                 to supper i' th' morning. So, so, so.

FOOL   And I'll go to bed at noon.

                                   Enter Gloucester.

GLOUCESTER Come hither, friend. Where is the King my master?

KENT   Here, sir; but trouble him not; his wits are gone.   80

63, 64. **lym:** a blood-hound. —**tyke:** A light word for "dog"—often used contemptuously (like *cur*). —
trundle-tail: a dog with a long drooping tail which he seems to "trundle" or drag along after him. 67. **the
hatch:** The entrance door of a house or shop often consisted of two parts, an upper and a lower, each moving on hinges. The upper part was frequently left open when the lower part—called "the hatch"—was
closed. 68. **Do de, de, de:** Perhaps words from a song. A *wake* was a night festival held on the vigil—the
eve—of a holy day. —**Sessa!** A mere interjection: "Come on!" Apparently a form of *sa, sa.* 69. **Poor Tom,
thy horn is dry:** A Poor-Tom formula in begging for drink. Beggars were said to have horns hung on
strings about their necks, in which they poured any drink they received when begging for alms. Edgar
implies that he feels scarcely able to maintain his part as poor Tom. 70. **anatomize:** dissect.—**about:** As
if there were some stony growth about her heart. 72. **entertain:** engage; take into my service. 73. **Persian:**
Edgar's strange garb has suggested to Lear two distant nations already—Theban and Athenian (3.4.133,
156). Persian attire was proverbially gorgeous. 76, 77. **the curtains:** Lear lies down "upon the cushions"
(3.6.30). The splendid bed, with its curtains, is a part of his delirium. —**So, so, so:** Spoken as he settles
down to rest: "Ah! well and good." —**supper in the morning:** He suddenly remembers that he has
had no supper—and remarks, madly, "Never mind! We'll have supper at breakfast time tomorrow." This
sounds like a jest to the Fool, who caps it with jester's logic: "Supper in the morning? Very well. Then
bedtime will come at noon!" Some critics have found deep meaning in this trifling jest—as if the Fool
were predicting his own death, or, at least, his final exit from the stage. Why he appears no more in the
play is not difficult to explain. At 4.6.80, Lear enters alone, having been separated in his madness from
all his followers and friends; and in the closing scenes there would be no place for the Fool, in fact. What
becomes of him Shakespeare has simply left to our imagination. (See note, 5.4.306).

GLOUCESTER Good friend, I prithee take him in thy arms.
    I have o'erheard a plot of death upon him.
    There is a litter ready; lay him in't
    And drive towards Dover, friend, where thou shalt meet
    Both welcome and protection. Take up thy master.   85
    If thou shouldst dally half an hour, his life,
    With thine, and all that offer to defend him,
    Stand in assured loss. Take up, take up!
    And follow me, that will to some provision
    Give thee quick conduct.

KENT   Oppressed nature sleeps.   90
    This rest might yet have balm'd thy broken senses,
    Which, if convenience will not allow,
    Stand in hard cure. [*To the Fool*] Come, help to bear thy master.
    Thou must not stay behind.

GLOUCESTER   Come, come, away! *Exeunt [all but Edgar].*

EDGAR When we our betters see bearing our woes,   95
    We scarcely think our miseries our foes.
    Who alone suffers suffers most i' th' mind,
    Leaving free things and happy shows behind;
    But then the mind much sufferance doth o'er skip
    When grief hath mates, and bearing fellowship.   100
    How light and portable my pain seems now,
    When that which makes me bend makes the King bow,
    He childed as I fathered! Tom, away!
    Mark the high noises, and thyself bewray
    When false opinion, whose wrong thought defiles thee,   105
    In thy just proof repeals and reconciles thee.
    What will hap more tonight, safe scape the King!
    Lurk, lurk.   [*Exit.*]

---

88. **Stand in assured loss:** are in a condition in which they are sure to be lost. 89, 90. **some provision:** some means of providing for safety. —**conduct:** escort, guidance. 93. **Stand in hard cure:** are in a condition in which cure is difficult. 95. **our woes:** i.e., the same kind of sorrows that *we* have to bear. 97. **Who alone suffers suffers most i' th' mind:** suffers in his mind more than one who has companions in his misery. Edgar's reflections are an elaboration of the familiar proverb: "Misery loves company." 98-100. **free:** carefree. —**happy shows:** happy looks; all appearances of happiness. —**sufferance:** suffering. —**o'er-skip:** escape, avoid. —**bearing:** endurance. 101. **portable:** endurable. 103. **He childed as I fathered!** *He* has children who are as cruel as the father that *I* have. 104-6. **Mark the high noises:** Give careful attention to the discord among the great and high.—**thyself bewray...reconciles thee:** reveal thyself—throw off thy disguise—when the false opinion that now mistakenly regards thee as a villain, shall, on proof that thou art guiltless, correct itself, and so shall recall thee to favor and make peace between thee and thy father. 107. **What:** whatsoever. 108. **Lurk, lurk:** Remain in hiding.

SCENE VII. [Gloucester's *Castle*.]

Enter Cornwall, Regan, Goneril, [Edmund the] Bastard, and Servants.

CORNWALL [*to Goneril*] Post speedily to my lord your husband, show him this letter. The army of France is landed.—Seek out the traitor Gloucester.
[*Exeunt some of the Servants.*]

REGAN Hang him instantly.

GONERIL Pluck out his eyes.

CORNWALL Leave him to my displeasure. Edmund, keep you our sister company.†
The revenges we are bound to take upon your traitorous father are
not fit for your beholding. Advise the Duke where you are going, to a
most festinate preparation. We are bound to the like. Our posts shall
be swift and intelligent betwixt us. Farewell, dear sister; farewell, my
Lord of Gloucester.   10

Enter [Oswald the] Steward.

How now? Where's the King?

OSWALD My Lord of Gloucester hath convey'd him hence.
Some five or six and thirty of his knights,
Hot questrists after him, met him at gate;
Who, with some other of the lord's dependants,   15
Are gone with him towards Dover, where they boast
To have well-armed friends.

CORNWALL   Get horses for your mistress.

GONERIL Farewell, sweet lord, and sister.

CORNWALL Edmund, farewell.   *Exeunt Goneril, [Edmund, and Oswald].*
Go seek the traitor Gloucester,

SCENE VII.
This scene takes place immediately after scene 6, apparently on the next day—the day following the
stormy night.
2. **France:** the French king. —**is landed.** See 3.3.8-10. **Advise...preparation:** Advise the Duke of
Albany, to whose palace you are going, to make the speediest possible preparation for war. —**festinate:** to
make haste. —**bound to the like:** on our way to the same speedy preparation. —**Our posts:** the couriers
between us and the Duke of Albany. —**intelligent:** giving information; furnished with all necessary
news of our warlike movements. 10. **my Lord of Gloucester:** i.e., Edmund. 14. **Hot questrists after
him:** who had been rapid and eager in their search for him.

---

†   In Michael Elliott's televised 1983 production with Laurence Olivier, the sexual attraction between Regan (Diana Rigg) and Edmund (Robert Lindsey) becomes blatant and is flaunted early
in the scene: Regan kisses Edmund just as her husband Cornwall begins to torture and then blind
Gloucester; later in the scene (4.7.80) she is obviously unperturbed by her husband's death when
the servant stabs him.

Pinion him like a thief, bring him before us.   20

                                                [*Exeunt other Servants.*]

Though well we may not pass upon his life
Without the form of justice, yet our power
Shall do a court'sy to our wrath, which men
May blame, but not control.

           Enter Gloucester, brought in by two or three.

                           Who's there? the traitor?

REGAN   Ingrateful fox! 'tis he.   25

CORNWALL   Bind fast his corky arms.

GLOUCESTER   What mean your Graces? Good my friends, consider
               You are my guests. Do me no foul play, friends.

CORNWALL   Bind him, I say.   [*Servants bind him.*]

REGAN   Hard, hard. O filthy traitor!

GLOUCESTER   Unmerciful lady as you are, I am none.   30

CORNWALL   To this chair bind him. Villain, thou shalt find—[*Regan plucks his beard.*]

GLOUCESTER   By the kind gods, 'tis most ignobly done
               To pluck me by the beard.

REGAN   So white, and such a traitor!

GLOUCESTER   Naughty lady,
               These hairs which thou dost ravish from my chin   35
               Will quicken, and accuse thee. I am your host.
               With robber's hands my hospitable favors
               You should not ruffle thus. What will you do?

CORNWALL   Come, sir, what letters had you late from France?

REGAN   Be simple-answer'd, for we know the truth.   40

CORNWALL   And what confederacy have you with the traitors
               Late footed in the kingdom?

REGAN   To whose hands have you sent the lunatic King?
               Speak.

GLOUCESTER   I have a letter guessingly set down,   45

---

20. **a thief:** a robber. A stronger word than in modern usage. 21. **pass upon:** pass judgment upon. 22-24.
yet our...control: yet our power shall act in accordance with the wrath we feel; and nobody can hinder
that action, though some may perhaps find it blameworthy. 26. **corky:** withered (by old age). 28. **foul
play:** This phrase was not, as in modern usage, confined to the sense of "murder." It is, in origin, the
antithesis to *fair play,* and suggests something that is out of accord with law and justice. 34. **Naughty:**
wicked. 36. **quicken:** come to life; become alive. 37, 38. **my hospitable favors:** "the features of me your
host." —**ruffle thus:** treat with such outrageous violence. A strong word. 40. **Be simple-answer'd:**
Answer without duplicity; tell the plain and simple truth. 42. **footed:** landed.

Which came from one that's of a neutral heart,
And not from one oppos'd.

CORNWALL   Cunning.

REGAN   And false.

CORNWALL   Where hast thou sent the King?

GLOUCESTER To Dover.

REGAN   Wherefore to Dover? Wast thou not charg'd at peril—   50

CORNWALL   Wherefore to Dover? Let him first answer that.

GLOUCESTER I am tied to th' stake, and I must stand the course.

REGAN   Wherefore to Dover, sir?

GLOUCESTER Because I would not see thy cruel nails
             Pluck out his poor old eyes; nor thy fierce sister   55
             In his anointed flesh stick boarish fangs.
             The sea, with such a storm as his bare head
             In hell-black night endur'd, would have buoy'd up
             And quench'd the stelled fires.
             Yet, poor old heart, he holp the heavens to rain.   60
             If wolves had at thy gate howl'd that stern time,
             Thou shouldst have said, "Good porter, turn the key."
             All cruels else subscrib'd. But I shall see
             The winged vengeance overtake such children.

CORNWALL   See't shalt thou never. Fellows, hold the chair.   65
             Upon these eyes of thine I'll set my foot.

GLOUCESTER He that will think to live till he be old,
             Give me some help!—O cruel! O ye gods!

REGAN   One side will mock another. Th' other too!

CORNWALL   If you see vengeance—

1. SERVANT   Hold your hand, my lord!   70
             I have serv'd you ever since I was a child;

---

50. **at peril:** under penalty (of death). 52. **tied...course:** A figure from bear-baiting. The bear was tied to a post and dogs were set on to attack him. A *course* (literally, a "running") was one such attack, lasting until the dogs were called off. 56. **anointed:** Anointing with holy oil was a part of the ceremony of coronation. Thus a king was a consecrated personage, whom it was sacrilege to attack. 58. **would have buoy'd up:** would have surged aloft in one great wave. 59. **the stelled fires:** the starry fires; the fires of the stars. Cf. Latin *stellatus* (from *stella,* star). 60. **holp:** helped. Both forms occur in Shakespeare. 61, 62. **Wolves:** Emphatic: "even wolves," the outlaws among wild animals. —**howl'd:** come howling for shelter. —**shouldst:** wouldst certainly. —**turn the key:** and let them in, out of the storm. 63. **All cruels else subscrib'd:** All other cruel creatures except you gave up their cruel natures in submission to the terror of the storm. 64. **The winged vengeance:** the vengeance of the gods, sweeping down upon them like a bird of prey.

But better service have I never done you
Than now to bid you hold.

REGAN   How now, you dog?

1. SERVANT   If you did wear a beard upon your chin,
I'ld shake it on this quarrel.

REGAN   What do you mean?   75

CORNWALL   My villain!   *Draw and fight.*

1. SERVANT   Nay, then, come on, and take the chance of anger.

REGAN   Give me thy sword. A peasant stand up thus?
She takes a sword and runs at him behind.

1. SERVANT   O, I am slain! My lord, you have one eye left
To see some mischief on him. O!   *He dies.*   80

CORNWALL   Lest it see more, prevent it. Out, vile jelly!
Where is thy lustre now?

GLOUCESTER   All dark and comfortless! Where's my son Edmund?
Edmund, enkindle all the sparks of nature
To quit this horrid act.

REGAN   Out, treacherous villain!   85
Thou call'st on him that hates thee. It was he
That made the overture of thy treasons to us;
Who is too good to pity thee.

GLOUCESTER   O my follies! Then Edgar was abus'd.
Kind gods, forgive me that, and prosper him!   90

REGAN   Go thrust him out at gates, and let him smell
His way to Dover.   *Exit [one] with Gloucester.*
How is't, my lord? How look you?

CORNWALL   I have receiv'd a hurt. Follow me, lady.
Turn out that eyeless villain. Throw this slave
Upon the dunghill. Regan, I bleed apace.   95
Untimely comes this hurt. Give me your arm.
Exit [Cornwall, led by Regan].

2. SERVANT   I'll never care what wickedness I do,

---

75. **this quarrel:** this cause—i.e., the cause for which I contend in this case; my defense of the old man. 76. **My villain!** My serf. Used rather as a term of abuse than in the literal sense. 80. **mischief:** harm, injury. 81. **more:** i.e., more harm than you have already done me. The servant has given Cornwall a fatal wound, as we learn from 4.2.70-72. —**prevent it:** forestall it; prevent it by anticipatory action. 84, 85. **nature:** natural affection. —**quit:** repay. —**Out:** Out upon thee! An interjection of cursing. 87. **overture:** disclosure. 89. **abus'd:** deceived (by Edmund). 90. **that:** my treatment of my son—the result of "my follies." 92. **How look you?** How do you seem to be (well or ill)?

If this man come to good.

3. SERVANT   If she live long,
And in the end meet the old course of death,
Women will all turn monsters.   100

2. SERVANT   Let's follow the old Earl, and get the bedlam
To lead him where he would. His roguish madness
Allows itself to anything.

3. SERVANT   Go thou. I'll fetch some flax and whites of eggs
To apply to his bleeding face. Now heaven help him!   *Exeunt.*   105

ACT IV

SCENE I. [*The heath.*]

Enter Edgar.

EDGAR   Yet better thus, and known to be contemn'd,
Than still contemn'd and flatter'd. To be worst,
The lowest and most dejected thing of fortune,
Stands still in esperance, lives not in fear.
The lamentable change is from the best;   5
The worst returns to laughter. Welcome then,
Thou unsubstantial air that I embrace!
The wretch that thou hast blown unto the worst
Owes nothing to thy blasts.

Enter Gloucester, led by an Old Man.

But who comes here?
My father, poorly led? World, world, O world!   10

---

98. **Untimely:** since it disables me when I should be leading my army against the invaders. 100. **Women will all turn monsters:** because they will lose all fear of vengeance from the gods for any misdeed, however flagrant. 101. **the bedlam:** the mad beggar, Edgar. 102, 103. **His roguish madness...anything:** The fact that he is a vagabond (a rogue) and a madman makes it possible for him to do anything without being called to account.

ACT IV. SCENE I.
This scene takes place on the same day as 3.7. It follows that scene almost immediately.
1. **thus:** in this beggarly condition. 3, 4. **most dejected:** most cast down—synonymous with *lowest*. Edgar comforts himself with the commonplace reflection that any change from the worst must be for the better. —**of fortune:** in my fortunes. —**Stands still in esperance:** is in condition that always admits of hope. 6. **The worst returns to laughter:** The worst condition, when it changes, marks one's return to happiness. 9. **Owes nothing to thy blasts:** and therefore need have no fear of what they can do to him. The figure is from the relation of creditor and debtor: when a man's debts are paid, he fears no creditor.

But that thy strange mutations make us hate thee,
Life would not yield to age.

OLD MAN   O my good lord,
I have been your tenant, and your father's tenant,
These fourscore years.

GLOUCESTER Away, get thee away! Good friend, be gone.   15
Thy comforts can do me no good at all;
Thee they may hurt.

OLD MAN   You cannot see your way.

GLOUCESTER I have no way, and therefore want no eyes;
I stumbled when I saw. Full oft 'tis seen
Our means secure us, and our mere defects   20
Prove our commodities. Ah dear son Edgar,
The food of thy abused father's wrath!
Might I but live to see thee in my touch,
I'ld say I had eyes again!

OLD MAN   How now? Who's there?

EDGAR   [aside] O gods! Who is't can say "I am at the worst"? 25
I am worse than e'er I was.

OLD MAN   'Tis poor mad Tom.

EDGAR   [aside] And worse I may be yet. The worst is not
So long as we can say "This is the worst."

OLD MAN   Fellow, where goest?

GLOUCESTER   Is it a beggarman?

OLD MAN   Madman and beggar too.   30

GLOUCESTER He has some reason, else he could not beg.
I' th' last night's storm I such a fellow saw,

11, 12. **But that...age:** The only thing that makes us grow old and die is our hatred of life in this world, and that hatred is caused by the strange vicissitudes of fortune. 16. **Thy comforts:** thy attempts to aid me in my misery. 18. **I have no way:** There is no path in life for me to follow—nothing left for me to do with myself in this world. 19-21. **I stumbled when I saw:** When I had my eyes, I walked recklessly and lost my footing. Gloucester refers to the terrible blunder he had made in believing Edmund's lies about Edgar, which, he thinks, ought to have been obvious to any clear-sighted judgment. —**Full oft 'tis seen...commodities:** Thus Gloucester interprets "I stumbled when I saw" and applies it as a general truth of common experience: "Prosperity makes us careless, and adversity ('our mere defects') proves to be an advantage, for it forces us to recognize the facts of life." Now, in his blindness, he sees the truth. —**secure:** make careless or over-confident (Latin *securus,* "without care"). —**mere:** absolute. **defects:** deprivations. —**commodities:** benefits. 22. **The food of thy abused father's wrath:** that on which his anger fed; the object of his anger. —**abused:** deceived. 23, 24. **Might I...again!** To hold thee in my embrace again would be as great a blessing as the restoration of eyesight. 27, 28. **The worst is not... worst:** for so long as we can take comfort in assuring ourselves that we are at the worst, that comforting reflection shows that we are not hopeless, and so not actually at the worst. 29. **goest?** goest thou?

Which made me think a man a worm. My son
Came then into my mind, and yet my mind
Was then scarce friends with him. I have heard more since. 35
As flies to wanton boys are we to th' gods.†
They kill us for their sport.

EDGAR   [*aside*] How should this be?
Bad is the trade that must play fool to sorrow,
Ang'ring itself and others.—Bless thee, master!

GLOUCESTER Is that the naked fellow?

OLD MAN   Ay, my lord.   40

GLOUCESTER Then prithee get thee gone. If for my sake
Thou wilt o'ertake us hence a mile or twain
I' th' way toward Dover, do it for ancient love;
And bring some covering for this naked soul,
Who I'll entreat to lead me.

OLD MAN   Alack, sir, he is mad!   45

GLOUCESTER 'Tis the time's plague when madmen lead the blind.
Do as I bid thee, or rather do thy pleasure.
Above the rest, be gone.

OLD MAN I'll bring him the best 'parel that I have,
Come on't what will.   *Exit.*   50

GLOUCESTER Sirrah naked fellow—

EDGAR   Poor Tom's acold. [*Aside*] I cannot daub it further.

GLOUCESTER Come hither, fellow.

EDGAR   [*aside*] And yet I must.—Bless thy sweet eyes, they bleed.

GLOUCESTER Know'st thou the way to Dover?   55

EDGAR   Both stile and gate, horseway and footpath. Poor Tom hath been
scar'd out of his good wits. Bless thee, good man's son, from the foul

---

33. **a worm.** *Job*, xxv, 6: "How much less man, that is a worm? and the son of man, which is a worm?"
34. **Came then into my mind:** because I thought that my son was doubtless a homeless wanderer like
that poor beggar. 35. **friends:** friendly. 36. **wanton:** sportive, playful. 38, 39. **play fool to sorrow:** act the
fool to one who is in sorrow (as my father is). **—Ang'ring:** distressing. **—master:** sir. 46. **'Tis...blind.**
Gloucester makes a kind of parable out of his own situation: "So it is in the world. When the leaders are
mad and the people themselves are blind—that is a sad time for humanity." 47. **do thy pleasure:** do what
you please. Gloucester is in no condition to give an order to anybody. 52. **I cannot daub it further:** "I
cannot carry on this miserable counterfeiting any longer." To *daub* is, literally, to plaster with mortar.

---

†   (*So are we to the gods*) In Trevor Nunn's production, the Earl of Gloucester (William Gaunt) is
      guided at first by a young woman (not an old man), wrapped in a hooded cloak. At these words,
      she weeps, tears gleaming on her face.

fiend! Five fiends have been in poor Tom at once: of lust, as Obidicut;
Hobbididence, prince of dumbness; Mahu, of stealing; Modo, of
murder; Flibbertigibbet, of mopping and mowing, who since possesses chambermaids and waiting women. So, bless thee, master!   61

GLOUCESTER Here, take this purse, thou whom the heavens' plagues
            Have humbled to all strokes. That I am wretched
            Makes thee the happier. Heavens, deal so still!
            Let the superfluous and lust-dieted man,   65
            That slaves your ordinance, that will not see
            Because he does not feel, feel your pow'r quickly;
            So distribution should undo excess,
            And each man have enough. Dost thou know Dover?

EDGAR   Ay, master.   70

GLOUCESTER There is a cliff, whose high and bending head
            Looks fearfully in the confined deep.
            Bring me but to the very brim of it,
            And I'll repair the misery thou dost bear
            With something rich about me. From that place   75
            I shall no leading need.

EDGAR   Give me thy arm.
            Poor Tom shall lead thee.   *Exeunt.*

58-61. **Five fiends:** Obidicut and the four other devils are from Harsnet's *Declaration* (see note, 3.4.95)
[K.S.R]. —**mopping and mowing:** grimacing and making faces.—**since:** i.e., since Flibbertigibbet
left me, he has possessed chambermaids and waiting women, who are for ever twisting their faces into
strange shapes in the attempt to put on elegant airs. A *flibbertigibbet* is a "flirt," a "frivolous creature."
Hence this is a good name for the demon that affects airs and graces. 63. **Have humbled to all strokes:**
have brought so low that thou sufferest every kind of misery. 64. **deal so still!** Gloucester calls upon the
gods to make his sufferings a common experience of the great and high when—as in his own case—they
have abused their prosperity. 65-69. **Let...enough:** Let the man who has far more than he needs and is
able to gratify every desire, feel your power quickly (as I have been made to feel it). In this way such men
will learn to distribute their superfluous wealth among the needy, and no one will be in want. Compare
Lear's expression of the same idea in 3.4.34-37. —**superfluous:** Cf.2.4.262. —**lust-dieted:** whose lusts
(i.e., desires of every kind) are fed to the full. —**That slaves your ordinance:** The gods have ordained
that one man shall be rich and another poor. Thus they have imposed upon the man who has a superfluity
the obligation to use his riches for the relief of his needy fellow-creatures. But he treats this ordinance of
the gods as if it were not an *obligation* but an *unlimited privilege.* 72. **fearfully:** so as to inspire terror in
one who looks over the edge. —**in:** down into. —**the confined deep:** the Strait of Dover. —**confined:**
shut in by land on both sides.

SCENE II. [*Before the* Duke of Albany's *Palace.*]

Enter Goneril and [Edmund the] Bastard.

GONERIL   Welcome, my lord. I marvel our mild husband
Not met us on the way.

Enter [Oswald the] Steward.

Now, where's your master?

OSWALD   Madam, within, but never man so chang'd.
I told him of the army that was landed:
He smil'd at it. I told him you were coming: 5
His answer was, "The worse." Of Gloucester's treachery
And of the loyal service of his son
When I inform'd him, then he call'd me sot
And told me I had turn'd the wrong side out.
What most he should dislike seems pleasant to him;   10
What like, offensive.

GONERIL   [*to Edmund*]   Then shall you go no further.
It is the cowish terror of his spirit,
That dares not undertake. He'll not feel wrongs
Which tie him to an answer. Our wishes on the way
May prove effects. Back, Edmund, to my brother.   15
Hasten his musters and conduct his pow'rs.
I must change arms at home and give the distaff
Into my husband's hands. This trusty servant
Shall pass between us. Ere long you are like to hear
(If you dare venture in your own behalf)   20
A mistress's command. Wear this.
[*Gives a favor.*]
                                    Spare speech.
Decline your head.† This kiss, if it durst speak,

SCENE II.
This scene follows scene 1 almost immediately—perhaps on the next day.
2. **on the way:** on the way from Gloucester's castle. 4. **the army that was landed.** See 3.3.9-10. 8. **sot:** fool. 9. **had turn'd the wrong side out:** because I should have said "Edmund's treachery" and "the loyal service of Gloucester." 12. **cowish:** cowardly. 13. **undertake:** show activity or enterprise in anything. 14, 15. **Our wishes:** Goneril and Edmund have been making love en route. —**May prove effects:** may perhaps be fulfilled. 16. **his pow'rs:** his troops. 17. **change:** exchange; for I must take the sword and give my husband the distaff (a staff used in spinning, the regular emblem of wifely industry, and also a woman's weapon.) 21. **A mistress's command:** a command from one who is not only your mistress in rank but your sweetheart as well.

---

†   (*Decline thy dead*) in Trevor Nunn's production, Goneril (Frances Barber) kisses Edmund deeply, and he returns her kiss, after the next line: "Yours in the ranks of death."

	Would stretch thy spirits up into the air.	
	Conceive, and fare thee well.	
EDMUND	Yours in the ranks of death!	*Exit.*
GONERIL	My most dear Gloucester!	25
	O, the difference of man and man!	
	To thee a woman's services are due;	
	My fool usurps my body.	
OSWALD	Madam, here comes my lord.	*Exit.*

Enter Albany.

GONERIL	I have been worth the whistle.	
ALBANY	O Goneril,	
	You are not worth the dust which the rude wind	30
	Blows in your face! I fear your disposition.	
	That nature which contemns it origin	
	Cannot be bordered certain in itself.	
	She that herself will sliver and disbranch	
	From her material sap, perforce must wither	35
	And come to deadly use.	
GONERIL	No more! The text is foolish.	
ALBANY	Wisdom and goodness to the vile seem vile;	
	Filths savor but themselves. What have you done?	
	Tigers, not daughters, what have you perform'd?	40
	A father, and a gracious aged man,	
	Whose reverence even the head-lugg'd bear would lick,	
	Most barbarous, most degenerate, have you madded.	
	Could my good brother suffer you to do it?	
	A man, a prince, by him so benefited!	45
	If that the heavens do not their visible spirits	

---

24. **Conceive:** understand my meaning. 25. **Yours...death!** Spoken with a flourishing gesture of devotion. 28. **My fool:** one who should rather be the court fool than be my husband. —**body:** Edmund has her *heart.* 29. **I have been worth the whistle:** Goneril implies that her husband has been slow in meeting her: "There *has* been a time when I was worth whistling for!" 31. **I fear your disposition:** Your disposition (character, temperament) is such as to make me anxious about you. 32. **it:** its. 33. **Cannot be...in itself:** can have no sure boundaries of conduct in its own character. There is no enormity that it may not perpetrate. 34, 35. **sliver and disbranch:** Synonymous: "sever." —**From her material sap:** from the tree whence she draws the vital element that constitutes and nourishes her frame. 36. **to deadly use:** to destruction—as the dead branches of a tree are of use only as fuel and so come to naught. 37. **No more! The text is foolish:** No more of this sermon! Since the text is foolish, we cannot expect the sermon to be worth hearing. 39. **Filths savor but themselves:** "To the filthy all things taste filthy." —**savor:** get the taste of. 41. **gracious:** kindly. 42. **Whose reverence...lick:** to whom even a sulky bear would do homage by licking his hand. —**head-lugg'd:** tugged along by the head. The slow lumbering gait of a bear gives one the impression of surly reluctance. 46-50. **visible:** in visible form.

Send quickly down to tame these vile offences,
It will come,
Humanity must perforce prey on itself,
Like monsters of the deep.

GONERIL   Milk-liver'd man!   50
That bear'st a cheek for blows, a head for wrongs;
Who hast not in thy brows an eye discerning
Thine honor from thy suffering; that not know'st
Fools do those villains pity who are punish'd
Ere they have done their mischief. Where's thy drum?   55
France spreads his banners in our noiseless land,
With plumed helm thy state begins to threat,
Whiles thou, a moral fool, sit'st still, and criest
"Alack, why does he so?"

ALBANY   See thyself, devil!
Proper deformity seems not in the fiend   60
So horrid as in woman.

GONERIL   O vain fool!

ALBANY   Thou changed and self-cover'd thing, for shame!
Bemonster not thy feature! Were't my fitness
To let these hands obey my blood,
They are apt enough to dislocate and tear   65
Thy flesh and bones. Howe'er thou art a fiend,
A woman's shape doth shield thee.

GONERIL   Marry, your manhood mew!

—**tame:** subdue, put down. —**It will come...itself:** The inevitable result will follow—all men will become ferocious animals and devour each other. 50. **Milk-liver'd:** white-livered. Cowardice was thought to be caused by lack of blood in the liver. 52, 53. **an eye discerning...suffering:** an eye that can discriminate between what one may honorably endure and what should spur one to noble resentment. 54-55. **Fools...mischief.** Goneril continues to upbraid him for inaction. "You do not understand that only a *fool* will pity such wretched creatures as are overtaken by punishment before they have summoned up energy enough to strike a blow." Albany's inaction, she implies, will be his ruin, and nobody will ever pity him. 56, 57. **France:** the King of France. —**noiseless:** quiet—i.e., passive and unresisting. —**thy state:** thy government; thy dominions. 58. **moral:** moralizing; i.e., arguing about the rights and wrongs of the matter instead of opposing the invader. 60. **Proper:** i.e., proper to the fiend—appropriate to his character, and therefore not so repulsive. 61. **vain:** silly. 62-65. **changed and self-cover'd:** transformed in thine appearance and with thy woman's self covered by the likeness of a fiend. —**Bemonster...feature!** Do not allow thy form and features to be thus transformed into those of a monster! *Feature* includes her whole shape. Albany knows that Goneril is a woman; yet she seems to be changing to a fiend before his eyes. —**Were't my fitness:** if it were right and proper for me. —**my blood:** my passionate impulse. —**apt:** ready. 66, 67. **Howe'er...shield thee:** Yet, after all, however much of a fiend thou art, I see that thy shape is still that of a woman; and so thou art safe from my attack. 68. **Marry:** Literally, an oath: by the Virgin Mary. Here used as a slight interjection, dismissing the subject: "Well, well." —**your manhood mew!** Your valor seems to be feeble—in need of nursing and tender care to restore it to vigor. Shut it up in the *mews* awhile, as we confine an ailing falcon that requires dieting and medicine. The *mews* was a building in which hawks were caged.

Enter a Gentleman.

ALBANY   What news?

GENTLEMAN   O, my good lord, the Duke of Cornwall's dead,   70
            Slain by his servant, going to put out
            The other eye of Gloucester.

ALBANY   Gloucester's eyes?

GENTLEMAN   A servant that he bred, thrill'd with remorse,
            Oppos'd against the act, bending his sword
            To his great master; who, thereat enrag'd,   75
            Flew on him, and amongst them fell'd him dead;
            But not without that harmful stroke which since
            Hath pluck'd him after.

ALBANY   This shows you are above,
            You justicers, that these our nether crimes
            So speedily can venge! But O poor Gloucester!   80
            Lost he his other eye?

GENTLEMAN   Both, both, my lord.
            This letter, madam, craves a speedy answer.
            'Tis from your sister.

GONERIL   [*aside*]   One way I like this well;
            But being widow, and my Gloucester with her,
            May all the building in my fancy pluck   85
            Upon my hateful life. Another way
            The news is not so tart.—I'll read, and answer.   *Exit.*

ALBANY   Where was his son when they did take his eyes?

GENTLEMAN   Come with my lady hither.

ALBANY   He is not here.

GENTLEMAN   No, my good lord; I met him back again.   90

ALBANY   Knows he the wickedness?

GENTLEMAN   Ay, my good lord. 'Twas he inform'd against him,

---

73. **remorse:** pity, compassion. 74, 75. **bending his sword To:** directing his sword against. 76. **fell'd:** they felled. 78. **pluck'd:** To *pluck* is the regular Elizabethan verb for to "pull." —**him:** Cornwall. 79. **our nether crimes:** our offenses in this world. 83. **One way I like this well:** In one respect Cornwall's death is good news, since it has removed an obstacle to Goneril's plans. Her hope was to get rid of her husband, marry Edmund, and seize Regan's half of the kingdom, thus becoming sole Queen of Britain. 85-87. **May…life:** may pull down the whole structure that I have raised in my imagination and bury the rest of my life in its ruins—so that my life will be hateful to me. If Regan wins Edmund as a husband, Goneril's plan will obviously fail and she will probably lose her own half of Britain. —**Another way:** Goneril returns to the first consideration. "Another way" is the same as the "one way" of line 83. —**tart:** disagreeable. 90. **back again:** as he was on his way back to Gloucester's castle.

And quit the house on purpose, that their punishment
Might have the freer course.

ALBANY   Gloucester, I live
To thank thee for the love thou show'dst the King,   95
And to revenge thine eyes. Come hither, friend.
Tell me what more thou know'st.   *Exeunt.*

[SCENE III. *The French camp near Dover.*]

Enter Kent and a Gentleman.

KENT   Why the King of France is so suddenly gone back know you the
            reason?

GENTLEMAN   Something he left imperfect in the state, which since his coming forth
            is thought of, which imports to the kingdom so much fear and dan-
            ger that his personal return was most required and necessary.   5

KENT   Who hath he left behind him general?

GENTLEMAN   The Marshal of France, Monsieur La Far.

KENT   Did your letters pierce the Queen to any demonstration of grief?

GENTLEMAN   Ay, sir. She took them, read them in my presence,
            And now and then an ample tear trill'd down   10
            Her delicate cheek. It seem'd she was a queen
            Over her passion, who, most rebel-like,
            Sought to be king o'er her.

KENT   O, then it mov'd her?

GENTLEMAN   Not to a rage. Patience and sorrow strove
            Who should express her goodliest. You have seen   15
            Sunshine and rain at once: her smiles and tears
            Were like, a better way. Those happy smilets

---

96. **revenge:** avenge.
SCENE III.
The Gentleman who enters in conversation with Kent is the same that he had sent to Dover with a message
to Cordelia (3.1.35 ff.). In the interval between this scene and scene 2, Lear has reached Dover (line 36).
The interval cannot be long, for Gloucester was being led toward Dover Cliff in 4.1, and he reaches the cliff
in 4.6. Scenes 4, 5 and 6 of this Act all occur on one and the same day. This scene is omitted in the Folios.
3-5. **the state:** the administration of the government. —**which imports...danger:** which, unless it
is attended to, will bring upon the French kingdom so much panic and danger. —**required:** imperative. 8. **letters:** letter. 12. **passion:** emotion, sorrow. —**rebel-like:** Impulse and passion or emotion are
often figured as rebelling against one's reason or self-control. 14, 15. **rage:** a violent outburst of grief,
not wrath. —**Patience:** self-control. —**express her goodliest:** give her the most beautiful expression.
17-19. **Were like, a better way:** were like sunshine and rain at once, but after a better fashion—i.e., the
comparison does her smiles and tears injustice; they were more beautiful than mingled sunshine and
rain. —**smilets:** little smiles.

That play'd on her ripe lip seem'd not to know
What guests were in her eyes, which parted thence
As pearls from diamonds dropp'd. In brief,   20
Sorrow would be a rarity most belov'd,
If all could so become it.

KENT   Made she no verbal question?

GENTLEMAN Faith, once or twice she heav'd the name of father
Pantingly forth, as if it press'd her heart;
Cried "Sisters, sisters! Shame of ladies! Sisters!   25
Kent! father! sisters! What, i' th' storm? i' th' night?
Let pity not be believ'd!" There she shook
The holy water from her heavenly eyes,
And clamor moisten'd. Then away she started
To deal with grief alone.

KENT   It is the stars,   30
The stars above us, govern our conditions;
Else one self mate and mate could not beget
Such different issues. You spoke not with her since?

GENTLEMAN No.

KENT   Was this before the King return'd?

GENTLEMAN   No, since.   35

KENT   Well, sir, the poor distressed Lear's i' th' town;
Who sometime, in his better tune, remembers
What we are come about, and by no means
Will yield to see his daughter.

GENTLEMAN   Why, good sir?

KENT   A sovereign shame so elbows him; his own unkindness,   40
That stripp'd her from his benediction, turn'd her
To foreign casualties, gave her dear rights
To his dog-hearted daughters—these things sting

—which: who—i.e., the guests in her eyes, the tears. 20. pearls from diamonds dropp'd: We should remember that it is a courtly gentleman who is speaking, and that elegant language was expected of courtiers. Shakespeare often calls tears "pearls." 22. If all could so become it: if it could be so becoming to *all* as it is to *her*. —Made she no verbal question? Did she actually say nothing *in words*? *Question* means "speech," not "interrogation." 27. believ'd: believed in (as existent in a world that sees such deeds). 29. And clamor moisten'd: and thus she moistened her lamentation—i.e., followed her cries of sorrow with tears. The Gentleman outdoes himself in this phrase, but the meaning is clear enough. 31, 32. our conditions: our characters. —one self: one and the same. 37. sometime: sometimes. —in his better tune: in a comparatively lucid interval. 40. sovereign: over-mastering, overpowering. —elbows him: stands by his side like a constant attendant. 41. stripp'd her from his benediction: deprived her of his blessing when they parted. 43. dog-hearted: Without pity [K.S.R].

His mind so venomously that burning shame
Detains him from Cordelia.

GENTLEMAN   Alack, poor gentleman!   45

KENT   Of Albany's and Cornwall's powers you heard not?

GENTLEMAN 'Tis so; they are afoot.

KENT   Well, sir, I'll bring you to our master Lear
And leave you to attend him. Some dear cause
Will in concealment wrap me up awhile.   50
When I am known aright, you shall not grieve
Lending me this acquaintance. I pray you go
Along with me.   *Exeunt.*

SCENE IV. [*The French camp.*]

Enter, with Drum and Colors, Cordelia, Doctor, and Soldiers.

CORDELIA   Alack, 'tis he! Why, he was met even now
As mad as the vex'd sea, singing aloud,
Crown'd with rank fumiter and furrow weeds,
With hardocks, hemlock, nettles, cuckoo flow'rs,
Darnel, and all the idle weeds that grow   5
In our sustaining corn. A century send forth.
Search every acre in the high-grown field
And bring him to our eye.   [*Exit an Officer.*]
          What can man's wisdom
In the restoring his bereaved sense?   10
He that helps him take all my outward worth

DOCTOR   There is means, madam.
Our foster nurse of nature is repose,
The which he lacks. That to provoke in him

---

46. **powers:** forces, troops. 47. **'Tis so:** The report is true. —**afoot:** in motion; on the move. 49-52. **dear:** important. —**aright:** in my true character. —**not grieve/Lending me:** not be sorry for having known me [K.S.R.].

SCENE IV.
Between this scene and scene 3 Lear has wandered away, and has to be rediscovered (lines 6-8). 3. **fumiter:** fumitory, a wild herb. 4-6. **Hardocks:** There is a weed called *hardhack* in New England. —**cuckoo flow'rs:** So called because they flower for the most part in April and May, when the Cuckoo begins to sing. —**Darnel:** tares [vetch or other such weeds. K.S.R]. —**idle:** useless. —**sustaining:** supporting—since bread is "the staff of life." —**corn:** wheat. —**A century:** a troop of a hundred soldiers. 9. **What can man's wisdom?** What power has science? 11. **worth:** property, possessions. 13. **Our... nature:** the foster nurse of our nature; that which fosters and sustains our life. 14-16. **provoke:** induce.

Are many simples operative, whose power   15
Will close the eye of anguish.

CORDELIA   All blest secrets,
All you unpublish'd virtues of the earth,
Spring with my tears! be aidant and remediate
In the good man's distress! Seek, seek for him!
Lest his ungovern'd rage dissolve the life   20
That wants the means to lead it.

Enter Messenger.

MESSENGER   News, madam.
The British pow'rs are marching hitherward.

CORDELIA   'Tis known before. Our preparation stands
In expectation of them. O dear father,
It is thy business that I go about.   25
Therefore great France
My mourning and important tears hath pitied.
No blown ambition doth our arms incite,
But love, dear love, and our ag'd father's right.
Soon may I hear and see him!   *Exeunt.*   30

SCENE V. [*Gloucester's Castle.*]

Enter Regan and [Oswald the] Steward.

REGAN   But are my brother's pow'rs set forth?

OSWALD   Ay, madam.

REGAN   Himself in person there?

OSWALD   Madam, with much ado
Your sister is the better soldier.

—**simples:** medicinal plants—so called in contradistinction to *compounds.* —**anguish:** extreme physical pain. 16, 17. **secrets.** In old times every distinguished physician claimed the knowledge of "secrets"— special remedies, unknown to the majority. The next line repeats the sense with elaboration of phrase. — **virtues:** efficacious medicinal plants. —**of the earth:** that grow in the earth. Medicine in Shakespeare's day was, for the most part, botanical medicine. 18. **be aidant and remediate:** act as aids and remedies. 20, 21. **rage:** frenzy. —**the means:** i.e., his reason. 22-24. **pow'rs:** forces. —**Our preparation...them:** Our troops stand ready to meet them. 27. **important:** importunate. 28. **blown:** puffed up, swollen.
SCENE V.
The scene seems to occur on the same day as scene 4. Oswald's fidelity to Goneril comes out clearly in this scene. Regan does not succeed in getting a sight of Goneril's letter.
1. **pow'rs:** troops. 2. **with much ado:** as the result of much effort. Albany's reluctance is made clear in 4.2.

REGAN	Lord Edmund spake not with your lord at home?
OSWALD	No, madam. 5
REGAN	What might import my sister's letter to him?
OSWALD	I know not, lady.
REGAN	Faith, he is posted hence on serious matter.
	It was great ignorance, Gloucester's eyes being out,
	To let him live. Where he arrives he moves 10
	All hearts against us. Edmund, I think, is gone,
	In pity of his misery, to dispatch
	His nighted life; moreover, to descry
	The strength o' th' enemy.
OSWALD	I must needs after him, madam, with my letter. 15
REGAN	Our troops set forth tomorrow. Stay with us.
	The ways are dangerous.
OSWALD	I may not, madam.
	My lady charg'd my duty in this business.
REGAN	Why should she write to Edmund? Might not you
	Transport her purposes by word? Belike, 20
	Something—I know not what—I'll love thee much—
	Let me unseal the letter.
OSWALD	Madam, I had rather—
REGAN	I know your lady does not love her husband;
	I am sure of that; and at her late being here
	She gave strange eliads and most speaking looks 25
	To noble Edmund. I know you are of her bosom.
OSWALD	I, madam?
REGAN	I speak in understanding. Y'are! I know't.
	Therefore I do advise you take this note.
	My lord is dead; Edmund and I have talk'd, 30
	And more convenient is he for my hand
	Than for your lady's. You may gather more.

---

4. **Lord Edmund…home?** We do not hear the whole of the conversation between Regan and Oswald. He has apparently already given her that information, and she then recalls his words and asks for confirmation. 6. **might import:** could signify.—**my sister's letter:** The letter with which Oswald was entrusted by Goneril. Regan is justly suspicious as to its contents. 8. **on serious matter:** on important business. 20. **Belike:** probably. 25. **eliads:** languishing looks. 26. **of her bosom:** in her confidence. 29. **take this note:** to take note of this; to receive and consider what I tell you. 30-32. **have talk'd:** i.e., practically, "have come to an understanding." —**more convenient:** more fitting. —**You may gather more:** You can draw a further inference from the hints that I have given you.

If you do find him, pray you give him this;
And when your mistress hears thus much from you,
I pray desire her call her wisdom to her.   ▸   35
So farewell.
If you do chance to hear of that blind traitor,
Preferment falls on him that cuts him off.

OSWALD   Would I could meet him, madam! I should show
What party I do follow.

REGAN   Fare thee well.   *Exeunt.*   40

SCENE VI. [*The country near Dover.*]

Enter Gloucester, and Edgar [like a Peasant].

GLOUCESTER When shall I come to th' top of that same hill?[†]

EDGAR   You do climb up it now. Look how we labor.

GLOUCESTER Methinks the ground is even.

EDGAR   Horrible steep.
Hark, do you hear the sea?

GLOUCESTER   No, truly.

EDGAR   Why then, your other senses grow imperfect   5
By your eyes' anguish.

GLOUCESTER   So may it be indeed.
Methinks thy voice is alter'd, and thou speak'st
In better phrase and matter than thou didst.

EDGAR   Y'are much deceiv'd. In nothing am I chang'd
But in my garments.

GLOUCESTER   Methinks y'are better spoken.   10

EDGAR   Come on, sir; here's the place. Stand still. How fearful
And dizzy 'tis to cast one's eyes so low!

---

33. **this.** Some love token—not a letter, for, when Oswald is searched by Edgar, only the letter from Goneril
is found (4.6.249 ff.). 34. **thus much:** i.e., what I have told you. 38. **Preferment:** promotion, advancement.
SCENE VI.
This scene must take place on the same day as scene 5. The interval between the present scene and scene
3 cannot be more than one day.

---

†   In this famous scene on the cliffs near Dover, Edgar leads his blind father to the edge of the cliff
       and persuades him that he is about to leap to his death. In the Edward Sherin version (with James
       Earl Jones), on stage at the outdoor theater in New York's Central Park there is a close approxima-
       tion to what must have been done on an bare Elizabethan stage, in order to hypnotize the audience
       into accepting the scene as plausible.

The crows and choughs that wing the midway air
Show scarce so gross as beetles. Halfway down
Hangs one that gathers sampire—dreadful trade!   15
Methinks he seems no bigger than his head.
The fishermen that walk upon the beach
Appear like mice, and yond tall anchoring bark,
Diminish'd to her cock; her cock, a buoy
Almost too small for sight. The murmuring surge   20
That on th' unnumb'red idle pebble chafes
Cannot be heard so high. I'll look no more,
Lest my brain turn, and the deficient sight
Topple down headlong.

GLOUCESTER   Set me where you stand.

EDGAR   Give me your hand. You are now within a foot   25
Of th' extreme verge. For all beneath the moon
Would I not leap upright.

GLOUCESTER   Let go my hand.
Here, friend, 's another purse; in it a jewel
Well worth a poor man's taking. Fairies and gods
Prosper it with thee! Go thou further off;   30
Bid me farewell, and let me hear thee going.

EDGAR   Now fare ye well, good sir.

GLOUCESTER   With all my heart.

EDGAR   [aside]. Why I do trifle thus with his despair
Is done to cure it.

GLOUCESTER   O you mighty gods!†   He kneels.
This world I do renounce, and, in your sights   35
Shake patiently my great affliction off.

13, 14. **choughs:** a kind of jackdaw, pronounced *chuffs.* —**gross:** large. 15. **sampire:** samphire (*herbe de Saint Pierre*)—an aromatic plant which, pickled in vinegar, was a favorite relish served with meat. It grows on the face of cliffs by the sea, and was gathered (as here described) by men who were lowered by a rope. Dover Cliff was famous for its samphire. 19. **cock:** cockboat. 21. **unnumb'red:** numberless, innumerable. —**idle:** useless, barren. 23, 24. **and the deficient sight Topple down headlong:** and I, my sight failing me, fall headlong. 27. **leap upright:** i.e., if I were as near the edge as you are at the moment. 29. **Fairies:** There are two superstitious notions about "fairy gold." One is that it merely seems to be gold, and resumes its real nature as rubbish when the finder has stored it away. The other is that hidden treasure is guarded by fairies and that they make it multiply miraculously in the possession of the discoverer. 33, 34. **Why I...it:** A very necessary "aside" for the enlightenment of the audience. Edgar is trying a dangerous experiment, for the agitation may be too great for Gloucester's strength; but the experiment succeeds.

---

† (*Oh you mighty gods*) As Gloucester prays, in Trevor Nunn's production the sound of cries of gulls becomes increasingly loud, as if he were near the edge of the cliff and the water below.

If I could bear it longer and not fall
To quarrel with your great opposeless wills,
My snuff and loathed part of nature should
Burn itself out. If Edgar live, O, bless him!   40
Now, fellow, fare thee well.   *He falls [forward and swoons].*

EDGAR   Gone, sir, farewell.—
And yet I know not how conceit may rob
The treasury of life when life itself
Yields to the theft. Had he been where he thought,
By this had thought been past.—Alive or dead?   45
Ho you, sir! friend! Hear you, sir? Speak!—
Thus might he pass indeed. Yet he revives.
What are you, sir?

GLOUCESTER   Away, and let me die.

EDGAR   Hadst thou been aught but gossamer, feathers, air,
So many fadom down precipitating,   50
Thou'dst shiver'd like an egg; but thou dost breathe;
Hast heavy substance; bleed'st not; speak'st; art sound.
Ten masts at each make not the altitude
Which thou hast perpendicularly fell.
Thy life's a miracle. Speak yet again.   55

GLOUCESTER But have I fall'n, or no?

EDGAR   From the dread summit of this chalky bourn.
Look up a-height. The shrill-gorg'd lark so far
Cannot be seen or heard. Do but look up.

GLOUCESTER Alack, I have no eyes!   60
Is wretchedness depriv'd that benefit
To end itself by death? 'Twas yet some comfort
When misery could beguile the tyrant's rage
And frustrate his proud will.

EDGAR   Give me your arm.
Up—so. How is't? Feel you your legs? You stand.   65

37, 38. **fall To quarrel with:** come to a state of rebellion against. Gloucester implies that such rebellion would be a greater sin than suicide. —**opposeless:** irresistible. 39. **My snuff:** The snuff is the burnt piece of wick which dims the light of a lamp or candle and causes a disagreeable smoke. The meaning here is explained by the phrase that follows. —**loathed part of nature:** the remnant of my natural life, which is hateful to me. 42-44. **how conceit...theft:** how powerful imagination may be in rifling life's treasury of all its stores (i.e., of vitality) when life itself does not resist such robbery. 46. **you, sir!** Edgar now plays the part of a man who, walking on the beach below, has seen Gloucester fall from the cliff. 47. **pass:** pass away, die. 49, 50. **gossamer:** a floating thread of spider's web. —**fadom:** fathoms. —**precipitating:** falling headlong. 53. **at each:** one on top of another. 57, 58. **bourn:** boundary. —**a-height:** on high. —**shrill-gorg'd:** shrill-throated, shrill-voiced. 62. **Yet:** "after all;" "when things were at the very worst." 63. **beguile:** deceive, cheat, elude—i.e., by suicide.

Cordelia sees her father "fantastically dressed with weeds"(4.6.80 SD)," his mind now wandering from sanity to madness. (Kozintsev, 1971)

GLOUCESTER Too well, too well.

EDGAR   This is above all strangeness.
        Upon the crown o' th' cliff what thing was that
        Which parted from you?

GLOUCESTER   A poor unfortunate beggar.

EDGAR   As I stood here below, methought his eyes
        Were two full moons; he had a thousand noses,   70
        Horns whelk'd and wav'd like the enridged sea.
        It was some fiend. Therefore, thou happy father,
        Think that the clearest gods, who make them honors
        Of men's impossibilities, have preserv'd thee.

GLOUCESTER I do remember now. Henceforth I'll bear   75
        Affliction till it do cry out itself
        "Enough, enough," and die. That thing you speak of,
        I took it for a man. Often 'twould say
        "The fiend, the fiend"—he led me to that place.

EDGAR   Bear free and patient thoughts.

            Enter Lear, mad, [fantastically dressed with weeds].
                            But who comes here?   80
        The safer sense will ne'er accommodate
        His master thus.

71. **whelk'd and wav'd:** rising on the surface into wave-like ridges. *Enridged* carries out the figure, but Edgar is not thinking of huge billows, but of the normal appearance of the surface of the ocean. 72. **father:** Common in addressing any venerable man. Edgar's use of the term, therefore, does not reveal his identity, but he takes comfort in thus addressing Gloucester. 73, 74. **clearest:** glorious. **—who make... impossibilities:** who win honor by helping men who cannot help themselves. "Man's extremities are God's opportunities." 75. **I do remember now:** Gloucester recalls strange action and speech on the part of the supposed Bedlam beggar. 80. **free:** free from sorrow, cheerful. 81, 82. **The safer sense...thus:** A sound mind would never let its possessor dress himself up in this fashion.

LEAR   No, they cannot touch me for coining.
            I am the King himself.

EDGAR   O thou side-piercing sight!   85

LEAR   Nature's above art in that respect. There's your press money. That fel-
            low handles his bow like a crow-keeper. Draw me a clothier's yard.
            Look, look, a mouse! Peace, peace; this piece of toasted cheese will
            do't. There's my gauntlet; I'll prove it on a giant. Bring up the brown
            bills. O, well flown, bird! i' th' clout, i' th' clout! Hewgh! Give the
            word.   91

EDGAR   Sweet marjoram.

LEAR   Pass.

GLOUCESTER I know that voice.

LEAR   Ha! Goneril with a white beard? They flatter'd me like a dog, and
            told me I had white hairs in my beard ere the black ones were there.
            To say "ay" and "no" to everything I said! "Ay" and "no" too was no
            good divinity. When the rain came to wet me once, and the wind to
            make me chatter; when the thunder would not peace at my bidding;
            there I found 'em, there I smelt 'em out. Go to, they are not men o'
            their words! They told me I was everything. 'Tis a lie—I am not ague-
            proof.   102

GLOUCESTER The trick of that voice I do well remember.
            Is't not the King?

83-91. Lear has wandered away from Dover (4.3.40). In his delirium he sees constables who try to arrest him as a coiner of counterfeit money. The next moment he is a captain engaged in the enlistment of
drafted men and in testing the recruits. Suddenly he catches sight of an imaginary mouse. Then he is a
champion defying all opponents; then a captain once more; then a spectator at an archery contest; then,
catching sight of Edgar, he becomes a sentry and challenges him: "Give the word." 83. **coining:** coining
counterfeit money. 85. **side-piercing:** that pierces one to the heart. 86. **Nature's above art in that respect:**
A madly philosophical reflection: "Art is said to improve nature; but that does not hold true in the case
of kingship, for a king's authority comes by nature and nothing can abrogate it." 86-91. **press money:** a
small sum paid to the recruit when he enlisted. —**like a crow-keeper:** like a boy stationed to guard a field
from crows—i.e., in clumsy fashion. —**a clothier's yard:** The standard English arrow was a cloth-yard
in length. —**prove it:** put my cause (signified by my gauntlet) to the test of combat. —**the brown bills:**
halberds or pikes (browned to prevent rust). —**bird:** as if the arrow were a falcon. —**the clout:** the wooden
peg in the centre of the target; the bull's-eye. —**Hewgh!** An imitation of the whizzing of the arrow. —**the
word:** the watchword; the countersign. 95, 96. **Goneril with a white beard?** Lear takes Gloucester for
Goneril in disguise. —**like a dog:** as a dog fawns on his master. —**told me...there:** when I was a beardless
boy they told me that I was as wise as an old man. 96, 98. **To say "ay" and "no" to everything I said!**
To agree with me always—saying "ay" or "no" as such agreement might require, without regard to the
truth. —**"Ay" and "no" too was no good divinity:** It was bad theology. The right doctrine is to let your
ay mean "ay" and your *no* mean "no" in accordance with the truth; but these flatterers were ready to use
both words without any conscientious discrimination, and to shift from one to the other whenever flattery
required it. 100-102. **Go to:** Here an exclamation of scornful reproof. —**ague-proof:** Lear is shivering
and has, in fact, taken a severe chill. 103. **trick:** peculiarity. 104. **Is't not the King?** Gloucester's question
recalls Lear to the subject with which he began—that of sovereignty.

LEAR   Ay, every inch a king!
When I do stare, see how the subject quakes.   105
I pardon that man's life. What was thy cause?
Adultery?
Thou shalt not die. Die for adultery? No.
The wren goes to't, and the small gilded fly
Does lecher in my sight.   110
Let copulation thrive; for Gloucester's bastard son
Was kinder to his father than my daughters
Got 'tween the lawful sheets.
To't, luxury, pell-mell! for I lack soldiers.
Behold yond simp'ring dame,   115
Whose face between her forks presageth snow,
That minces virtue, and does shake the head
To hear of pleasure's name.
The fitchew nor the soiled horse goes to't
With a more riotous appetite.   120
Down from the waist they are Centaurs,
Though women all above.
But to the girdle do the gods inherit,
Beneath is all the fiend's.

There's hell, there's darkness, there's the sulphurous pit; burning,
scalding, stench, consumption. Fie, fie, fie! pah, pah! Give me an
ounce of civet, good apothecary, to sweeten my imagination. There's
money for thee.   128

GLOUCESTER   O, let me kiss that hand!

LEAR   Let me wipe it first; it smells of mortality.   130

GLOUCESTER   O ruin'd piece of nature! This great world
Shall so wear out to naught. Dost thou know me?

LEAR   I remember thine eyes well enough. Dost thou squiny at me? No, do
thy worst, blind Cupid! I'll not love. Read thou this challenge; mark
but the penning of it.   135

GLOUCESTER   Were all the letters suns, I could not see one.

---

105. **the subject:** my subjects. 106. **thy cause?** the offense which caused thy sentence; your offense. 114.
luxury: lascivious- ness. 117. **minces virtue:** counterfeits virtue by her mincing airs—her pretence
of delicate prudery. 118. **pleasure's name:** It shocks her to hear even the word mentioned. 119. **fitchew:**
polecat. **—soiled:** full-fed with grass in the spring. 121. **Centaurs:** wildly lustful creatures. 123. **inherit:**
possess; hold sway. 131. **piece of nature!** masterpiece of Nature's workmanship. **—This great world:**
the universe—so called in contrast with the "little world of man." See 3.1.10. 133. **squiny:** squint; look
with half-shut eyes. 134. **this challenge:** Lear's mind jumps back to the idea of defying an enemy (lines
89, 90); but now that enemy is "blind Cupid." Gloucester does not know that the written challenge
exists only in Lear's mad fancy.

EDGAR   [*aside*] I would not take this from report. It is,
          And my heart breaks at it.

LEAR   Read.

GLOUCESTER What, with the case of eyes?   140

LEAR   O, ho, are you there with me? No eyes in your head, nor no money
          in your purse? Your eyes are in a heavy case, your purse in a light. Yet
          you see how this world goes.

GLOUCESTER I see it feelingly.

LEAR   What, art mad? A man may see how the world goes with no eyes.
          Look with thine ears. See how yond justice rails upon yond simple
          thief. Hark in thine ear. Change places, and, handy-dandy, which is
          the justice, which is the thief? Thou hast seen a farmer's dog bark at a
          beggar?   149

GLOUCESTER Ay, sir.

LEAR   And the creature run from the cur?

          There thou mightst behold the great image of authority: a dog's
               obey'd in office.
          Thou rascal beadle, hold thy bloody hand!
          Why dost thou lash that whore? Strip thine own back.   155
          Thou hotly lusts to use her in that kind
          For which thou whip'st her. The usurer hangs the cozener.
          Through tatter'd clothes small vices do appear;
          Robes and furr'd gowns hide all. Plate sin with gold,
          And the strong lance of justice hurtless breaks;   160
          Arm it in rags, a pygmy's straw does pierce it.
          None does offend, none—I say none! I'll able 'em.

---

137. **take:** credit, believe. **—this:** Edgar refers to the whole situation—this meeting between the mad King and the blind Duke. 140. **the case of eyes:** "Am I to read with the *sockets* of eyes?" 141, 142. **are you there with me?** Is that what you mean? Is that what you are trying to tell me? **—in a heavy case:** in a sad condition (with a pun on *case* and on *heavy*). 144. **I see it feelingly:** Gloucester uses *feelingly* in a double sense: (1) by means of my sense of feeling; (2) with the keenest feeling—in a way that pierces me to the heart. 146. **simple:** ordinary, mere. 147. **handy-dandy:** The formula in a game. You show a child your hands—one empty and one with a toy or a coin or a sweetmeat in it; then, after putting your hands behind your back, you hold them out again, both closed, and offer him his choice, repeating a formula. 152. **image:** likeness, figure. **—dog:** "even a *dog*." 154-56. **beadle:** a minor constable, one of whose duties was to punish offenders by whipping. **—kind:** manner, way. 157. **The usurer hangs the cozener:** Lear implies that justices are often guilty of usury, and thus are far greater criminals than the cozeners (sharpers, petty cheats) whom they sentence to be hanged. 158, 159. **Through...appear:** Even trivial faults are visible when a man's clothes are full of holes and cannot hide his real self. **—Robes and furr'd gowns:** Lear is still thinking of judges and their robes of office. **—Plate sin with gold:** Attire sin in armor made of plates of gold. 162. **None does offend...I'll able 'em:** In the interest of justice, Lear—as king—issues a royal edict: "I abolish all punishment. Nobody shall be regarded as guilty of any offense against the law. I will give everybody a license to act as he pleases." To *able* is to "authorize," "warrant," "vouch for."

	Take that of me, my friend, who have the power	
	To seal th' accuser's lips. Get thee glass eyes	
	And, like a scurvy politician, seem	165
	To see the things thou dost not. Now, now, now, now!	
	Pull off my boots. Harder, harder! So.	
EDGAR	O, matter and impertinency mix'd!	
	Reason in madness!	
LEAR	If thou wilt weep my fortunes, take my eyes.	170
	I know thee well enough; thy name is Gloucester.	
	Thou must be patient. We came crying hither.	
	Thou know'st, the first time that we smell the air	
	We wawl and cry. I will preach to thee. Mark.	
GLOUCESTER	Alack, alack the day!	175
LEAR	When we are born, we cry that we are come	
	To this great stage of fools. This' a good block.	
	It were a delicate stratagem to shoe	
	A troop of horse with felt. I'll put't in proof,	
	And when I have stol'n upon these sons-in-law,	180
	Then kill, kill, kill, kill, kill, kill!	

Enter a Gentleman [with Attendants].

GENTLEMAN	O, here he is! Lay hand upon him.—Sir,	
	Your most dear daughter—	
LEAR	No rescue? What, a prisoner? I am even	
	The natural fool of fortune. Use me well;	185
	You shall have ransom. Let me have a surgeon;	
	I am cut to th' brains.	
GENTLEMAN	You shall have anything.	
LEAR	No seconds? All myself?	
	Why, this would make a man a man of salt,	
	To use his eyes for garden waterpots,	190

---

163. **Take that of me:** Lear imagines that Gloucester is a criminal, and makes a gesture as if he were handing him a pardon signed and sealed. 165. **scurvy:** vile. A general term of contempt. 166, 167. **Now... boots:** Lear imagines that he has just come back from hunting or from a journey. —**So:** Ah, well and good! My boots are off at last. 168. **matter and impertinency:** good sense and incoherent talk. 174. **wawl and cry:** Synonymous. 177. **stage:** Life as a stage play was a popular metaphor [K.S.R]. —**This' a good block:** This is a hat of a good fashion. Cf. "Your hat is of a better block then mine." The action here is left to the discretion of the actor. The hat which Lear commends is probably imaginary. He wears no hat in this scene. 179. **felt:** woolen material of which hats were made. —**put't in proof:** try the experiment. 182. The Gentleman is one of the band sent out by Cordelia to search for her father (4.4.6-8). 155. **The natural fool of fortune:** Someone controlled by Fortune, her natural child or dupe [K.S.R.]. Lear's phrase is even more emphatic: the sport of Fortune. 189. **a man of salt:** That tears are salty is a fact which Shakespeare never forgets.

	Ay, and laying autumn's dust.	
GENTLEMAN	Good sir—	
LEAR	I will die bravely, like a smug bridegroom. What! I will be jovial. Come, come, I am a king; My masters, know you that?	
GENTLEMAN	You are a royal one, and we obey you.	195
LEAR	Then there's life in't. Nay, an you get it, you shall get it by running. Sa, sa, sa, sa! *Exit running. [Attendants follow.]*	
GENTLEMAN	A sight most pitiful in the meanest wretch, Past speaking of in a king! Thou hast one daughter Who redeems nature from the general curse Which twain have brought her to.	200
EDGAR	Hail, gentle sir.	
GENTLEMAN	Sir, speed you. What's your will?	
EDGAR	Do you hear aught, sir, of a battle toward?	
GENTLEMAN	Most sure and vulgar. Every one hears that Which can distinguish sound.	
EDGAR	But, by your favor, How near's the other army?	205
GENTLEMAN	Near and on speedy foot. The main descry Stands on the hourly thought.	
EDGAR	I thank you, sir. That's all.	
GENTLEMAN	Though that the Queen on special cause is here, Her army is mov'd on.	
EDGAR	I thank you, sir. *Exit [Gentleman].*	210
GLOUCESTER	You ever-gentle gods, take my breath from me; Let not my worser spirit tempt me again	

---

192. **bravely:** in fine attire. *Smug* repeats the idea; it means "spick and span." Lear is thinking of his floral adornments. 194. **My masters:** gentlemen. 196. **there's life in't:** The case is not yet desperate. 196, 197. **Nay....running:** A defiant challenge: "Catch me if you want me!" —**Sa, sa, sa, sa!** French *çà, çà!* ("here, here!") was an old hunting cry to call a hound or to urge the dogs forward in chase of the hare. It was also in common use as a rallying cry, or as an interjection of challenge and defiance. Here the King challenges his pursuers: "Come on! come on! Catch me if you can!" And so he runs off the stage, waving his arm in a defiant gesture. 200. **general:** universal. 202. **gentle:** noble, honorable. —**speed you:** God prosper you! 203. **toward?** in preparation; in the near future. 204. **vulgar:** common; i.e., a matter of common knowledge. 207, 208. **The main descry...thought:** The main body of the army is expected soon [K.S.R.]. To *stand on* is, literally, to "depend on." 209, 210. **Though that:** though. —**on:** because of, on account of. 211, 212. **take my breath from me:** i.e., when the appointed time comes. —**my worser spirit:** the evil side of my nature; or, perhaps, "my evil genius." There is at least an allusion to the old idea that every man is attended by two spirits, one good and one bad.

To die before you please!

EDGAR   Well pray you, father.

GLOUCESTER Now, good sir, what are you?

EDGAR   A most poor man, made tame to fortune's blows,   215
             Who, by the art of known and feeling sorrows,
             Am pregnant to good pity. Give me your hand;
             I'll lead you to some biding.

GLOUCESTER   Hearty thanks.
             The bounty and the benison of heaven
             To boot, and boot!

                    Enter [Oswald the] Steward.

OSWALD   A proclaim'd prize! Most happy!   220
             That eyeless head of thine was first fram'd flesh
             To raise my fortunes. Thou old unhappy traitor,
             Briefly thyself remember. The sword is out
             That must destroy thee.

GLOUCESTER   Now let thy friendly hand
             Put strength enough to't.   [*Edgar interposes.*]

OSWALD   Wherefore, bold peasant,   225
             Dar'st thou support a publish'd traitor? Hence!
             Lest that th' infection of his fortune take
             Like hold on thee. Let go his arm.

EDGAR   Chill not let go, zir, without vurther 'cagion.

OSWALD   Let go, slave, or thou diest!   230

EDGAR   Good gentleman, go your gait, and let poor voke pass. An chud ha'
             bin zwagger'd out of my life, 'twould not ha' bin zo long as 'tis by a
             vortnight. Nay, come not near th' old man. Keep out, che vore ye,
             or Ise try whether your costard or my ballow be the harder. Chill be
             plain with you.   235

OSWALD   Out, dunghill!   *They fight.*

EDGAR   Chill pick your teeth, zir. Come! No matter vor your foins.

---

213. **father:** See line 72, and note. 215. **tame:** humbly submissive. 216, 217. **feeling:** heartfelt. —**pregnant to:** readily susceptible of. 218. **some biding:** some place of permanent refuge. 219, 220. **The bounty...To boot, and boot!** Besides giving you my thanks, I pray heaven to favor and bless you, and may that favor and blessing be your reward! 223. **Briefly thyself remember:** Recall your past offenses and refer yourself to Heaven [K.S.R.]. 224. **friendly:** since I long for death. 229 ff. **Chill not...foins:** Edgar assumes the lingo that, from the Elizabethan time to the end of the eighteenth century, served as the stage dialect of rusticity. It accords well enough with the dialect of Somersetshire, but the dramatists were not finicky. We may note, in this regard, the "Irish brogue," the "cockney English" and the "Yankee dialect" still found on the modern stage.

[Oswald falls.]

OSWALD   Slave, thou hast slain me. Villain, take my purse.
         If ever thou wilt thrive, bury my body,
         And give the letters which thou find'st about me   240
         To Edmund Earl of Gloucester. Seek him out
         Upon the British party. O, untimely death!
         Death!   *He dies.*

EDGAR   I know thee well. A serviceable villain,
         As duteous to the vices of thy mistress   245
         As badness would desire.

GLOUCESTER What, is he dead?

EDGAR   Sit you down, father; rest you.
         Let's see his pockets; these letters that he speaks of
         May be my friends. He's dead. I am only sorry   250
         He had no other deathsman. Let us see.
         Leave, gentle wax; and, manners, blame us not.
         To know our enemies' minds, we'ld rip their hearts;
         Their papers, is more lawful.   *Reads the letter.*

            "Let our reciprocal vows be rememb'red. You have many op-
         portunities to cut him off. If your will want not, time and place
         will be fruitfully offer'd. There is nothing done, if he return the
         conqueror. Then am I the prisoner, and his bed my jail, from
         the loathed warmth whereof deliver me, and supply the place for
         your labor.   260
            Your (wife, so I would say) affectionate servant,

                                                            GONERIL."

         O indistinguish'd space of woman's will!
         A plot upon her virtuous husband's life,
         And the exchange my brother! Here in the sands
         Thee I'll rake up, the post unsanctified   265
         Of murtherous lechers; and in the mature time
         With this ungracious paper strike the sight
         Of the death-practis'd Duke. For him 'tis well
         That of thy death and business I can tell.

GLOUCESTER The King is mad. How stiff is my vile sense,   270
         That I stand up, and have ingenious feeling

---

240. **letters:** Oswald was carrying a letter from Edmund to Goneril. 242. **Upon the British party:** on the side of the British. 251. **deathsman.** executioner. 252. **Leave.** Give me leave, allow me. 262. **O indistinguish'd space of woman's will!** O woman's lust, how limitless is thy range! 265. **rake up:** bury hastily and without ceremony. —**post:** messenger. 266. **in the mature time:** when time is ripe. 267. **ungracious:** abominable. 268. **the death-practis'd Duke:** the Duke whose death is plotted. 271. **ingenious feeling:** acute mental consciousness.

Of my huge sorrows! Better I were distract.
So should my thoughts be sever'd from my griefs,
And woes by wrong imaginations lose
The knowledge of themselves.   *A drum afar off.*

EDGAR   Give me your hand.   275
Far off methinks I hear the beaten drum.
Come, father, I'll bestow you with a friend.   *Exeunt.*

SCENE VII. [*A tent in the French camp.*]

Enter Cordelia, Kent, Doctor, and Gentleman.

CORDELIA   O thou good Kent, how shall I live and work
To match thy goodness? My life will be too short
And every measure fail me.

KENT   To be acknowledg'd, madam, is o'er-paid
All my reports go with the modest truth;   5
Nor more nor clipp'd, but so.

CORDELIA   Be better suited.
These weeds are memories of those worser hours.
I prithee put them off.

KENT   Pardon, dear madam.
Yet to be known shortens my made intent.
My boon I make it that you know me not   10
Till time and I think meet.

CORDELIA   Then be't so, my good lord. [*To the Doctor*] How does the King?

DOCTOR   Madam, sleeps still.

CORDELIA   O you kind gods,
Cure this great breach in his abused nature!   15
Th' untun'd and jarring senses, O, wind up
Of this child-changed father!

DOCTOR   So please your Majesty

---

272. **distract:** distracted, insane. 277. **bestow you:** provide a refuge for you.
SCENE VII.
Perhaps on the day after scene 6, Lear has been found by the searchers sent out in scene 4. He has been
brought to Cordelia's camp and put to bed.
3. **every measure fail me:** since thy goodness is unmeasurable. 5. **All my reports...truth:** Everything
that I have told you (about the King and his sufferings) corresponds exactly with a moderate expression
of the facts. 6, 7. **suited:** clothed. Kent is still disguised as a serving-man. See 1.4.1-4. —**weeds:** clothes.
—**memories:** reminders. 9. **Yet...intent:** If I reveal myself now, I shall come short of the plan that I have
formed. 10. **My boon I make it:** I ask it of you as a special favor. 17. **child-changed:** changed to a child.

That we may wake the King? He hath slept long.

CORDELIA Be govern'd by your knowledge, and proceed
I' th' sway of your own will. Is he array'd?   20

Enter Lear in a chair carried by Servants.

GENTLEMAN Ay, madam. In the heaviness of sleep
We put fresh garments on him.

DOCTOR Be by, good madam, when we do awake him.
I doubt not of his temperance.

CORDELIA   Very well.   *[Music.]*

DOCTOR Please you draw near. Louder the music there!   25

CORDELIA O my dear father, restoration hang
Thy medicine on my lips, and let this kiss
Repair those violent harms that my two sisters
Have in thy reverence made!

KENT   Kind and dear princess!

CORDELIA Had you not been their father, these white flakes   30
Had challeng'd pity of them. Was this a face
To be oppos'd against the warring winds?
To stand against the deep dread-bolted thunder?
In the most terrible and nimble stroke
Of quick cross lightning? to watch—poor perdu!—   35
With this thin helm? Mine enemy's dog,
Though he had bit me, should have stood that night
Against my fire; and wast thou fain, poor father,
To hovel thee with swine and rogues forlorn,
In short and musty straw? Alack, alack!   40
'Tis wonder that thy life and wits at once
Had not concluded all.—He wakes. Speak to him.

DOCTOR Madam, do you; 'tis fittest.

CORDELIA How does my royal lord? How fares your Majesty?

---

19. **your knowledge:** your understanding of such cases. 24. **temperance:** normal self-control. 25. **the music:** The beneficial effect of music in the treatment of madness is an ancient theory. 29. **in thy reverence:** in thee, to whom all reverence is due. 30, 31. **been:** "Even if you had not *been* their father." — **flakes.** Lear's white hair hangs down in long straight strands. —**challeng'd:** claimed. —**of:** from. 33. **dread-bolted:** with its terrible thunderbolts. 35. **cross:** zigzag. —**perdu:** a solitary sentinel keeping watch far away from the main body, and therefore in a very dangerous position. 36. **this thin helm:** his scanty locks. 38. **wast thou fain:** wast thou glad. 39, 40. **hovel.** See 3.4.150. —**rogues:** vagabonds. —**straw?** *Short* in this passage has worried some critics, and Moberly actually suggests "dirt" as an emendation. Long, clean straw would make a good bed. The straw in the hovel was damp and musty and had been broken up into short lengths by constant use as bedding. 42. **concluded all:** come to a complete end.

LEAR	You do me wrong to take me out o' th' grave. 45
	Thou art a soul in bliss; but I am bound
	Upon a wheel of fire, that mine own tears
	Do scald like molten lead.
CORDELIA	Sir, do you know me?
LEAR	You are a spirit, I know. When did you die?
CORDELIA	Still, still, far wide! 50
DOCTOR	He's scarce awake. Let him alone awhile.
LEAR	Where have I been? Where am I? Fair daylight?
	I am mightily abus'd. I should e'en die with pity,
	To see another thus. I know not what to say.
	I will not swear these are my hands. Let's see. 55
	I feel this pin prick. Would I were assur'd
	Of my condition!
CORDELIA	O, look upon me, sir,
	And hold your hands in benediction o'er me.
	No, sir, you must not kneel.
LEAR	Pray, do not mock me.
	I am a very foolish fond old man, 60
	Fourscore and upward, not an hour more nor less;
	And, to deal plainly,
	I fear I am not in my perfect mind.
	Methinks I should know you, and know this man;
	Yet I am doubtful; for I am mainly ignorant 65
	What place this is; and all the skill I have
	Remembers not these garments; nor I know not
	Where I did lodge last night. Do not laugh at me;
	For (as I am a man) I think this lady
	To be my child Cordelia.
CORDELIA	And so I am! I am! 70
LEAR	Be your tears wet? Yes, faith. I pray weep not.
	If you have poison for me, I will drink it.
	I know you do not love me; for your sisters
	Have, as I do remember, done me wrong.

---

47. **that:** so that. 50. **wide!** wide of the mark, distracted. 51. **scarce awake:** We should observe that Lear is no longer delirious. He merely needs a few minutes to adjust himself to the present situation, for he has no memory of what has happened in the interval. His confusion is well understood by the Doctor. 53. **abus'd:** deceived, deluded. Lear cannot trust the evidence of his senses. 60. **fond:** doting. 65. **mainly:** very, absolutely. 66. **skill:** power of mind. 71. **Be your tears wet?** Lear still fears that he is suffering from a delusion.

You have some cause, they have not.

CORDELIA   No cause, no cause.   75

LEAR   Am I in France?

KENT   In your own kingdom, sir.

LEAR   Do not abuse me.

DOCTOR   Be comforted, good madam. The great rage
You see is kill'd in him; and yet it is danger
To make him even o'er the time he has lost.   80
Desire him to go in. Trouble him no more
Till further settling.

CORDELIA   Will't please your Highness walk?

LEAR   You must bear with me.
Pray you now, forget and forgive. I am old and foolish.

Exeunt. Manent Kent and Gentleman.

GENTLEMAN   Holds it true, sir, that the Duke of Cornwall was so slain?   85

KENT   Most certain, sir.

GENTLEMAN   Who is conductor of his people?

KENT   As 'tis said, the bastard son of Gloucester.

GENTLEMAN   They say Edgar, his banish'd son, is with the Earl of Kent in Germany.

KENT   Report is changeable. 'Tis time to look about; the powers of the kingdom approach apace.   91

GENTLEMAN   The arbitrement is like to be bloody.
Fare you well, sir.   [*Exit.*]

KENT   My point and period will be throughly wrought,
Or well or ill, as this day's battle 's fought.   *Exit.*   95

---

77. **abuse:** deceive. 78. **The great rage:** the violent delirium. 80. **To make…lost:** to make him fill up the gap in his memory by recalling what happened while he was delirious. 83. **walk:** withdraw. 85. **Holds it true?** Is the report confirmed? 90. **powers:** forces, armies. 92. **The arbitrement:** the decision of the case. 94, 95. **My point…fought:** The completion of my lot in life will be worked out, for good or ill, according as this battle results in victory or defeat. —**period.** Cf. 5.3.204. —**throughly:** thoroughly, completely.

Act V

Scene I. [*The British camp near Dover.*]

Enter, with Drum and Colors, Edmund, Regan, Gentlemen, and Soldiers.

EDMUND   Know of the Duke if his last purpose hold,
Or whether since he is advis'd by aught
To change the course. He's full of alteration
And self-reproving. Bring his constant pleasure.   [*Exit an Officer.*]

REGAN   Our sister's man is certainly miscarried.   5

EDMUND   'Tis to be doubted, madam.

REGAN   Now, sweet lord,
You know the goodness I intend upon you.
Tell me—but truly—but then speak the truth—
Do you not love my sister?

EDMUND   In honor'd love.

REGAN   But have you never found my brother's way   10
To the forfended place?

EDMUND   That thought abuses you.

REGAN   I am doubtful that you have been conjunct
And bosom'd with her, as far as we call hers.

EDMUND   No, by mine honor, madam.

REGAN   I never shall endure her. Dear my lord,   15
Be not familiar with her.

EDMUND   Fear me not.
She and the Duke her husband!

Enter, with Drum and Colors, Albany, Goneril, Soldiers.

ACT V. SCENE I.
Manifestly the same day as 4.7. Cf. 4.6.274, with the first stage direction in the present scene. The battle mentioned as "this day's battle" in 4.7.95 occurs in 5.2.
1-4. **his last purpose:** i.e., to join us in the battle against Cordelia's forces. —**advis'd by aught:** instructed by (induced by consideration of) anything. —**constant:** "Bring information of what he has finally determined as his course of action." 5, 6. **Our sister's man:** Oswald. —**miscarried:** come to harm. Cf. line 45. When Regan parted with Oswald he was on his way to Edmund, and he has not arrived (4.5). —**doubted:** feared. 9. **honor'd:** honorable. 11. **forfended:** forbidden. —**That thought abuses you:** If you think so, you are mistaken. 12. **I am doubtful:** I suspect. —**conjunct:** united. 13. **bosom'd:** intimate. —**as far...hers:** in the fullest sense of the word; in respect to all that she has and is. 16. **Fear me not:** Don't worry about me in that regard.

GONERIL   [*aside*] I had rather lose the battle than that sister
           Should loosen him and me.

ALBANY   Our very loving sister, well bemet.   20
           Sir, this I hear: the King is come to his daughter,
           With others whom the rigor of our state
           Forc'd to cry out. Where I could not be honest,
           I never yet was valiant. For this business,
           It toucheth us as France invades our land,   25
           Not bolds the King, with others whom, I fear,
           Most just and heavy causes make oppose.

EDMUND   Sir, you speak nobly.

REGAN   Why is this reason'd?

GONERIL   Combine together 'gainst the enemy;
           For these domestic and particular broils   30
           Are not the question here.

ALBANY   Let's then determine
           With th' ancient of war on our proceeding.

EDMUND   I shall attend you presently at your tent.

REGAN   Sister, you'll go with us?

GONERIL   No.   35

REGAN   'Tis most convenient. Pray you go with us.

GONERIL   [*aside*] O, ho, I know the riddle.—I will go.
           [*As they are going out,*] enter *Edgar* [*disguised*].

EDGAR   If e'er your Grace had speech with man so poor,
           Hear me one word.

ALBANY   I'll overtake you.—Speak.   40

                    Exeunt [*all but Albany and Edgar*].

EDGAR   Before you fight the battle, ope this letter.
           If you have victory, let the trumpet sound
           For him that brought it. Wretched though I seem,
           I can produce a champion that will prove

---

20. **well bemet:** well met. 22, 23. **state:** government, administration. —**to cry out:** to protest loudly.
—**be honest:** be honorable; act with a good conscience. 25-27. **as…oppose:** insofar as the French king
is invading Britain, but not insofar as he is supporting King Lear and others who (as I fear) have just
cause to oppose us. Albany implies that the government of Britain has been tyrannical of late. 28. **Why
is this reason'd?** Why do you waste time thus in arguing with yourself about the justice of our cause?
30. **domestic and particular:** family and personal. 32. **th' ancient of war:** our veteran officers, who are
men of experience. 36. **convenient:** proper, fit. 37. **I know the riddle:** I understand her hidden meaning;
she is afraid to leave Edmund and me together. 43. **For him:** to summon him.

What is avouched there. If you miscarry,   45
Your business of the world hath so an end,
And machination ceases. Fortune love you!

ALBANY   Stay till I have read the letter.

EDGAR   I was forbid it.
When time shall serve, let but the herald cry,
And I'll appear again.   50

ALBANY   Why, fare thee well. I will o'erlook thy paper.   *Exit [Edgar].*

Enter Edmund.

EDMUND   The enemy's in view; draw up your powers.
Here is the guess of their true strength and forces
By diligent discovery; but your haste
Is now urg'd on you.

ALBANY   We will greet the time.   *Exit.*   55

EDMUND   To both these sisters have I sworn my love;
Each jealous of the other, as the stung
Are of the adder. Which of them shall I take?
Both? one? or neither? Neither can be enjoy'd,
If both remain alive. To take the widow   60
Exasperates, makes mad her sister Goneril;
And hardly shall I carry out my side,
Her husband being alive. Now then, we'll use
His countenance for the battle, which being done,
Let her who would be rid of him devise   65
His speedy taking off. As for the mercy
Which he intends to Lear and to Cordelia—
The battle done, and they within our power,
Shall never see his pardon; for my state
Stands on me to defend, not to debate.   *Exit.*   70

45-47. **avouched:** asserted. —**miscarry:** A euphemism for "are defeated and killed." —**machination:** all plotting against your life. 51. **o'erlook:** look over, read. 53-55. **Here:** Edmund hands Albany a paper. —**diligent discovery:** careful reconnoitering. —**your haste...on you:** rapid action on your part is urgently necessary. —**greet the time:** meet the crisis promptly. 57. **jealous:** suspicious. 62. **carry out my side:** bring my plans to a successful issue. Edmund aspires to the kingship. 63, 64. **countenance:** authority and support. 69, 70. **Shall:** they shall. —**my state...debate:** the condition of my affairs is such that it is incumbent on me to protect myself by action; it leaves me no time to consider rights and wrongs.

SCENE II. [*A field between the two camps.*]

Alarum within. Enter, with Drum and Colors, the Powers of France over the stage,
Cordelia with her Father in her hand, and exeunt.

Enter Edgar and Gloucester.

EDGAR   Here, father, take the shadow of this tree
             For your good host. Pray that the right may thrive.
             If ever I return to you again,
             I'll bring you comfort.

GLOUCESTER   Grace go with you, sir!   *Exit [Edgar].*

Alarum and retreat within. Enter Edgar.

EDGAR   Away, old man! give me thy hand! away!   5
             King Lear hath lost, he and his daughter ta'en.
             Give me thy hand! come on!

GLOUCESTER No further, sir. A man may rot even here.

EDGAR   What, in ill thoughts again? Men must endure
             Their going hence, even as their coming hither;   10
             Ripeness is all. Come on.

GLOUCESTER   And that's true too.   *Exeunt.*

SCENE III. [*The British camp, near Dover.*]

Enter, in conquest, with Drum and Colors, Edmund; Lear and Cordelia as prisoners;
Soldiers, Captain.

EDMUND   Some officers take them away. Good guard
             Until their greater pleasures first be known
             That are to censure them.

CORDELIA   We are not the first
             Who with best meaning have incurr'd the worst.

SCENE II.
This scene takes place on the same day as scene 1—the day of the battle.
1. **Alarum:** a trumpet call to the onset (*all' arme*). 4. **Grace:** the favor of the gods. —**retreat:** a trumpet signal giving the order to retreat. —**within:** behind the scenes. In the interval between the exit and the reëntrance of Edgar the battle has been fought. This is a good instance of "dramatic condensation." 11. **Ripeness is all:** The only thing that is important in life is to be ready for death when it comes.
SCENE III.
The scene takes place on the same day as scenes 1 and 2—the day of the battle.
2, 3. **their greater pleasures:** the wishes of those persons of higher rank. —**censure them:** pass judgment on them.

For thee, oppressed king, am I cast down;   5
Myself could else outfrown false Fortune's frown.
Shall we not see these daughters and these sisters?

LEAR   No, no, no, no! Come, let's away to prison.
We two alone will sing like birds i' th' cage.
When thou dost ask me blessing, I'll kneel down   10
And ask of thee forgiveness. So we'll live,
And pray, and sing, and tell old tales, and laugh
At gilded butterflies, and hear poor rogues
Talk of court news; and we'll talk with them too—
Who loses and who wins; who's in, who's out—   15
And take upon 's the mystery of things,
As if we were God's spies; and we'll wear out,
In a wall'd prison, packs and sects of great ones
That ebb and flow by th' moon.

EDMUND   Take them away.

LEAR   Upon such sacrifices, my Cordelia,   20
The gods themselves throw incense. Have I caught thee?
He that parts us shall bring a brand from heaven
And fire us hence like foxes. Wipe thine eyes.
The goodyears shall devour 'em, flesh and fell,
Ere they shall make us weep! We'll see 'em starv'd first.   25
Come.   *Exeunt [Lear and Cordelia, guarded].*

EDMUND   Come hither, Captain; hark.
Take thou this note [*gives a paper*]. Go follow them to prison.
One step I have advanc'd thee. If thou dost
As this instructs thee, thou dost make thy way
To noble fortunes. Know thou this, that men   30
Are as the time is. To be tender-minded
Does not become a sword. Thy great employment
Will not bear question. Either say thou'lt do't,
Or thrive by other means.

13. **rogues:** wretched creatures. 16, 17. **take upon 's…spies:** assume (in our talk) that we can explain all the mysteries of human affairs, as if God had so endowed us. 18. **packs and sects:** "parties," "sets." 19. **by th' moon:** The moon is not only the mistress of tides but also the emblem of change. 20, 21. **Upon such sacrifices…incense:** Upon such sacrifices as thou hast made for my sake the gods themselves attend as priests. 22, 23. **He…heaven:** No human power shall ever part us again. —**fire…foxes:** as foxes are driven from their holes by fire and smoke. 24. **The goodyears:** A phrase of uncertain origin [The sense seems to that as long as we're together, the "good years" will destroy our enemies before we will ever weep. K.S.R.]. —**fell:** skin. 27. **this note:** This is Edmund's writ ordering the death of Lear and Cordelia. See lines 245-46. He has special authority as Regan's commissioned substitute in the campaign (lines 63, 64). 30, 31. **men Are as the time is:** i.e., they may be merciful in time of peace but must be savage in war. 33. **bear question:** admit discussion. 34. **by other means:** since you will be out of favor with *me*.

CAPTAIN	I'll do't, my lord.
EDMUND	About it! and write happy when th' hast done. 35
	Mark—I say, instantly; and carry it so
	As I have set it down.
CAPTAIN	I cannot draw a cart, nor eat dried oats;
	If it be man's work, I'll do't. *Exit.*

Flourish. Enter Albany, Goneril, Regan, Soldiers.

ALBANY
Sir, you have show'd today your valiant strain, 40
And fortune led you well. You have the captives
Who were the opposites of this day's strife.
We do require them of you, so to use them
As we shall find their merits and our safety
May equally determine.

EDMUND   Sir, I thought it fit 45
To send the old and miserable King
To some retention and appointed guard;
Whose age has charms in it, whose title more,
To pluck the common bosom on his side
And turn our impress'd lances in our eyes 50
Which do command them. With him I sent the Queen,
My reason all the same; and they are ready
Tomorrow, or at further space, t' appear
Where you shall hold your session. At this time
We sweat and bleed: the friend hath lost his friend; 55
And the best quarrels, in the heat, are curs'd
By those that feel their sharpness.
The question of Cordelia and her father
Requires a fitter place.

ALBANY   Sir, by your patience,
I hold you but a subject of this war, 60

35, 36. **write happy:** write down thy name as that of a fortunate man; call thyself fortunate (on account of my favor). **—carry it:** manage the affair. 38, 39. **I cannot...I'll do't:** A bit of rough humor based on the proverbial contrast between a man and a horse (thought of as a stupid animal and a beast of burden). 40. **strain:** lineage. Albany implies that Edmund has shown himself worthy of being a legitimate son of Gloucester. 42. **the opposites:** our opponents. 43. **require:** See 1.1.186, note. 47. **To some retention and appointed guard:** to a place where they could be held in custody by guards designated for that purpose. 49. **To pluck...side:** to attract strongly the feelings of the rank and file of men to take his part. To *pluck* is, literally, to "pull." 50. **impress'd:** enlisted by conscription. 56. **quarrels:** causes. 59. **Requires a fitter place:** requires for its settlement a fitter place than the camp. **—by your patience:** if you will not be offended at my frankness. A phrase of courteous apology (like "by your leave") for plain language.

Not as a brother.

REGAN   That's as we list to grace him.
Methinks our pleasure might have been demanded
Ere you had spoke so far. He led our powers,
Bore the commission of my place and person,
The which immediacy may well stand up   65
And call itself your brother.

GONERIL   Not so hot!
In his own grace he doth exalt himself
More than in your addition.

REGAN   In my rights
By me invested, he compeers the best.

GONERIL   That were the most if he should husband you.   70

REGAN   Jesters do oft prove prophets.

GONERIL   Holla, holla!
That eye that told you so look'd but asquint.

REGAN   Lady, I am not well; else I should answer
From a full-flowing stomach. General,
Take thou my soldiers, prisoners, patrimony;   75
Dispose of them, of me; the walls are thine.
Witness the world that I create thee here
My lord and master.

GONERIL   Mean you to enjoy him?

ALBANY   The let-alone lies not in your good will.

EDMUND   Nor in thine, lord.

ALBANY   Half-blooded fellow, yes.   80

---

61. **That's…grace him:** That question—whether he is to be regarded by you as a subject or as a brother in this war—depends upon my will to do him honor. Regan uses the "royal we," speaking as a sovereign. —**list:** choose, please. 62, 63. **pleasure:** wishes. —**demanded:** asked. —**powers:** troops. 64, 65. **Bore…person:** had the authority belonging to my rank and represented me personally. —**The which immediacy:** and the fact that he was thus my immediate representative, clothed with all my authority. 67, 68. **grace:** merit and honor. —**your addition:** *Addition* often means "title" (something added to one's name) or "honor." 69. **compeers:** is the peer of; equals. 70. **That were the most:** Such investment in your rights would be most fully accomplished. 71. **Jesters do oft prove prophets:** A form of the proverb, "There's many a true word spoken in jest." 72. **look'd but asquint:** did not see straight. 74. **a full-flowing stomach:** a full tide of angry resentment. *Stomach* for "wrath" is common. 76. **the walls are thine:** You have won the walls; you have taken my defenses by storm. The metaphor by which a woman or a woman's heart is identified with a castle or walled town defending itself against besiegers was common in the Middle Ages and had become conventional long before Shakespeare's time. 78. **enjoy:** possess. 79. **The let-alone…good will:** The prohibition does not depend upon *your* will and pleasure; you have no authority to forbid her taking him as her husband. *Let it alone* is a regular prohibitory phrase—a command not to do something. 80. **Half-blooded fellow:** bastard.

REGAN	[*to Edmund*] Let the drum strike, and prove my title thine.

ALBANY Stay yet; hear reason. Edmund, I arrest thee
On capital treason; and, in thine attaint,
This gilded serpent [*points to Goneril*]. For your claim, fair sister,
I bar it in the interest of my wife.   85
'Tis she is subcontracted to this lord
And I, her husband, contradict your banes.
If you will marry, make your loves to me;
My lady is bespoke.

GONERIL   An interlude!

ALBANY Thou art arm'd, Gloucester. Let the trumpet sound.   90
If none appear to prove upon thy person
Thy heinous, manifest, and many treasons,
There is my pledge [*throws down a glove*]! I'll prove it on thy heart,
Ere I taste bread, thou art in nothing less
Than I have here proclaim'd thee.

REGAN   Sick, O, sick!   95

GONERIL [*aside*] If not, I'll ne'er trust medicine.

EDMUND There's my exchange [*throws down a glove*]. What in the world he is
That names me traitor, villain-like he lies.
Call by thy trumpet. He that dares approach,
On him, on you, who not? I will maintain   100
My truth and honor firmly.

ALBANY A herald, ho!

EDMUND   A herald, ho, a herald!

ALBANY Trust to thy single virtue; for thy soldiers,
All levied in my name, have in my name
Took their discharge.

---

81. **prove:** i.e., by combat, if necessary. 83. **On capital treason:** on a charge of high treason. —**in thine attaint:** as a sharer in the treason of which thou art guilty. Treason was a crime that "corrupted the blood" of the traitor—i.e., deprived his kindred of their civil rights. 84-89. Elaborate irony. "As for your claim to Edmund, sister Regan, I bar it, acting in my wife's interest. It is *she* that is contracted to marry this lord, and I—as a husband asserting my wife's rights—forbid your marriage." The *banes* (or *banns*) were the notice of intended marriage given out in church in order that anyone who knew of a legal impediment (such as a contract of intended marriage with another person) might protest. Neither Shakespeare nor his audience worried about the anachronism involved in Albany's speech. 86. **subcontracted:** bound by a contract which depends for its validity on the fulfillment or abrogation of a previous contract. 89. **bespoke:** promised; betrothed; engaged to be married. —**An interlude!** What a farce! An *interlude* was a brief play, usually comical, so called from its coming in an interval of festivities. Goneril's contempt for her husband's elaborate irony seems well deserved. 90 ff. **Thou art arm'd:** Edmund still wears the armor that he wore in the battle. —**Let...sound:** Albany is acting in accordance with the instructions that he has received from Edgar in the letter mentioned in 5.1.41. 94. **in nothing:** in no respect; in no one detail. 96. **medicine:** Goneril has poisoned her sister. 97. **What:** whoever and of whatever rank. 103. **virtue:** strength, ability. 105. **grows upon me:** begins to overpower me.

REGAN	My sickness grows upon me.	105
ALBANY	She is not well. Convey her to my tent.	[*Exit Regan, led.*]

Enter a Herald.

Come hither, herald. Let the trumpet sound,
And read out this.

CAPTAIN   Sound, trumpet!   *A trumpet sounds.*

HERALD   (*reads*) "If any man of quality or degree within the lists of the
army will maintain upon Edmund, supposed Earl of Gloucester,
that he is a manifold traitor, let him appear by the third sound of
the trumpet. He is bold in his defence."   113

EDMUND   Sound!   *First trumpet.*

HERALD   Again!   *Second trumpet.* 115

HERALD   Again!   *Third trumpet.*

Trumpet answers within.

Enter Edgar, armed, at the third sound, a Trumpet before him.

ALBANY   Ask him his purposes, why he appears
Upon this call o' th' trumpet.

HERALD   What are you?
Your name, your quality? and why you answer
This present summons?

EDGAR   Know my name is lost;   120
By treason's tooth bare-gnawn and canker-bit.
Yet am I noble as the adversary
I come to cope.

ALBANY   Which is that adversary?

EDGAR   What's he that speaks for Edmund Earl of Gloucester?

EDMUND   Himself. What say'st thou to him?

EDGAR   Draw thy sword,   125
That, if my speech offend a noble heart,
Thy arm may do thee justice. Here is mine.
Behold, it is the privilege of mine honors,

---

107. **trumpet:** trumpeter. 110. **quality or degree:** rank or high position. —**lists:** limits. 121. **cankerbit:**
eaten away, as it were, by the canker—the "worm in the bud," a caterpillar that, being hatched inside
the rosebud, destroys it before it opens. The figure is here particularly appropriate because of Edmund's
duplicity. 123. **cope:** cope with; meet in combat. 127. **arm:** weapon, sword. 128. **the privilege:** Edgar
means that, being a knight, he has the privilege of his knighthood—namely, to challenge to single
combat anyone whom he has reason to accuse of an offense against knightly honor. Treason is the most
flagrant of all such offenses.

My oath, and my profession. I protest—
Maugre thy strength, youth, place, and eminence,   130
Despite thy victor sword and fire-new fortune,
Thy valor and thy heart—thou art a traitor;
False to thy gods, thy brother, and thy father;
Conspirant 'gainst this high illustrious prince;
And from th' extremest upward of thy head   135
To the descent and dust beneath thy foot,
A most toad-spotted traitor. Say thou "no,"
This sword, this arm, and my best spirits are bent
To prove upon thy heart, whereto I speak,
Thou liest.

EDMUND   In wisdom I should ask thy name;   140
But since thy outside looks so fair and warlike,
And that thy tongue some say of breeding breathes,
What safe and nicely I might well delay
By rule of knighthood, I disdain and spurn.
Back do I toss those treasons to thy head;   145
With the hell-hated lie o'erwhelm thy heart;
Which—for they yet glance by and scarcely bruise—
This sword of mine shall give them instant way
Where they shall rest for ever. Trumpets, speak!

Alarums. Fight. [Edmund falls.]†

---

129. **My oath:** the oath that I swore when I was dubbed knight. —**profession:** i.e., of knighthood. 130, 131. **Maugre:** in spite of. —**victor:** victorious (in the recent battle). —**fire-new:** brand-new—just finished on the smith's forge. Edgar refers to Edmund's recent elevation to the rank of Earl of Gloucester (3.5.14). 132. **heart:** courage. Synonymous with *valor*. 134. **Conspirant:** engaged in a conspiracy. —**prince:** i.e., Albany. 135, 136. **from…foot:** An elaboration of the familiar "from head to foot" or "from top to toe." —**To the descent…foot:** to the sole of your foot and the dust beneath it. 137. **toad-spotted:** spotted with treason as the toad is marked with spots that exude venom. That the toad is venomous is still a popular notion. 138. **my best spirits are bent:** all my strength and courage is directed. 139. **whereto I speak:** Edgar's accusation comes from the heart and is addressed to the heart and conscience of Edmund. 140. **In wisdom I should ask thy name:** to determine if you are a worthy opponent [K.S.R.]. 142. **that:** since that; since. **some say of breeding breathes:** shows some touch of a gentleman's education. —**say:** "indication," "sign." 143, 144. **What safe…spurn:** I scorn to delay the combat, as I might in accordance with the code of chivalry, if I cared to insist on the strict rules of that code. —**safe:** safely: i.e., lawfully, without infringing the rules. —**nicely:** punctiliously; with insistence on details. The rule of knighthood which Edmund scorns to take advantage of is expressed by Goneril in lines 152, 153: he was not bound to accept a challenge from an anonymous opponent, for such an opponent might not be a gentleman. 145. **those treasons:** those accusations of treason. 146. **hell-hated:** as hateful as hell—since treason is the most odious of all crimes. 147. **Which:** "Which accusations of treason—since, being false, they do not harm me—my sword shall instantly cause to return to you, with whom they shall remain forever, for the combat will prove that *you* are the traitor." —**for:** because.

---

†   In Richard Eyre's production the epic duel scene between Edgar and Edmund, when the two men engage in an ultimate struggle, is accomplished without the drums and spears appearing in the expansive sets of both Brook and Kozintsev. Instead, Eyre manages to enclose the terror of an entire war into the tiny space of his sparsely furnished studio stage.

ALBANY Save him, save him!

GONERIL   This is mere practice, Gloucester. 150
By th' law of arms thou wast not bound to answer
An unknown opposite. Thou art not vanquish'd,
But cozen'd and beguil'd.

ALBANY   Shut your mouth, dame,
Or with this paper shall I stop it. [*Shows her her letter to Edmund.*]—
[*To Edmund*]. Hold, sir.   155
[*To Goneril*] Thou worse than any name, read thine own evil.
No tearing, lady! I perceive you know it.

GONERIL Say if I do—the laws are mine, not thine.
Who can arraign me for't?

ALBANY   Most monstrous!
Know'st thou this paper?

GONERIL   Ask me not what I know.   *Exit.* 160

ALBANY Go after her. She's desperate; govern her.   [*Exit an Officer.*]

EDMUND What you have charg'd me with, that have I done,
And more, much more. The time will bring it out.
'Tis past, and so am I.—But what art thou
That hast this fortune on me? If thou'rt noble,   165
I do forgive thee.

EDGAR   Let's exchange charity.
I am no less in blood than thou art, Edmund;
If more, the more th' hast wrong'd me.
My name is Edgar and thy father's son.
The gods are just, and of our pleasant vices   170
Make instruments to scourge us.
The dark and vicious place where thee he got
Cost him his eyes.   *The whore he slept with*

EDMUND   Th' hast spoken right; 'tis true.
The wheel is come full circle, I am here.

150-52. **Save him, save him!** Albany desires that Edmund's life may be spared in order to obtain his confession. —**mere practice:** out-and-out trickery. *Mere* often has the sense of "unmixed," "pure." — **answer…opposite:** to accept the challenge of an unknown opponent. 155. **Hold, sir:** like the modern "Just a moment!" Before he can show the paper to Edmund he must give attention to Goneril. 156. **evil:** wickedness. 158, 159. **the laws…thine:** I am the sovereign, not you! Who can arraign me? For a sovereign cannot be brought to trial. 160. **Know'st…paper?** Albany insists on a direct answer, though the evidence is clear enough. 161. **govern:** restrain. Albany fears that she may kill herself. Cf. lines 222-26, 292. 168. **If more:** Since Edmund is only "half-blooded" (line 80). 172. **got:** begot. 174. **The wheel… here:** I began life at the very lowest point on Fortune's wheel. As the wheel revolved, I rose to the summit. Now its revolution is completed, and here I am—at the very bottom, where I was at the beginning. On this wheel are mortals, who are therefore sometimes rising, sometimes at the summit, and sometimes descending or at the very bottom of their fate.

ALBANY	Methought thy very gait did prophesy	175
	A royal nobleness. I must embrace thee.	
	Let sorrow split my heart if ever I	
	Did hate thee, or thy father!	
EDGAR	Worthy prince, I know't.	
ALBANY	Where have you hid yourself?	
	How have you known the miseries of your father?	180
EDGAR	By nursing them, my lord. List a brief tale;	
	And when 'tis told, O that my heart would burst!	
	The bloody proclamation to escape	
	That follow'd me so near (O, our lives' sweetness!	
	That with the pain of death would hourly die	185
	Rather than die at once!) taught me to shift	
	Into a madman's rags, t' assume a semblance	
	That very dogs disdain'd; and in this habit	
	Met I my father with his bleeding rings,	
	Their precious stones new lost; became his guide,	190
	Led him, begg'd for him, sav'd him from despair;	
	Never (O fault!) reveal'd myself unto him	
	Until some half hour past, when I was arm'd,	
	Not sure, though hoping of this good success,	
	I ask'd his blessing, and from first to last	195
	Told him my pilgrimage. But his flaw'd heart	
	(Alack, too weak the conflict to support!)	
	'Twixt two extremes of passion, joy and grief,	
	Burst smilingly.	
EDMUND	This speech of yours hath mov'd me,	
	And shall perchance do good; but speak you on;	200
	You look as you had something more to say.	
ALBANY	If there be more, more woful, hold it in;	
	For I am almost ready to dissolve,	
	Hearing of this.	
EDGAR	This would have seem'd a period	
	To such as love not sorrow; but another,	205
	To amplify too much, would make much more,	
	And top extremity.	

---

183. **The bloody proclamation:** See 2.1.61-64, 111-13. 185-86. **That...at once!** How strange it is that we prefer to suffer the pain of death every hour rather than to die at once and be at rest! 192. **fault!** error in judgment; mistake. 196. **flaw'd:** i.e., on account of what it had already suffered. 198. **passion:** strong emotion. 201. **as:** as if. Cf. line 213. 203. **dissolve:** melt in tears. 204, 205. **This would have seem'd a period:** It would have seemed that sorrow had run its course. —**love not:** are not in love with. —**another:** another woe.

Whilst I was big in clamor, came there a man,
Who, having seen me in my worst estate,
Shunn'd my abhorr'd society; but then, finding   210
Who 'twas that so endur'd, with his strong arms
He fastened on my neck, and bellowed out
As he'd burst heaven; threw him on my father;
Told the most piteous tale of Lear and him
That ever ear receiv'd; which in recounting   215
His grief grew puissant, and the strings of life
Began to crack. Twice then the trumpets sounded,
And there I left him tranc'd.

ALBANY   But who was this?

EDGAR   Kent, sir, the banish'd Kent; who in disguise
Followed his enemy king and did him service   220
Improper for a slave.

               Enter a Gentleman with a bloody knife.

GENTLEMAN   Help, help! O, help!

EDGAR   What kind of help?

ALBANY   Speak, man.

EDGAR   What means that bloody knife?

GENTLEMAN   'Tis hot, it smokes.
It came even from the heart of—O, she's dead!

ALBANY   Who dead? Speak, man.   225

GENTLEMAN   Your lady, sir, your lady! and her sister
By her is poisoned; she hath confess'd it.

EDMUND   I was contracted to them both. All three
Now marry in an instant.

                    Enter Kent.

EDGAR   Here comes Kent.

ALBANY   Produce their bodies, be they alive or dead.   [*Exit Gentleman.*]   230
This judgment of the heavens, that makes us tremble,
Touches us not with pity. O, is this he?
The time will not allow the compliment
That very manners urges.

208, 209. **big in clamor:** loud in my lamentations. —**estate:** condition. 213. **threw him on my father:** threw himself on the body of my father. 216-18. **puissant:** powerful, overmastering. —**the strings of life:** his heartstrings. —**tranc'd:** in a swoon. 221. **Improper for a slave:** unfitting even for a slave. 228, 229. **All...marry:** are all united in death. 233. **compliment:** ceremony.

KENT   I am come
       To bid my king and master aye good night.   235
       Is he not here?

ALBANY   Great things of us forgot!
       Speak, Edmund, where's the King? and where's Cordelia?

The bodies of Goneril and Regan are brought in.

       Seest thou this object, Kent?

KENT   Alack, why thus?

EDMUND   Yet Edmund was belov'd.
       The one the other poisoned for my sake,   240
       And after slew herself.

ALBANY   Even so. Cover their faces.

EDMUND   I pant for life. Some good I mean to do,
       Despite of mine own nature. Quickly send
       (Be brief in't) to the castle; for my writ   245
       Is on the life of Lear and on Cordelia.
       Nay, send in time.

ALBANY   Run, run, O, run!

EDGAR   To who, my lord? Who has the office? Send
       Thy token of reprieve.

EDMUND   Well thought on. Take my sword;   250
       Give it the Captain.

ALBANY   Haste thee for thy life.   [*Exit Edgar.*]

EDMUND   He hath commission from thy wife and me
       To hang Cordelia in the prison and
       To lay the blame upon her own despair
       That she fordid herself.   255

ALBANY   The gods defend her! Bear him hence awhile.

[Edmund is borne off.]

Enter Lear, with Cordelia [dead] in his arms, [Edgar, Captain, and others following].

---

235. **aye:** forever. 236. **Great thing...forgot!** This amnesia on everybody's part is necessary for the climax that follows, but—though the audience thinks little of it—the reader always feels a shock. **—of:** by. 238. **this object:** this sight. In Elizabethan English *object* often means all that one sees at the moment. 239. **Yet:** "after all—bastard and villain though he is." 250. **my sword:** as proof that you are the bearer of orders from me. 255. **fordid:** destroyed.

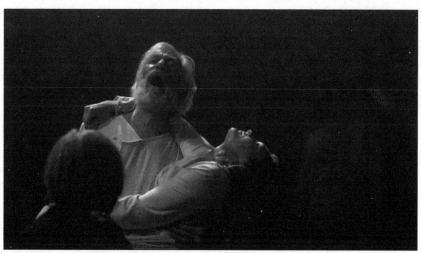

The image of the old King (Ian McKellen) carrying his daughter, dead in his arms, is sometimes suggestive of Michelangelo's *Pieta*. (Nunn, 2008)

LEAR	Howl, howl, howl, howl! O, you are men of stone.[†]
	Had I your tongues and eyes, I'ld use them so
	That heaven's vault should crack. She's gone for ever!
	I know when one is dead, and when one lives. 260
	She's dead as earth. Lend me a looking glass.
	If that her breath will mist or stain the stone,
	Why, then she lives.
KENT	Is this the promis'd end?
EDGAR	Or image of that horror?
ALBANY	Fall and cease!
LEAR	This feather stirs; she lives! If it be so, 265
	It is a chance which does redeem all sorrows
	That ever I have felt.
KENT	O my good master!
LEAR	Prithee away!
EDGAR	'Tis noble Kent, your friend.

262. **stone:** the surface of the mirror [If Cordelia still lived, her faint breath would fog the mirror. K.S.R.]. 263, 264. **the promis'd end:** the Day of Doom that the prophets foretell. —**image:** exact likeness. **Fall and cease!** Addressed to the universe: "Let the end of all things come!" 266. **redeem:** repay in full; atone for.

---

†   In this celebrated moment, Lear enters the stage bearing the broken body of Cordelia, and crying out in terrible pain. At the close of the Peter Brook film, Lear falls further and further back, and then simply vanishes from the screen (see also Production Note 5.3.309). The screen becomes a blank white, as if to symbolize the eternity into which the old king has disappeared. The scene's blocking seems to imitate the ending of Frederick B. Warde's 1916 silent version of *King Lear*.

Kozinstsev's film shows Cordelia hanging from a rope, while Shakespeare's play leaves room for her father's brief hope that, even after hanging, she still might be alive.

LEAR	A plague upon you, murderers, traitors all!
	I might have sav'd her; now she's gone for ever! 270
	Cordelia, Cordelia! stay a little. Ha!
	What is't thou say'st? Her voice was ever soft,
	Gentle, and low—an excellent thing in woman.
	I kill'd the slave that was a-hanging thee.
CAPTAIN	'Tis true, my lords, he did.
LEAR	Did I not, fellow? 275
	I have seen the day, with my good biting falchion
	I would have made them skip. I am old now,
	And these same crosses spoil me. Who are you?
	Mine eyes are not o' th' best. I'll tell you straight.
KENT	If fortune brag of two she lov'd and hated, 280
	One of them we behold.
LEAR	This' a dull sight. Are you not Kent?
KENT	The same—
	Your servant Kent. Where is your servant Caius?
LEAR	He's a good fellow, I can tell you that. 285
	He'll strike, and quickly too. He's dead and rotten.
KENT	No, my good lord; I am the very man—
LEAR	I'll see that straight.

270. **I might have sav'd her:** We are not to suppose that Cordelia was alive when Lear brought her in. He was deluded by his desperate hope. 278. **these same crosses:** these troubles of mine. A *cross* is anything that vexes or thwarts one. 279. **straight:** straightway; in a moment. 280, 281. **If Fortune...behold:** In the whole course of human history we cannot find a stranger example of Fortune's inconstancy than Lear's life affords. 282. **This':** this is. *This* means "this sight of mine." 288. **I'll see that straight:** I'll attend to that in a moment. Lear's mind is wandering, not from insanity, but merely at the approach of death.

KENT	That from your first of difference and decay Have followed your sad steps.
LEAR	You're welcome hither. 290
KENT	Nor no man else! All's cheerless, dark, and deadly. Your eldest daughters have fordone themselves, And desperately are dead.
LEAR	Ay, so I think.
ALBANY	He knows not what he says; and vain is it That we present us to him.
EDGAR	Very bootless. 295

Enter a Captain.

CAPTAIN	Edmund is dead, my lord.
ALBANY	That's but a trifle here. You lords and noble friends, know our intent. What comfort to this great decay may come Shall be applied. For us, we will resign, During the life of this old Majesty, 300 To him our absolute power; [*to Edgar and Kent*] you to your rights; With boot, and such addition as your honors Have more than merited.—All friends shall taste The wages of their virtue, and all foes The cup of their deservings.—O, see, see! 305
LEAR	And my poor fool is hang'd!† No, no, no life! Why should a dog, a horse, a rat, have life, And thou no breath at all? Thou'lt come no more, Never, never, never, never, never!

---

289. **from your first of difference and decay:** from the very beginning of your decline in fortunes. *Decay* is synonymous with *difference*. 291. **Nor no man else!** No, I am not welcome, nor is any one else welcome! Kent implies that this is a time when no one can be greeted as a guest—this is no occasion for the courtesies of normal life. 298. **comfort:** help and support. —**this great decay:** this great man, thus fallen into weakness. Such use of an abstract noun to describe a person was common in Elizabethan English. —**may:** can. 299. **For:** as for. —**us, we.** The "royal *we*" since Albany is to all intents and purposes King of Britain. 301. **our absolute power:** all the sovereign power that is in my hands. 302. **boot.** Synonymous with *addition*. —**honors:** noble deeds. 306. **my poor fool:** i.e., Cordelia [not Lear's Fool, who last appeared in 3.6. K.S.R.]. *Fool* was often used as a term of affection.

---

†   Since the word "fool" was sometimes used to mean "child," Lear's reference to the "fool" in line 305 could mean Cordelia. But this is not certain—it could just as well be a reference to the Court Fool. There is a tradition that the actor who played the Fool also played Cordelia, since we never see the two of them on stage at the same time—an example of Shakespearean "doubling," where one actor might play two or more roles.

The Fool disappears from the play (see 5.3.306 footnote) but survives in Kozintsev's film, where this images shows him playing his flute, as other survivors make efforts to rebuild.

Pray you undo this button.[†] Thank you, sir.   310
Do you see this? Look on her! look! her lips!
Look there, look there![‡]   *He dies.*

EDGAR   He faints! My lord, my lord!

KENT   Break, heart; I prithee break!

EDGAR   Look up, my lord.

KENT   Vex not his ghost. O, let him pass! He hates him
That would upon the rack of this tough world   315
Stretch him out longer.

EDGAR   He is gone indeed.

KENT   The wonder is, he hath endur'd so long.
He but usurp'd his life.

ALBANY   Bear them from hence. Our present business
Is general woe. [*To Kent and Edgar*] Friends of my soul, you twain
Rule in this realm, and the gor'd state sustain.   321

---

314. **his ghost:** his departing spirit. 315. **the rack:** A common torture in Shakespeare's time. The victim was extended and bound upon a frame and levers were applied to stretch his joints even to dislocation. 318. **usurp'd:** "He lived beyond the rightful (alloted) term of mortality." Lear's uncommon vigor is more than once emphasized. 319. **business:** Kent feels unable to survive the death of the master to whom he was so devoted. We are not to take his words literally, as if he were soon to die.

---

†   (*Undo this button*) In Trevor Nunn's production, King Lear himself struggles to undo the button, before asking for assistance. In a different production, however, the button referred to could be Cordelia's, and would then become part of King Lear's effort to save his daughter or to determine if she were still alive.

‡   (*Look there*) In Peter Brook's version, King Lear *and* the audience see an image of Cordelia standing in the distance, as if awaiting her father. As he dies, Lear simply and silently falls out of the frame, as a sinking ship might slowly slip under the sea.

KENT   I have a journey, sir, shortly to go.
                   My master calls me; I must not say no.

ALBANY   The weight of this sad time we must obey,†
                   Speak what we feel, not what we ought to say.   325
                   The oldest have borne most; we that are young
                   Shall never see so much, nor live so long.

Exeunt with a dead march

324-27. The final speech is given to Albany in the Quartos; to Edgar in the Folios. The Quartos are correct, for such a concluding speech (serving as an epilogue) would, in a tragedy, regularly be assigned to the person of highest rank who survives. 324. **weight:** Compare the common use of *heavy* for "sad," "sorrowful."

---

†   In Kozintsev's film, Lear's Fool does not vanish in the third act, as he does in the play, but returns again at the end to help with the visual commentary on the desperate fate of mankind. Now transformed into the village idiot, the Fool sits amidst the rubble, playing mournfully upon his pipe. Devastated by the loss of his master, he shares with all suffering mankind—and the audience—Edgar's "image of that horror." And as the credits roll, a passerby kicks the Fool aside.

HOW TO READ *KING LEAR* AS PERFORMANCE

Productions of Shakespeare's plays, even after four hundred years, continue to delight audiences all over the world. And because these plays include some of the greatest poetry ever written, many people delight in reading passages aloud or listening to them read professionally on recordings. But since the plays were composed for performance, witnessing a theatrical production is really the best and most thrilling introduction. When this is impossible, however, one can still derive much pleasure and gain surprising insights by simply reading the script, either alone or with friends, while at the same time visualizing ways it might work on stage. This can be accomplished easily, in fact, when one begins thinking about the choices that directors and actors have to make at various moments in the action, especially choices regarding the characters' speeches, soliloquies, exchanges, and even the silences they often must assume.

Consider for example the opening moments of *King Lear*. The first stage direction indicates that during the time that the Earl of Kent and Earl of Gloucester are talking, Gloucester's son "Edmund stands back." But just how far back should he stand? Should Edmund, who is silent for most of the sequence, stand "back" at some distance or close enough to the speakers that he overhears his father's crude joke about his illegitimacy and about the fun he and Edmund's mother had during the boy's conception (1.1.6-17)? This eavesdropping could provide a motive for some of Edmund's behavior later in the play. What is to be gained (or lost) by placing Edmund out of hearing? And how might his facial expressions and body language during his silence signal his emotions to the audience?

Another character who is mainly silent a little later in this same scene is King Lear's youngest daughter Cordelia, who listens quietly to her sisters Goneril and Ragan, as they compete for their father's love, which both they and he measure solely in words and land. The reader notes that the actor playing Cordelia speaks only a few words, yet those words suggest that her feelings are strong and deep. The actor must convey these feelings, moreover, while taking in the hollow praise her two sisters heap upon their credulous old father. Should the actor show surprise, contempt, or some other emotion? And how is that emotion conveyed silently?

The answers to such questions sometimes can be found in *asides* (implicit stage directions spoken to the audience), suggesting or instructing certain actions or expressions of feeling. In this first scene, for example, Cordelia speaks two *asides* to the audience, both conveying her emotions but neither suggesting specific actions. In the first, she questions the audience: "What shall Cordelia speak?"(1.1.53); thus we are engaged as confidents, allied in her decision (expressed in the same line, presumably after a pause) to "Love and be silent." Her second aside, a few lines later, defines her particular silence as a *true* expression of love, distinguishing it from the *false* expression so obvious in her sisters' loquacious hyperbole: "I am sure my love's more richer than my tongue" (70-71). Yet while we accept the honesty of Cordelia's love, we still must imagine how an actor can convey that by facial expressions, body language, and movement. Elizabethan actors used popularly-understood symbolic gestures to signal shifting emotions; but such gestures would appear ludicrous now, and so directors must find more subtle ways to display feelings and emotions.

Since this is true for each character in the play, in the absence of rhetorical clues such as *asides*, it often becomes necessary, for directors and readers to imagine how someone under particular circumstances *might* credibly react and then to experiment with possibilities. For example, in Trevor Nunn's 2009 BBC Great Performances production, starring Ian McKellen, King Lear's middle daughter Regan (Monica Dolan) and her new husband Cornwall (Guy Williams) are portrayed as heavy drinkers, both steadily sipping wine, with the frequency increasing as the tension mounts. Since this wine business is unsupported by the script, we must accept or reject it on the basis of whether or not we believe along with the director that this is a credible response to stress and perhaps to guilt, of which there is more than plenty in *King Lear*. Indeed most productions, whether staged or filmed, show some sort of directorial intervention, additional business, or pruning or rearrangement of the script; though very few directors add their own lines to Shakespeare's.

Readers will find, however, that there are directorial clues all throughout the play script, in sites other than stage directions and spoken *asides*. For example, two seemingly random remarks made by two different characters can shed light on King Lear's physical appearance, certainly the most obvious of casting questions. The King himself says that he is "a very foolish fond old man, / Fourscore and upward" (4.7.60-61), making him over eighty years old—quite aged, especially in Shakespeare's time; and the Earl of Gloucester, also quite old, is said to have "corky arms" (3.7.26); that is to say that his arms are easily broken, thus linking old age and fragility. In Gregori Kozintsev's 1969 Russian film, Uri Yarvet's King Lear is especially fragile, thin, and almost gnome-like, but reveals an inner dynamism the moment he speaks. In contrast, Paul Scofield's Lear, in the Peter Brook 1971 movie, is in no way fragile but is a gruff, laconic, bipolar type, more depressive than manic, while Michael Hordern's Lear, in the 1982 BBC televised production, looks like an exhausted ex-alcoholic, but tackled the storm scene like a pro linebacker. The point is that even with textual cues available, directors often take liberties, knowing that variety in the physical appearance of King Lear makes each embodiment of the character unique, always inviting comparisons with predecessors.

Whether or not one begins by reading the script at once or by first experiencing stage or film productions, such as those under discussion, the more that one knows about the play in advance the more satisfying it will be in the long run. It's a good idea to have a plot outline available, for getting the major events in mind, and a Xerox copy of the play's *dramatis personae* (cast list) helps one avoid having to thumb back in search of a forgotten character. And many find it rewarding to read along with a recording of the play, such as the Arkangel Audiobook, with Trevor Peacock as King Lear.

Today's readers of Shakespeare benefit from an incredible electronic revolution that has produced a galaxy of televised and cinematic productions, so that multiple productions of many of Shakespeare's plays, including *King Lear*, are readily available on line, if not at local rental outlets. The most ambitious undertaking in the twentieth-century, the complete BBC/Time/Life recording of Shakespeare plays, are now available on DVD and even newer technologies such as iPod, Google, and YouTube, have subsequently scanned unbelievable amounts of data found in the past only in remote research libraries. YouTube, for example, provides a feast of televised images of famous actors like Laurence Olivier, Michael Hordern, Ian Holm, and James Earl Jones, all enacting scenes from *King Lear.*

Yet perhaps the most important thing to remember when reading drama is that it is language that provides the catalyst for bringing together the interaction between plot and character that together establish the play's major themes. Until a character is actually tested in a conflict of some sort there is, as in life, really no character, only a hollow vessel. Plus the process of reading allows time to grasp this interaction and to understand the full meaning of any given passage, which in the theater may scoot by unheard, either through an actor's poor enunciation, or the listener's own inattention.

Another thing to keep in mind, when thinking about language, is that Shakespeare wrote in early Modern English (c.1500-present), not in Middle English (1066-1500), the language of Geoffrey Chaucer, and certainly not in Old English (500 AD to 1066), the language of *Beowulf.* That way you will avoid making a fool of yourself by declaring in front of people who know better that "Shakespeare wrote his plays in Old English." Indeed, our language is always changes constantly. And a convenient glossary of difficult words will prove a Godsend, as you navigate through words whose meanings have shifted over time, so that when a character says he will come "presently," he means "right away" not when he jolly well gets around to it, as we tend to think nowadays. There are many such glossaries available, though one the best and least expensive is David and Ben Crystal's *Shakespeare's Words: A Glossary and Language Companion* (2002). A glance at many of the words' roots, moreover, may show that they are simply upholstered versions of contemporary usage.

Sometimes the difficulties of Shakespearean language get exaggerated. A good deal of it remains simple, monosyllabic, as, for example, "Let copulation thrive; for Gloucester's bastard son, / Was kinder to his father than my daughters/Got 'tween the lawful sheets' (4.6.112-13). There are no enormous, jaw-breaking, polysyllabic words here.

There is a rugged simplicity, however, which conceals the labyrinth of Elizabethan cultural codes underlying Lear's thinking. The way that he blurts out an unpleasant word like "copulation" resonates today as over the top. He grants more decency to Edmund as a son of Gloucester, bastard as he is, than he gives his own daughters. His stipulation that the daughters were "got" ("begotten") between "lawful" sheets brings in a weird trope in which the domestic paraphernalia of sheets becomes entangled with oppressive laws against adultery. It is difficult to think of anyone today comparing "lawful" and "unlawful" sheets." But when you think about it, this kind of expression is delightfully fresh. Shakespeare can be both entertaining and at the same time serious. And a major diversion for a theater audience is detecting how well the actors comprehend the words they are speaking, for nothing is more boring than an actor who has no idea of what he is saying.

Another example of Shakespearean language is an aphoristic style, though of course these "styles" are always triggered by the personality of the speaker. Lear says to Gloucester, "Plate sin with gold, /And the strong lance of justice hurtless breaks; / Arm it in rags, a pygmy's straw does pierce it" (4.6.159-61). This is simply a timeless cliché about how prosperous appearances protect the rich from the invasive police tactics used on the scruffy poor. People who understand the literal text will have better luck in thinking about the implications, of a speech, the "subtext," not so much what the actor *says* an as what he *thinks*. To put it another way, the meaning *between* the lines can be as important as the meaning *in* the lines A very important clue can also be teased out from the way that an actor responds to another actor's words through non-verbal facial expressions and body language, as was first noted above.

One way to orient oneself to reading as performance is first to examine the stage setting, or *mise en scéne*, as the French say. An RSC production at Stratford-upon-Avon, for example, featured a spectacular blood-red map of England covering nearly the entire stage floor. From time to time during the performance, it was ripped and torn to signify important moments in the deterioration of the social hierarchy. In Laurence Olivier's *Lear*, one setting becomes the mysterious Stonehenge ruin, deeply embedded in British mythology. Good directors will often seek, moreover, to invent some new innovative way of designing the play's décor and costuming. But since the story of King Lear and his daughters takes place in a remote, pre-historic past, costumers have not been inclined to do anything elaborate, though the women are often handsomely dressed in fur-trimmed, ankle-length gowns with long sleeves. The timeless comic-opera style costumes in Trevor Nunn's 2009 BBC production tends to squash questions about the precise historical period.

This production is notable also because in his passion for order and harmony the director never ignores the text but makes a marvelous synthesis that leave both Nunn's and Shakespeare's genius unsullied. Like a great orchestra leader, Nunn interprets the score creatively but with precise discipline. Thus he never leaves in doubt the fate of the Fool, who is soon seen dangling from the end of a noose. And even though Lear's ambiguous line, "My poor Fool is hang'd," (5.3.306), correctly refers to Cordelia, Nunn uses it also as a surrogate for the hanging of the Fool. There is even an attempt to plug another hole, the purpose of Kent's final journey, with a flash cut to a concealed hand gun as he exits. Ian McKellen's performance as Lear steers a middle ground between Olivier's sacerdotal approach (who is sanctified in white robes, so to speak), and Holm's more direct and aggressive style, making all the more remarkable McKellen's achievement in filling the role of an octogenarian king.

Much of what has been said relates to theatrical performance, and it is understood that there are differences between theater and film, a fundamental difference being that theater puts a live actor in front of a live audience. When successful, it creates an electric atmosphere, as the audience grows increasingly absorbed and becomes part of the stage dynamic. It's a commonplace to say, moreover, that all of this is absent from a film version, since the actors are only phantoms, images, detached from the audience. On the other hand, too much can be made of "differences," which often get exaggerated; there are in fact common issues and overlapping agendas. A production captured on film provides a stable, verifiable text; and the truth is that a film screening, or even a television production, can be even more thrilling than a theatrical event.

Regardless of the performance medium, it should be clear that Shakespeare's plays always allow for multiple, often opposed directorial interpretations, as suggested by the stage and screen versions of *King Lear* referenced in the discussion above. Those readers who are willing to explore the play closely enough to envision its enactment become *de facto* directors, each with defensible interpretive judgments and the potential to illuminate some conundrum in Shakespeare's timeless script.

TIMELINE

1000 BC-55BC	Unrecorded history. Briton ruled by warring tribes. Possible period for King Lear's reign.
55BC-450 BC	Invasion of and occupation of British isles by Roman legions initially led by Julius Caesar. There is no reference in the play to the Romans, though the Roman gods are invoked.
1138-1139	Geoffrey of Monmooth, *History of the Kings of Britain*. A source for *King Lear*.
1485	Battle of Bosworth Field ends Wars of the Roses between red rose of the House of York and white rose of Lancaster. Henry Tudor (1457-1509) defeats Richard III and establishes Tudor dynasty, dominated by Queen Elizabeth I from 1549 to 1603.
1509	Erasmus publishes *In Praise of Folly*, and *Education of a Christian Prince* (1516).
1533	Michel de Montaigne born, *Essais* (1580)
1564	Birth of William Shakespeare in Stratford-upon-Avon, England (Baptised April 26)
1567	Establishment of the Red Lion theater, which possibly preceded The Theatre, in Shoreditch, traditionally cited as London)'s first public playhouse.
1572	John Donne born (d.1631)
1576	The Theatre, built by Burbages in Shoreditch, long credited as London's first public playhouse.
1582	William Shakespeare marries Ann Hathaway.
1586	Timothy Bright's *A Treatise of Melancholia*, first treatise by an English physician on melancholy, influenced Robert Burton's *Anatomy of Melancholy* (1621).
1592-94	Plague years when Shakespeare turned to writing poetry during the closing of the theatres.
1604-05	*King Lear written*

1605	Quarto of *King Lear* published
1616	Death of William Shakespeare (April 23)
1621	Robert Burton *The Anatomy of Melancholy*
1623	First Folio Published

NKS Topics for Discussion
and Further Study of *King Lear*

Study Questions

1. Does it make any difference to the outcome of the play whether Edmund overhears, or does not overhear, his father's boasting about the "good sport" with his mother in his son's "making" (1.1)?

2. How does Shakespeare make the play grow from a mere "domestic" drama (a soap opera) to acquire the emotional scale of authentic tragedy?

3. Does *King Lear* fit the classical definition of a tragedy in which a suffering person profits from learning a great truth?

4. An obsession with cruelty seems to be a major motif in the play. Who among the characters inflicts the most cruelty on others and for what reasons?

5. At what point in the play is there a high point in the action (a climax) when it can be said that all the action has arced into a converging design, and from there on out the story inevitably unfolds? Or can it be said there is no clear-cut climax in this play? Why?

6. Why did Shakespeare elect to have Cornwall and Regan travel to Gloucester's castle rather than stay at their own castle?

7. Is Edmund the most villainous character? If so what are his motives for inflicting evil on others? Is he justified? How consistent is his final behavior with his attitudes at the beginning of the play?

8. Compare and contrast the good daughter of Lear, Cordelia, with the good son of Gloucester, Edgar. What strengths and weaknesses does each display?

9. Although at the end of the play Edgar becomes the monarch, is there any possibility that Albany or Kent might have been better qualified?

10. Edmund, the villain, makes a clever attack on the assumptions of the astrologists that the confluence of the stars governs man's behavior (see *Romeo and Juliet* as "star-crossed lovers"). Make a case for Edmund as an evil but bold genius.

11. Is it true as many have thought that Gloucester's pessimistic statement "as flies to wanton boys, are we to th' Gods; They kill us for their sport" (4.1.36-37). sums up the theme of the play? What possible exceptions in the play are there to his pessimism?

12. At 3.4.28, the old king suddenly expresses pity for "the poor naked wretches" who inhabit the earth. What specific events have occurred to bring him to this recognition of the misery of other human beings? Does his prior attitude lead logically to this outcome?

NKS Performance Questions for *Lear*

1. How far should a director go in encouraging sympathy for Regan and Goneril's outrage over their father's thoughtlessness in imposing his one hundred knights on them? Is there any truth in the daughters' charges that the knights are rude and out of control?

2. In the Kozintsev version of *King Lear*, the principal actor, Yuri Yarvet, bears little resemblance to the traditional image of the king as a huge, blustering war lord. Is Yarvet miscast, or an actor who brings a fresh approach to the role?

3. Write an analysis of the banter that goes on between Fool and King Lear. Should the Fool's put-downs consistently reveal him to be more intelligent than the king?

4. Imagine that you are a well-financed and well connected producer in Hollywood and that you're considering the production of a *King Lear* film. Which Hollywood actors would be your first choice for such key roles as Lear, Gloucester, Cordelia, Edmund? Why would you select them as your choices?

5. Write a critique of the continuity in the play. That is to say, how does event A lead to event B to event C? Is there a possibility that the movement of the action from Albany's to Gloucester's castle may confuse the audience? Where there are gaps in the action, what devices does Shakespeare employ to fill them?

6. Is the Fool as big a "fool" as his name implies or is there wisdom in his utterances? In what sense is the Fool an inner consciousness of the king?

7. How might this idea be captured in performance?

8. Do you feel as Nahum Tate did, that the play would be more acceptable if the ending were less grim, and therefore it should be made over into a tragi-comedy?

9. Should the actor playing King Lear be allowed to declaim his greatest speeches in the sonorous tones of an oracle, or would understatement work more effectively with most audiences?

10. If you were director would you allow Edmund to overhear the act one, scene one, conversation between Kent and Gloucester?

11. Although it has been attempted, what difficulties arise in presenting a "modernized" version of *Lear*? What elements in the play are timeless; which ones completely absent in modern society?

BIBLIOGRAPHY

Anon. *The History of King Leir*, 1605. The Malone Society Reprints, Oxford: Oxford UP, n.d. This *King Leir* is not to be confused with Shakespeare's *King Lear*, for which it may have provided some inspiration. To see to what extent *Leir* influenced Shakespeare's *Lear*, this reprint is a handy resource.

Bates, Jonathan and Russell Jackson, eds. *Shakespeare: An Illustrated Stage History*. Oxford: Oxford UP, 1992. A handsome and useful book for getting Shakespearean stage history in perspective.

Black, James, ed. *Nahum Tate. The History of King Lear*. Lincoln: U of Nebraska Press, 1975. A full text of Tate's play with a thoughtful introduction by James Black. It is fascinating to discover shards of Shakespeare embedded in Tate's version.

Booth, Stephen. *King Lear, Macbeth, Indefinition, and Tragedy*. New Haven: Yale University Press, 1983. Booth examines the special effects of tragedy upon audiences and the ways it helps us situate ourselves in the world.

Bradley, A.C. *Shakespearean Tragedy* (1904). New York: World Publishing Co., 1962 (reprint). Although often thought of today as dated because of its heavy reliance on "character criticism," Bradley's book remains a most eloquent and powerful commentary on Shakespeare.

Browne, Sir Thomas. *Religio Medici* (1642). Boston: Ticknor and Fields, 1863 (reprint). Sir Thomas Browne's *Religion of a Doctor* offers an insight into the thought of the Jacobean period.

Burton, Robert. *The Anatomy of Melancholy* (1621). Holbrook Jackson, ed. London: J.M. Dent, 1972. Despite the intimidating title, Burton's book remains one of the most delightful ever written and gives modern readers an insight into the "cult of melancholia."

Danby, J. F. *Shakespeare's Doctrine of Nature: A Study of* King Lear. London: Faber & Faber, 1949. Danby's break with the fashionable New Criticism dogma that criticism could not stray outside the boundaries of aesthetics made his exploration of major themes in *King Lear* especially interesting.

Elton, W. R. King Lear *and the Gods*. San Marino: Huntington Library, 1966. Elton argues energetically against the popular Victorian insistence that Lear was a "Christian" play.

Foakes, Reginald. *King Lear*. The Arden Shakespeare, Third Series. Walton-on-Thames: Thomas Nelson and Sons Ltd., 1997. This edition effectively supplements Kenneth Muir's earlier Arden volume by taking full account of the editorial and staging issues that have absorbed scholars in the years between the editions, while commenting insightfully on the issue of violence in *King Lear*.

Gianetti, Louis D. *Understanding Movies*, second edition. Englewood: Prentice Hall, 1976. A great help for anyone who feels uncomfortable with cinematic terminology.

Hawkes, Terence. *William Shakespeare: King Lear*. Plymouth, England: Northcote Publishers, 1995. Hawkes brings New Historical concerns to bear upon *King Lear*.

Heilman, Robert B. *This Great Stage: Image and Structure in "King Lear."* Baton Roufe: Louisiana State University Press, 1948. Heilman highlights the play's concern with generational conflict and issues of aging.

Hunter, G. K., ed. *King Lear: Nahum Tate's Edition, Elliston, 1820*. London: Cornmarket Press, 1970. The nineteenth century edition of Tate's play shows how Shakespeare's original intentions were gradually creeping back into the play.

Greenblatt, Stephen. *Shakespeare's Negotiations: The Circulation of Social Energy in Renaissance England*. Berkeley: U of California Press, 1988. Greenblatt shows in detail how the Catholic belief in the exorcism of devils, and Samuel Harsnett's attack on it, shaped the exotic language of Mad Tom.

Halio, Jay, ed. *The Tragedy of King Lear*, updated edition. Cambridge: Cambridge UP, 2005. An edition that includes many valuable supporting materials.

Jackson, Russell, ed. *Victorian Theatre: The Theatre in its Time*. New York: New Amsterdam Books, 1989. Jackson's collection of essays by Victorian theater people gives the reader a first-hand view of life among the players on the nineteenth-century stage.

Leggatt, Alexander. *King Lear: Shakespeare in Performance*. Manchester: Manchester UP, 1991. Leggatt's concise history describes the major productions, though there is no pretense to cover the vast subject in its entirety.

Lusardi, James and June Schleuter. *Reading Shakespeare in Performance: King Lear*. Madison: Fairleigh Dickinson University Press, 1991. Outlines the principles of performance analysis and insightfully compares two notable film versions of *King Lear*.

Mack, Maynard. *King Lear in Our Time*. Berkeley: University of California Press, 1972. Mack's study displays an acute interest in performance issues while connecting the play's themes to contemporary concerns.

Muir, Kenneth, ed. *King Lear. The Arden Shakespeare*. Eighth edition. London: Methuen and Co., 1959. Muir's edition continues to be a valuable research resource.

Rosenberg, Marvin. *The Masks of* King Lear. Berkeley: U of California Press, 1972. It is not clear how the author managed the impossible task of collecting and synthesizing the immense amount of data he has assembled. For microanalysis based on evidence of different parts of the play from different productions, the book remains unexcelled.

Rothwell, Kenneth S. *A History of Shakespeare on Screen: A Century of Film and Television*. Second edition. Cambridge: Cambridge UP, 2004. The book is based for the most part on first-hand screenings of archival Kinescope, 35mm and 16mm films, before the invention of videotapes and DVDs.

Styan, J. L. *The English Stage: A History of Drama and Performance*. Cambridge: Cambridge UP, 1996. A concise and useful overview of the history of the English stage.

Weise, René. *King Lear: A Parallel Text Edition*. New York: Longman, 1993. Weise's side-by-side format makes comparisons of the Folio and the Quarto texts a pleasurable experience.

Urkowitz, Steven. *Shakespeare's Revision of* King Lear. Princeton: Princeton UP, 1980. Urkowitz makes a through and even passionate case in favor of the "Two Text" theory of *King Lear*.

FILMOGRAPHY

King Lear (USA, 1909). Dir. William Ranous. Vitagraph Company, black & white, silent. Runtime: 10 mins. One of a dozen or so one-reel Shakespeare films made in Brooklyn under the supervision of J. Stuart Blackton, a magician turned film producer. By cramming key episodes of the play into the action, an effort has been made to go beyond abbreviation into abridgement.

Re Lear (Italy, 1910). Dir. Gerolamo Savio. Filme d'Arte Production, black & white, silent. Runtime: 17 mins. Cast; King Lear (Ernest Novelli), Cordelia (Francesca Bertini). With the help of title cards and the exaggerated acting styles of the silent era, the film manages to convey the main thrust of the play, though subtleties and nuances are lacking. The removal of the Gloucester plot helps to focus the film on Lear and his daughters.

King Lear (USA, 1916). Dirs. Edwin Thanhouser and Ernest Wade. Thanhouser Films, black & white, silent. Runtime: 43 mins. Cast: King Lear (Frederick B. Warde), Cordelia (Lorraine Huling), Fool (Ernest Warde). This best and most ambitious of the *Lear* silents was filmed in New Rochelle, New York, by the Thanhouser company (Edwin and his wife), who ventured outdoors for what in those days were spectacular cavalry shots and sprawling battle scenes. The expatriate British actor, Frederick B. Warde, as the king brought old-world style to the performance.

King Lear (USA, 1948). Dir. Royston Morley, BBC Television, black & white. Runtime: 200 min. (in two parts, first televised Sunday, August 22 and Sunday, August 29, 1948. Cast: King Lear (William Devlin), Cordelia (Ursula Howards). The most expensive and thorough mounting of *King Lear* on television after the Luftwaffe missions of World War Two. Royston Morley poured all of his talent into this trail-blazing production.

King Lear (USA, 1953). Dirs. Peter Brook and Andrew McCullough. Composer: Virgil Thomson. TV Radio Workshop of the Ford Foundation, black & white. Runtime: 73 mins. (first televised on *Omnibus*, Oct. 18, 1953). Cast: King Lear (Orson Welles), Cordelia (Natasha Perry), Albany (Arnold Moss), Goneril (Beatrice Straight). The Ford Foundation, at the height of its power during the culturally desolate 1950s, financed this truncated but remarkable production of *King Lear*. Under Peter Brook's direction, Orson Welles as the king was his usual blustering but attention-getting persona. Despite its flaws, it richly deserves to remain undisturbed in the Hall of Fame for *Lear* in moving images.

Karol Lear (USSR, 1969). Dir. Grigori Kozintsev. Translation: Boris Pasternak. Music: Dimitri Shostakovich. Lenfilm, black & white. Runtime: 140 mins. Russian with English subtitles. Cast: King Lear (Yuri Yarvet), Cordelia (Valentina Shendrikova), Fool (Øleg Dal). Kozintsev won wide acclaim for this superb film that bypasses ideology, including Marxism, in favor of a philosophical approach steeped in humanitarian values. His book, *The Space of Tragedy*, should be read while studying this movie.

King Lear (*Peter Brook's film of William Shakespeare's* King Lear). (UK/Denmark, 1971). Dir. Peter Brook. Producer: Lord Michael Birkett. Filmways (London), Aherne/Lanterna Films (Copenhagen), black & white. Runtime: 137 mins. Cast; King Lear (Paul Scofield), Cordelia (Annelise Gabold), Edmund (Ian Hogg), Goneril (Irene Worth), Fool (Jack McGowan), Gloucester (Alan Webb). Brook's art-house film triggered roars of disapproval from the critics who did not understand his modernist approach, in which he sought to ferret out the primal truths embedded in the play. Being released almost simultaneously with Kozintsev's film of King Lear, it joined in what was the high point in the history of Shakespearean filmmaking. Some critics "hated it", but others realized that Brook was forcing the audience to "share in the last bitter dregs of geriatric experience."

King Lear (USA, 1973). Dir. Edward Sherin. Producer: Joseph Papp. Broadway Theatre Archive, taped at the Delacorte Theater, New York City. Runtime: 120 mins. Cast: King Lear (James Earl Jones), Kent (Douglas Watson), Edmund (Raul Julia). Jones received very favorable reviews for the range of emotions he showed in this stage production, now widely available on DVD.

Harry and Tonto (USA, 1974). Dir. Paul Mazursky. Twentieth Century Fox, color. Runtime: 117 mins. Cast: Harry (Art Carney), Shirley (Ellen Burstyn). As he also did with the film *Tempest* (1982), director Mazursky took on the challenging task of appropriating Shakespearean themes and motifs into a modern version of the old story. Muzursky's "recontextualization" of a Shakespeare play fits into the pattern followed by movies like *A Thousand Acres*, based on Jane Smiley's best-selling novel set on a farm in Iowa, and the 2002 televised *King of Texas*, which moved the action to a Texas ranch owned by a mean old man (Patrick Stewart). Unfortunately, the plethora of such interesting movies inspired by *King Lear* makes full discussion here impossible.

King Lear (UK, 1982). Dir. Jonathan Miller. The Shakespeare Play Series, British Broadcasting Company, colr. Runtime: 180 mins. Cast: King Lear (Michael Horden), Cordelia (Brenda Blethyn), Fool (Frank Middlemass). In Zeffirelli's

The Taming of the Shrew, Michael Horden as the father, old Baptista, mediates comically between the feuding Bianca and Kate; in this Miller *Lear*, he mediates ineptly but tragically among his three daughters. Horden has always had a gift for playing the overwhelmed father, as he does again here.

King Lear (UK, 1983). Dir. Michael Elliott. Granada Television, color. Runtime: 158 mins. Cast: King Lear (Laurence Olivier), Goneril (Dorothy Tutin), Regan (Diana Rigg), Cordelia (Anna Calder-Marshall), Dool (John Hurt), Cornwall (Jeremy Kemp), Gloucester (Leo McKern). With such a talented cast, this production cannot help but vie for top honors among the filmed versions of *King Lear*. Elliott confidently sets the time for his action in ninth century Britain, which cures much of the anxiety for those deeply concerned with the play's precise chronological slot in history. The placement of Stonehenge's stone pillars in the *mise en scene* further embellishes this inspired guesswork. Olivier's fine acting in the last great role of his career makes the experience immensely valuable.

Ran (Japan, 1985). Dir. Akira Kurosawa. Orion/Nippon, color. Runtime: 160 mins. Japanese with English subtitles. Cast: Lord Hidetora Ichimonji (tatsuya Nakadai), Lady Kaede (Mieko Harada). As Kurosawa did with his adaptation of *Macbeth* (*Throne of Blood*, 1957) he relocates Shakespeare's play in feudal Japan, with its hierarchical clans and ritualized codes of conduct. In full color and lavishly costumed, the film's visual splendor offers a peephole into a lost culture.

King Lear (USA/Switzerland, 1987) Dir. Jean-Luc Godard. Cannon Films, color. Runtime: 95 mins. Cast: William Shakespeare Jr. the 5th (Peter Sellars), Don Learo (Burgess Meredith), Cordelia (Molly Ringwald), Himself (Norman Mailer), Film Editor (Woody Allen). Those expecting to see Shakespeare's play on film will be gravely disappointed, but those in search of an original postmodernist approach will find the play dismembered but reconstituted in a pattern of meaningful and beautiful fragments.

King Lear (UK, 1999). Dir. Richard Eyre. BBC Video, color. Shown on Masterpiece Theater, USA. Cast: king Lear (Ian Holm), Goneril (Barbara Flynn), Regan (Amanda Redman), Gloucester (Timothy West), Edgar (Paul Rhys), Cordelia (Victoria Hamilton). An absorbing presentation of the play, led by Ian Holm as a forceful but not a nuanced king.

The Tragedy of King Lear (UK, 2008) Dirs. Trevor Nunn, Chris Hunt. Released on DVD 2009 by PBS Home Video, color. Cast: King Lear (Ian McKellen), Cordelia (Romola Garai), Fool: (Sylvester McCoy), Regan (Monica Dolan), Goneril (Frances Barker), Kent (Jonathan Hyde), Albany (Julian Harries), Gloucester (William Gaunt), Edmund (Philip Winchester), Cornwall (Guy Williams), Edgar (Ben Meyjes). Ian McKellen's award-winning Royal Shakespeare Company stage performance as King Lear was made into a film by director Trevor Nunn and broadcast on Channel Four television in the UK and PBS in the USA in 2008.